הגדה של פסח
HAGGADAH

With commentary compiled and adapted
from the writings of

Samson Raphael Hirsch

FELDHEIM PUBLISHERS *Jerusalem & New York*

Adapted from *Haggadah Nachlas Hasar*
(ed., Rabbi Mordechai ben Shamshon Breuer)
and translated from the original German
by Karin Paritzky, with portions translated
from the Hebrew by Rabbi Leonard Oschry

typesetting: Astronel, Jerusalem

First published 1988
Second, corrected edition 1989

Hardcover edition: ISBN 0-87306-461-5
Paperback edition: ISBN 0-87306-462-3

Feldheim Publishers Ltd.
POB 6525/Jerusalem, Israel

Philipp Feldheim Inc.
200 Airport Executive Park
Spring Valley, NY 10977

Printed in Israel

הגאון כמוהר"ר **שמשון** בן כמוהר"ר **רפאל הירש** זללה"ה
כ"ז טבת תרמ"ט

Preface

יודע ה' ימי תמימים ונחלתם לעולם תהיה

*God knows the days of "whole" men —
their inheritance shall remain forever*

"God is close to men of total integrity who subordinate all their strivings to the Divine dictate. Every day of their existence is lived under God's special care; every day is pregnant with meaning and significance. Yet the particular achievements of the individual cannot be measured by the outward appearance of their lives. ונחלתם לעולם תהיה — their work, their accomplishments, their influence belong to eternity" (Hirsch Commentary on *Psalms* 37:18).

With these words, R. Samson Raphael Hirsch unwittingly provided a precise assessment of his own unique life and work. It is difficult to gauge the impact of a great leader and thinker in his lifetime, for a true evaluation of his role in history is only possible in the light of retrospective analysis. The contemporary reaction to Hirsch's revolutionary ideology and course of action often came in the form of strong opposition to the concept of total independence of the Torah-true communal organizational structure.

In our time, almost one hundred years after the master's passing, the worldwide "Hirsch Kehillah" has grown to astounding proportions. The 19th century confrontation between the dissident camp and the adherents to the uncompromising way of life intensified in the last fifty years, years marked by the ravages of the Holocaust and an unprecedented materialization of our technology-dominated age. This in turn brought about an equally unprecedented return to Judaism's eternal sources in the form of the vast proliferation of the Yeshivah and Ba'alei Teshuvah movements. The inevitable conflict between these phenomena and the world's headlong plunge into secular vulgarization led straight to — Hirsch.

This explains the fascination with the Hirschian re-defined and re-applied Talmudic doctrine "Torah Im Derech Eretz" which, far from being a compromise or reconciliation, or even a synthesis, called for the full and uncompromising sovereignty of the Torah over whichever prevailing Derech Eretz. The Torah is immortal, unchangeable, permanent, eternally itself; Derech Eretz, literally "the way of the world", is transient, temporary, eternally changing its colors. Looking at life through the lens of Torah, we accept that which fits into its framework — everything else we reject.

The Rabbi Samson Raphael Hirsch Publications Society and its

vii

sister organ, the Rabbi Dr. Joseph Breuer Foundation, warmly welcome the long-awaited *Hirsch Haggadah* in English. Available for a number of years in the Hebrew version and thus not accessible to the non-Hebrew-speaking reader, it offers a matchless wealth of material invaluable for one's Pesach preparation and presentation at the Seder table. This new work is the latest in a long series of publications in English and Hebrew of the enormous output of Hirsch's writings meticulously prepared by Feldheim Publishers — the firm which has truly earned the title of "Hirsch Publishers". It is in no mean measure due to their concentration on the dissemination of the Hirsch literary legacy in the world of Jewish thought that the Hirschian approach to the Torah exegesis, the granite foundation of his ideology, and the overwhelming fervor of his mission to liberate the Torah from the deadly entanglement of a decaying Derech Eretz, have uplifted and inspired the hearts and minds of our people in our time, and most especially the younger generation.

Adding to our expression of profound gratitude to Mr. Yaakov Feldheim, head of Feldheim Publishers, for his and his co-workers' dedicated and professional work on this and the previous Hirsch publications, we would like to pay special tribute to the patriarch of the Feldheim family, the founder and mentor of this successful publishing house, Mr. Philipp Feldheim לאי״ט, in whose honor, and that of his wife, his faithful life companion, this work is presented to the public. From small beginnings, Mr. Feldheim built a concern of international repute, bringing to an ever-increasing loyal circle of readers a wide range of Judaica and Hebraica, with emphasis also on belletristic and juvenile literature.

The crowning glory of Mr. Feldheim's endeavors was his early and lasting ties with Rav Breuer, זצ״ל, perpetuator of the Hirschian heritage, spiritual father and founder of the model Kehillah in Washington Heights, New York, which he constructed and guided for forty blessed years on the principles and in the spirit of his illustrious grandfather. Their collaboration led to Mr. Feldheim's early resolve to become the "Hirsch Publisher", a title which he never relinquished and which will always be associated with his name. Rav Breuer, זצ״ל, greatly valued his friend's longtime membership in the Kehillah's Board of Trustees, where he was truly עוסק בצרכי צבור באמונה. Surely, in his years of richly deserved retirement, he derives great נחת רוח ושבע רצון from the continued involvement of his sons, Yaakov and Yitzchok, in the dissemination of the Hirschian literature in which his voice and views are still heard with respect and admiration. May הקב״ה grant him and his wife years of vigor and inner fortitude לאורך ימים טובים.

Jacob Breuer

viii

Publisher's Foreword

ויותר מהמה בני הזהר עשות ספרים הרבה אין קץ
ולהג הרבה יגעת בשר.

"And furthermore, my son, be admonished:
Of making many books there is no end;
and much study is a weariness of the flesh."

(*Koheles* 12:12)

To anyone familiar with the history of Hebrew book publishing, it is evident that more commentaries on the Pesach Haggadah have been written and published than on any other Jewish book. The reader, then, might reasonably ask why Feldheim Publishers has chosen to produce yet *another* Haggadah, when the existing selection is not only ample but includes numerous attractive volumes and excellent commentaries.

But surely Shlomo Hamelech's admonition concerning "making many books" does not apply to Haggados, for our Sages teach: וכל המרבה לספר ביציאת מצרים הרי זה משובח — "He who elaborates upon the story of the departure from Egypt is worthy of praise." Moreover, the vast wisdom, the profound insights and the countless Torah novellae contained in *The Hirsch Haggadah* make the publication of this unique work imperative.

To the wider Jewish public, Samson Raphael Hirsch, the renowned 19th century Torah scholar and leader of German Jewry, is noted for his historic role as a foremost opponent of Reform Judaism in Germany and as the man who succeeded in rejuvenating Torah-true Judaism at the time of its lowest ebb. His influence, in fact, spread far beyond his own borders and had an almost immediate impact on Central- and Eastern-European Jewry. *The Nineteen Letters*, his first, momentous work, was translated into many languages and, in 1890, was published in English in the United States (Rabbi B. Drachman, Funk and Wagnalls, New York).

To the Torah world, Hirsch is known as the leading proponent of the ideology of "Torah and Derech Eretz." But what is sometimes overlooked, especially by the yeshivah community, is Hirsch's greatness as an outstanding, unique interpreter of Torah. He is the only exegete to provide a comprehensive, detailed ta'am* for each and every mitzvah, elucidating even the finest points of halachah. We are confident that many readers of this Haggadah will be astounded and moved by Hirsch's ideas and inspired to delve further into his other writings, particularly his commentary on the Chumash (Judaica Press, New York, in six volumes and in a single-volume anthology).

Samson Raphael Hirsch never wrote a commentary on the Haggadah *per se*, but the extracts from his Chumash, Tehillim and Siddur commentaries constitute the very elements of which the bulk of the Haggadah text is comprised. His keen insights decode cryptic verses of Tanach and render the Sages' often-enigmatic words clear and comprehensible. In 1961, these enlightening commentaries, along with some of Hirsch's most brilliant essays on Pesach themes and on the fundamentals of Judaism, were translated into Hebrew and compiled to form the Haggadah *Nachlas Hasar*. The concept, proposed by Rabbi Yehuda Amital, was carried out by Rabbi Mordechai Breuer in consultation with his father, Prof. Samson Breuer, ל"ז, a grandson of Hirsch. This excellent edition has been reprinted many times over the years and is used and studied in thousands of homes in Israel.

As one of the most widely read Jewish books, the Pesach Haggadah is an ideal means by which to introduce Hirsch's ideas to those not familiar with his work and thereby arouse their interest in his other writings. To this end, we undertook the publication of this English adaptation of *Nachlas Hasar*. Using Rabbi Breuer's selection of commentaries as our primary guide, we translated and adapted almost all the material from the original German. This work was admirably executed by Karin Paritzky and edited by Howard Shapiro. Some portions were translated from the Hebrew by Rabbi Leonard Oschry.

Many talented individuals participated in the preparation of *The Hirsch Haggadah* for publication but it is to Rabbi Benzion Sobel's credit, first and foremost, that this volume is now seeing the light of

---

* Rabbi Shimon Schwab, שליט"א, commenting on why explanations of the mitzvos are called "ta'amei hamitzvos" and not "sibos hamitzvos," drew an analogy to eating. The reason, *sibah*, that one eats food, he said, is not because of its *taam*, its good taste, but because food provides health and nourishment. The good taam, the flavor and spices, add an element of pleasure to what is, in essence, a necessity.

Similarly, explanations of the mitzvos do not constitute their "sibos," the *reasons* that we perform them. Our devotion to Hashem is not dependent upon our understanding or enjoyment of His commandments. We are His servants, and as such, remain ready and willing to do His bidding under any and all circumstances. However, while performing the mitzvos uncompromisingly, an understanding of their taamim is a vital ingredient in the spiritual enjoyment and intensity of our kiyum ha-mitzvos. (See footnote to Hirsch's commentary on the Four Sons, page 72.)

day. He conscienciously researched every detail of the text and Hirsch commentary and prepared the halachic introduction and instructions which appear throughout the Haggadah.

It is important to note that, since this book was conceived as a compilation and *adaptation* of Hirsch's works, certain liberties were taken with his writings in order to clarify his thoughts for the modern reader. Hirsch's insightful commentaries, originally expressed in complex Germanic sentence structure, have been rendered here into clear, pleasing language. Now, Hirsch's beautiful imagery, his love of symmetry and his emotional intensity are no longer obscured in linguistic circumlocutions, but revealed in all their glory. (For comparison, see the Sources at the end of this volume. Most of Hirsch's works are now available in English translation.)

This laudable accomplishment was achieved by the present Feldheim editorial staff under the direction of Marsi Tabak. The fresh, clean, easily-readable appearance of this Haggadah is due to the efforts of Anita (Bracha) Steinberg, who designed the book and coordinated production, and Debbie Ismailoff, who copyedited and styled the text.

In this Haggadah, the reader will find Hirsch's ideas on subjects which encompass the essence of Judaism: emunah, bitachon, chinuch, the Jewish home, geulah, the true meaning of freedom and independence, Yisrael's mission in the world, and more. The reader should bear in mind the historic context of these essays: they were written well over one hundred years ago, and yet are startlingly contemporary in their applicability to the Jewish challenges of our time. Were Hirsch to write his essay on "The Wicked Son" today, for example (see page 77), he would surely write it differently, but his grasp of the heart of the problem is indisputable. Some chillingly prophetic ideas are expressed here as well, especially those put forth in the essay on "The Fourth Cup of Redemption" (see page 281).

The Hirsch Haggadah is a source of tremendous nachas for Feldheim Publishers and we are grateful that Hashem Yisbarach has enabled us to see the labors of many years and many individuals brought to fruition. We are confident that this volume will increase its readers' Torah knowledge, deepen their comprehension of the fundamentals of our faith and inspire them to "stride forward" toward the lofty ideals of Samson Raphael Hirsch.

The Feldheim-Hirsch Connection

The Feldheim family's association with Hirsh's works began with the close friendship — more accurately, the relationship of a chassid to his rebbe — between my father, Mr. Philipp Feldheim (Reb Shraga Yehuda ben Tzvi Mordechai, לאי״ט), may Hashem grant him many more years of fruitful activity in this world, and לבח"ל Rabbi Josef Breuer, of blessed memory.

In 1948, my father published the introduction to Hirsch's commentary to the Torah (originally written in German by Rabbi Josef Breuer and translated by Jacob Breuer) and in 1951, שמש מרפא על חומש בראשית by Rabbi Shimon Schwab, שליט"א. The latter was one of the first attempts to present Hirsch's ideas in Hebrew. *Horeb* in Hebrew was printed in 1953.

In the 1940s and '50s, Feldheim — in close cooperation with the Samson Raphael Hirsch Publication Society, headed by the Breuer family — published two anthologies of Hirsch's works in English, *Fundamentals of Judaism* (New York, 1949), and *Timeless Torah* (New York, 1957), both edited by Jacob Breuer. These works were reprinted many times and served as the primary vehicles for disseminating Hirsch's ideas until the time came for producing his complete works in English translation.

In 1960 we published an English translation of *The Nineteen Letters of ben Uziel*, prepared by Jacob Breuer and based on the translation of Rabbi Bernard Drachman. (A new edition of this work, with commentary and annotations by Rabbi Joseph Elias, is in preparation.)

In 1960-66 we published *The Psalms*, תהילים, with Hirsch's commentary in a superb English translation by Gertrude Hirschler.

In 1967 Hirsch's commentary on *Pirkey Avos* was released and in 1969, *The Hirsch Siddur*.

In 1976 we published *From the Wisdom of Mishle*, a collection of essays by Hirsch on the Book of Proverbs, translated by Karin Paritzky. This work had never been published in German in book form.

After the passing of Rabbi Joseph Breuer, the Rabbi Joseph Breuer Foundation, in cooperation with Feldheim Publishers, undertook the publication of the complete *Collected Writings of Samson Raphael Hirsch*. Four volumes of the planned eight-volume set have appeared thus far and the fifth will אי"ה be published this year. Commentaries on Yirmeyahu and Yechezkel by Rabbi Joseph Breuer, זצ"ל, who continued Hirsch's tradition of Tanach exegesis, are also in preparation. In addition, Feldheim Publishers produced and distributes *The Hirsch Chumash* in Hebrew, the publication of which was sponsored by Mossad Yitzchak Breuer, directed by Prof. Mordecai (ben Yitzchak) Breuer. With Hashem's help, the final volume, דברים, will be released this year, to coincide with the one hundredth yahrtzeit of Rabbi Hirsch, זצ"ל.

Obviously, we at Feldheim could not have built this beautiful edifice had we not been able to utilize the foundations laid by all those who labored to transmit Hirsch's ideas to the modern English-reading public. Dayan I. Grunfeld, Isaac Levy, Rabbi Joseph Breuer, זכר צדיקים לברכה and יבל"ח, Jacob Breuer, Rabbi Ephraim Oratz and Gertrude Hirschler were the pioneers; we merely followed the trail they blazed.

Yaakov Feldheim
Adar 5748

The Pesach Seder

Prologue

The fourteenth day of Nissan has arrived, and, as at the annual dinner of an ancient, worldwide fraternity, the table is set and the "fraternity symbols" are made ready for each member. No single hall can contain the entire membership, so the festive table is set in every house, each a link in a chain extending all over the world. A single thought, a single festive meal unites them all at one and the same time. In each house, the father of the family presides as master of ceremonies and the Founder of the fraternity, the Unique, Ancient and Eternal One, is also present wherever a Seder may be.

For weeks, the members of this fraternity have been busily engaged in preparing for this event. The special 'bread' of the society has been delivered to all brothers, no matter how distant, and even those who are in prison can derive comfort and encouragement from this bread of brotherhood.

No member will willingly absent himself from the yearly banquet. Even those who have remained aloof from the aims and functions of the society during the rest of the year now find themselves reminded of their old ties and obligations by the feverish preparations going on around them. And so, year after year, this solemn occasion challenges them: *Do you wish to share in the responsibilities and duties of your fellow Jews? You may perhaps conveniently forget these duties but surely you can never free yourself from them.*

All members are greeted by an identical program: The meal proceeds in conformity with the Seder instituted by our Sages of old. Four times the cups will be filled and raised to the fourfold theme of the Festival: freedom in its four manifestations, comparable to the tree with roots, trunk, branches and fruit.

God has shown us the meaning of freedom with four expressions of redemption:

1

והוצאתי אתכם מתחת סבלת מצרים	"I shall bring you out from under the burdens of Egypt"
והצלתי אתכם מעבדתם	"I shall deliver you from their bondage"
וגאלתי אתכם בזרוע נטויה ובשפטים גדולים	"I shall redeem you with an outstretched arm and with great punishing judgments"
ולקחתי אתכם לי לעם והייתי לכם לאלקים	"I shall take you to Me for a people and I will be your God"

(Shemos 6:6-7)

Thus spoke the ever-living Founder of the fraternity — and He kept His promise. He lifted the burdens from Yisrael's bent backs, unshackled their fetters, and with His outstretched arm brought about their everlasting liberation. He raised them up, He took them to be a people unto Him and gave them their destiny: They were to become heralds of liberty and deliverance, redemption and sanctity to the ranks of dispirited and degenerate mankind. Deliverance and liberation, then, constitute their common bond and vocation, uniting them into a people.

(This essay on the four cups of redemption is continued on page 258.)

The Search for Chametz

The Exodus from Egypt, the Divine revelation which laid the foundation of Yisrael, is effective only if it is perceived as such — as an act revealing God's work, as an additional "Let there be..." in the annals of mankind. However, if the Exodus is perceived only as one more episode in the history of humanity — an episode in which the human being is the primary focus and the presence of a hidden Guiding Hand is, at most, suspected — then its effectiveness is lost.

To accept the first premise is to attest to God's existence and His involvement in the affairs of nations. This acceptance endows Yisrael, in spite of its relative smallness and weakness, with the ability to stand firmly as the one nation acquired by God, to inspire the world with its spiritual power. Through this fulfillment of its Divine mission, that tiny nation *becomes* Yisrael.

To accept the second premise, however, is to deny all the above and Yisrael, detached from its Divine component, may go and lament its dream and its millennia of misery.

The first premise alone, which is eternally true and eternally new, must be impressed upon our hearts. It was the word of God alone that struck off the Egyptian chains and fetters. We must not deceive ourselves that, after years of slavery, a new spirit awoke in our forefathers, that they rose up and heroically wrested their freedom by defeating their oppressors. As slaves they went out, powerless captives — their freedom won solely through the power of God's word! Thus, just as every being belongs to God individually, Yisrael, the nation, belongs to God collectively.

"And Moshe said unto the people: 'Remember this day when you came out of Egypt, out of the house of bondage, that by strength of hand did Hashem bring you out of here and [therefore] nothing leavened shall be eaten'" (*Shemos* 13:3).

3

The juxtaposition of these two directives in one Torah verse indicates that by refraining from eating any chametz, leaven, during the days of our Festival of Freedom, by not deriving any use from it in any way, and by removing from our possession (even before the Festival commences) anything leavened,* we attest — for ourselves and for the world — to the fact that it was only by the strength of God's hand that our forefathers were brought out of Egypt. Indeed, this symbol was presented to Yisrael at the very time of the Exodus.

At noon on the 14th of Nissan, with the time of redemption drawing near, the Israelites were prevented from seizing their freedom by force. They were forbidden to leave their homes and had to wait — loins girded, walking sticks in hand — until God's call heralded their liberation. Freedom was not won through any human struggle; it came when it was earned, when our forefathers demonstrated their dedication to God. And they did so by fulfilling the commandment of the Pesach Sacrifice.

At the very hour of their redemption the Pesach Sacrifice had to be eaten together with matzah** — the unleavened bread of dependence — and maror — the bitter herbs which symbolized their affliction. By eating the unleavened bread which their Egyptian oppressors had compelled them to eat during their enslavement, the Israelites were to remember — even at the hour of redemption — the time of their subjugation and dependence. For slaves they remained until God, and God alone, restored their freedom. The Israelites did not march out of Egypt; they were driven out (see *Shemos* 12:33, 39), hastened to such a degree that the dough for the bread which was to sustain them on their journey did not have time to rise. Thus Yisrael was to realize it had contributed nothing directly towards its own liberation.

At that moment, the matzah was transformed into an everlasting memorial to the purely Divine character of the Exodus, and it remains a symbol of Yisrael's complete

---

* For the symbolic meanings of these three types of prohibitions, see page 67.
** See commentary on page 142 for an in-depth explanation.

4

helplessness during the redemption.

Accordingly, each year when the time comes for remembering the redemption from Egypt, we are forbidden to eat or enjoy anything leavened, or to retain any chametz in our possession. We must, in fact, rid our property of all leaven and leavened products by the very first hour that commemorates the redemption — that is, noon of the 14th of Nissan — and keep it free of chametz until the last day of the Festival, the day when the redemption culminated in the crossing of the Sea of Reeds. The abstention from and removal of chametz serves as a lesson for all time that our freedom and our entire mission as Jews were conferred upon us by God as a gift.

Conversely, any Jew who indulges in chametz on Pesach demonstrates his denial of the very basis of his People's destiny. He denies that Yisrael as a nation is God's creation, His acquired People, who must consequently be subservient to Him. The soul of such a Jew, the Torah declares, "shall be cut off from the congregation of Yisrael" (*Shemos* 12:19).

בְּדִיקַת חָמֵץ, בִּטוּלוֹ וּבְעוּרוֹ

The Search for Chametz
Annulling and Destroying Chametz

On the evening of the 14th of Nissan (or, if this falls on Friday night, on the evening of the 13th), every corner of the house must be searched for chametz. Although some families have the custom of putting out ten (well-wrapped) pieces of bread to be found during the search, this is by no means a substitute for making a thorough search for all chametz present. The search is made by the light of a candle. However, in places where it is more convenient, a flashlight may be used.

Before starting the search, one is required to make the appropriate berachah. All those who will help in the search should be present and attentive when the berachah is recited by the head of the household or whoever is leading the search, having in mind that it is being said for them, too. Immediately after the recitation of the berachah, one may not speak or delay before beginning the search, and it is preferable not to speak at all until the search has been completed, except when necessary for the performance of the search. One should have the intention that this berachah is not only for the search but also for the annulling of the chametz immediately afterward, the burning of the chametz the next morning and the final annulling after that. The berachah is as follows:

בָּרוּךְ אַתָּה יהוה אֱלֹהֵינוּ מֶלֶךְ הָעוֹלָם אֲשֶׁר קִדְּשָׁנוּ בְּמִצְוֹתָיו וְצִוָּנוּ עַל בְּעוּר חָמֵץ:

Blessed be You, Hashem our God, King of the universe, Who has sanctified us by His commandments and commanded us concerning the removal of chametz.

After the search, one should wrap the chametz which he intends to burn the following morning and store it in a place where it is safe from children and pests. Likewise, any chametz which he intends to eat until the permitted time expires should be similarly stored in a secure place.

6

At this point, all remaining chametz which is unknown to the head of the household is to be annulled. The following declaration is not a prayer but an act which, in order to be valid, must be understood. Therefore, it should be said in a language understood by the one reciting it.

כָּל חֲמִירָא וַחֲמִיעָא דְּאִכָּא בִרְשׁוּתִי. דְּלָא חֲמִיתֵהּ וּדְלָא בִעַרְתֵּהּ וּדְלָא יָדַעְנָא לֵיהּ. לִבָּטֵל וְלֶהֱוֵי הֶפְקֵר כְּעַפְרָא דְאַרְעָא:

All leaven and leavened products in my possession, which I have neither seen nor removed nor know about, shall be deemed of no value and ownerless like the dust of the earth.

On the morning of the 14th of Nissan (if it is not Shabbos) during the fifth hour of the day (see tables on pages 286-9 for local times), all chametz previously put aside or left over from breakfast is to be burned. After it has been burned, a declaration annulling all remaining chametz must be said in a language understood by the one reciting it. If erev Pesach is on Shabbos, then the chametz from the search is burned on Friday morning, and the declaration is said on Shabbos morning, at the regular time, after disposing of any leftover chametz from the meal by flushing it down the drain. The declaration is as follows:

כָּל חֲמִירָא וַחֲמִיעָא דְּאִכָּא בִרְשׁוּתִי. דַּחֲזִתֵהּ וּדְלָא חֲזִתֵהּ דַּחֲמִתֵּהּ וּדְלָא חֲמִתֵּהּ דְּבִעַרְתֵּהּ וּדְלָא בִעַרְתֵּהּ. לִבָּטֵל וְלֶהֱוֵי הֶפְקֵר כְּעַפְרָא דְאַרְעָא:

All leaven and leavened products in my possession, whether I have seen them or not, whether I removed them or not, shall be deemed of no value and ownerless like the dust of the earth.

The Pesach Sacrifice

ויאמר אליו קחה לי עגלה משולשת ועז משולשת ואיל משולש ותור וגוזל:
ויקח־לו את־כל־אלה ויבתר אותם בתוך ויתן איש־בתרו לקראת רעהו ואת־
הצפור לא בתר: וירד העיט על־הפגרים וישב אותם אברם: ויהי השמש לבוא
ותרדמה נפלה על־אברם והנה אימה חשכה גדולה נופלת עליו: ויאמר לאברם
ידוע תדע כי־גר יהיה זרעך בארץ לא להם ועבדום וענו אותם ארבע מאות
שנה:

And He said to him: 'Take unto Me three times a heifer and three
times a goat, and three times a ram, and a turtledove and a young
pigeon.' And He took all these unto Him, and He divided them in
the center and laid each piece opposite its corresponding piece, but
the birds He did not divide. Then the birds of prey came down
upon the carcasses and Avram drove them away. And when the sun
was going down a deep sleep fell upon Avram, and, lo, dread, a
great darkness fell upon him. And He said to Avram: 'Know for
sure that your seed shall be a stranger in a land that is not theirs and
they will enslave them and afflict them four hundred years'
(*Bereishis* 15:9-13).

Some three thousand years ago, there was a proud and mighty
state, in whose midst lived a minority which all the rest of the
population despised as being the dregs of humanity. The dire
prediction made to their forefather Avraham many years before
had come true in all its terrible reality.

For hundreds of years, these people had been homeless; indeed,
they had never had a homeland. The vision of a better future, a
land of their own, existed only in their dreams, but as yet not
one of their children had ever been born in this homeland.
Their only property — the field in which their forefathers had
been buried — was far away, in a distant country.

And, so, they were aliens. The ground under their feet was "not theirs" and supported them only grudgingly. Their landless status sealed their fate in the eyes of the indigenous population, for as a consequence they had no standing and were not even entitled to the air they breathed. In exchange for being tolerated, it was considered justified to extract from them inhuman labor and demand the total subjugation of their existence to "the good of the state." In Egypt, he who *had* nothing — *was* nothing. Property ownership determined a man's rights and worth instead of it being a man's right to own property. By this inversion of all concepts of justice, human beings had forfeited their freedom; they were "owned" by the state, had become its chattels. To further the "national interest," they were molded from birth by the state for its presumed benefit: priests, soldiers, artisans, farmers — but not human beings. In Egypt, equality of justice, attesting to the God-given dignity of man, had ceased to be even a faint memory. No trace remained of the rights to which every man was entitled by virtue of his being human.

Certainly in the midst of this nation, where each citizen was born and bred to his caste, there was no place for the homeless, landless foreigners — those Ivrim "from the other side." They were doomed to servitude and allowed only so much space and freedom of movement as the "rightful" population permitted them. They were aliens in a land which did not belong to them and therefore they were enslaved and oppressed for four hundred years.

Avram's vision in the night, the Covenant between the Portions, had become a horrible reality.

As decreed in this Divine Covenant, three generations had yielded up their strength: their creative force, as symbolized by the bull; their wealth, as symbolized by the ram; and their power of resistance, as symbolized by the goat. Yet, they maintained their ability to soar aloft, as reflected in the turtledove and the young pigeon.*

* For an in-depth explanation of these symbolic meanings, see commentary on page 90.

9

The bull's force had been broken by *enslavement*; as *aliens* they had been robbed of the ram's wealth that Yaakov's family had once enjoyed, while *affliction* had stifled their power of resistance. Three generations had been subjected to the helplessness of slavery and to every torment evil fantasies could devise. Three generations had been slaughtered, and already the severed limbs seemed destined to become prey to the rapacious vulture of despotism. But the vulture did not notice the Hand of God, revealing itself even in the death-throes of this people. It never noticed that each piece was laid "opposite its corresponding piece" and even in their severed state were merely waiting for reunification. It did not realize that tyranny had not succeeded in destroying everything, for the bird's ability to soar aloft, to fly above and beyond torment and oppression, remained. Nor did this vulture see the guardian spirit which hovered over the severed bodies, expectantly waiting for their resurrection, that is, the covenant and promise made to Avram and the merit of our forefathers. And, finally, it did not see that during the period "when the sun was going down" the severed bodies did not decompose and rot; rather a purifying fire and a torch of enlightenment passed between them to prepare the sons of Avraham for their great future.

And when the darkness of the night had intensified and the Holy One, Blessed be He, calculated the end of their exile, He commanded the carcasses to come to life. He raised them from the ground, unified the severed members into a living entity — and created a nation. He infused this entity with the spirit by which henceforth it was to remain immortal even as other nations rise and fall.

Surely now, when we, the sons of this immortal nation, celebrate the Festival of our own resurrection during the time when nature celebrates her revival — shall we not look into the document with which God has formed the character of this immortal national body and breathed into it the breath of His eternal spirit?

What terms introduced the Jewish nation's four hundred

years of agonized rebirth? "Take unto Me"! Not merely *give to Me*, but "take." Fully understanding with what you are parting, give up everything which the three generations following you will have to offer: their creative force, prosperity, and power of resistance.

And, now, upon this nation's emergence from the painful travails of birth, the first words were: "they shall *take* to them."

ויקחו להם איש שה לבית־אבות שה לבית: ואם־ימעט הבית מהיות משה ולקח הוא ושכנו הקרוב אל־ביתו במכסת נפשות איש לפי אכלו תכוסו על־ השה: שה תמים זכר בן־שנה יהיה לכם מן־הכבשים ומן־העזים תקחו:

"...they shall take to them every man a lamb, according to their fathers' houses, a lamb for a household. And if the household be too small for a lamb, then shall he and his neighbor who is near to his house take one according to the counting up of souls, according to every man's eating you shall make your count for the lamb. Your lamb shall be complete, without blemish, a male of the first year; you may take it from the sheep or the goats" (*Shemos* 12:3-5).

God had begun to restore to the fourth generation, what the three preceding ones had willingly surrendered to Him.

Every man. This is the first trait in the character-formation of this newly resurrected nation: each and every man. The foundation of God's nation rests on the personality of every individual. God has not built His nation on the basis of "national consciousness," for this, in the final analysis, is only an abstraction, as distinct from the strong conviction living in a citizen's heart. God does not envision this spiritual task as dependent upon one group among all the people, whether this group be the aristocracy or the leaders of the ecclesiastical and national bodies, who thereby absolve the "masses" of their individual responsibility. The foundation of God's nation does not rest in the hands of its representatives.

The rousing call which woke Yisrael from deathly darkness

11

is: *Each one*. Even if the children of Yisrael are as numerous as the sand on the seashore, their nation is represented by each individual. God calls upon every single person to participate in building the nation; no one is dispensable.

God knows His people only through its individuals, as He counts and recounts them now and in their subsequent wanderings, thereby instilling in the heart of each and every one of them an awareness of the individual's own worth and significance.

By the same token, the Pesach Sacrifice, the declaration of independence of the Jewish people, was, at one and the same time, both a communal sacrifice and an individual sacrifice. It was a national act, not performed by national representatives, but by each individual Jew. What made it communal was that the sacrifice was offered by each member of the nation at the same time and in the same manner.

The first fundamental trait, then, of the Jewish national character is pride. It is the self-respect of a person proudly conscious of his intrinsic human worth, not because of something he is, but because of his having been singled out to fulfill a task. This awareness, that the pinnacle of ethical perfection is accessible to him exactly as it is to everyone else, will never let him sink to the lowest level but will always motivate him to work towards greater achievements.

A lamb. We have seen that three generations had surrendered their creative energy, wealth and power of resistance, as symbolized by the bull, the ram and the goat, respectively. The first thing which God now restores to His people, newly raised to independence, is the lamb, cheerfully following its shepherd. Yisrael had already learned to accept suffering patiently during the years of their mortification. Now they had to be taught obedience to the guidance of their Shepherd and compliance with His leadership.

If the restoration of their strength was to be complete, if they wanted to regain the powers which they had sacrificed, they would have to entrust themselves to God, to become His "flock, the flock of My pasture" (*Yechezkel* 34:31). Only then could

12

they be led back to life by Him with the same confidence that they followed Him into death.

This compliance is the second characteristic of the Divine people. All are independent and conscious of their equal worth and dignity, but, at the same time, one and all are also equal in subordination to God — *every man a lamb.*

The third and fourth characteristics of Yisrael are that each person, with complete self-reliance and in total compliance with God's will, intimately relates back to his parental home and forward to his own household, as it says: *according to their fathers' houses, a lamb for each household.* This is the cornerstone of the Jewish nation: to bring the tradition of yesterday into the world of today. Every Jew emerging from the loving care his parents gave his body and soul must realize that the aim of his own aspirations is to build a home in his turn. By attending to his own children's physical and spiritual development, he repays the measure of love which he owes to his parents.

Is it any coincidence, then, that family purity is the first precondition of Jewish national development and, indeed, that in the merit of their adherence to the precepts of family purity they were redeemed from Egypt? "They did not behave immorally, and [consequently,] they did not change their Hebrew names or their language" (*Mechilta, Bo*). In the midst of their harsh exile they did not lose awareness of their unique mission. They did not forget the unique outlook and concepts that are embodied in their traditional language. Surely this feat could not have been achieved other than by preserving the purity of their families, by the fact that no child was haphazardly fathered or raised. It was achieved solely through each Jewish child having *a father and a mother* who, united in love, set an example for him by their actions and speech, transmitting to him throughout his childhood and adolescence all the impressions and influences which make up his education. Thus the child's physical development, initiated by conception and birth, is completed through the spiritual and ethical formation of his character by his parents.

13

Judaism depends on every Jew. To be a Jew means to be born and bred to this particular vocation. Can our Divinely revealed legacy be transferred from one generation to the next — can Judaism be realized — if the child has no parent, if he has no home in which his spiritual heritage is transmitted to him and where he can thrive in a morally pure and formative atmosphere?

To inherit a home and to build a home — this encompasses a Jew's entire happiness and ethical vocation on earth. And, in truth, is it not also the foundation of all human welfare? Is it not the *sine qua non* for the hopes and perfection of all nations? If only this first page of the founding charter of God's nation were read in all the conference halls and palaces where the fates and fortunes of nations are deliberated! If only this great "Magna Carta" were consulted wherever education and culture, peace and the salvation of men and mankind are discussed. For the fate of men, their success or failure, is decided neither in the chambers of rulers nor on the battlefield. It is not decided in business concerns, in colleges and institutes of arts and sciences or in houses of worship. It is sealed only in one place — in the parental home. Conceive children in purity, see to it that every child, whether he is born in a palace or a hut, is welcomed and nurtured by the love of a mother and a father who have preserved their purity for parenthood, endeavor to facilitate and strengthen the establishment of sanctified homes — then the foundation for the welfare of the people will have been laid and the nation will be assured from the start that all its affairs, at every level, will be dealt with by men of pure hearts and undefiled hands. If one wishes the spirit of ethical integrity to permeate his society, then there is only one way: "build houses" (*Yirmeyahu* 29:5), for such a spirit can flourish only in the dedicated atmosphere of a home. *There exists no substitute for the home*, and if one is looking elsewhere for the source of peace and prosperity, he is searching in vain.

All of a nation's politics and diplomacy, its theories of national economy and institutions for mass education, its trade and industry, its schools and community centers — none of these

14

will save the people from extinction if they let the parental home become a parody. Are children born for the sake of the state's false concern instead of the warm love of parents? Does the census show ever-growing numbers of children without parents and parents without children? Does the nation's high society make a mockery of moralty and modesty? If so, then all the palaces it is building are founded on quicksand.

Surely, the Sages of old perceived the core of a nation's welfare when, commenting on the repeated genealogies of Yisrael according to their families and houses, they explained (*Yalkut Shimoni, Bemidbar* 1:1):

> When Yisrael received the Torah, the nations of the world were envious. "Why were the Israelites deemed better suited to come near to God than the other nations?" The Holy One, Blessed be He, silenced them. He said to them: "Bring Me your genealogical tables, as it says [in *Divrei Hayamim I* 16:28]: 'Render unto Hashem, o' families of peoples,' in the same manner that My sons bring theirs and declare themselves [as it says in *Bemidbar* 1:18] 'according to their birth after their families '." Therefore He numbered them at the beginning of this Book [Bemidbar] immediately after the conclusion of the commandments [in the previous books]... For Yisrael merited to receive the commandments of the Torah solely because of the purity of their family lineage...Then they came to Shittim, "and the people began to commit harlotry" (*ibid.* 25:1). When the nations heard this, they rejoiced: "Now the crown they wore has been confiscated. The praise that they received is silenced. They are the same as we"...God smote all who had defiled themselves and restored their purity, as it says: "And it came to pass after the plague and Hashem spoke to Mosheh and Elazar...'take the sum of all the congregation of the children of Yisrael'" (*ibid.* 26:1).

The individuals who make up God's nation are like lambs, and as such, they may confidently follow His lead and entrust themselves to His guidance. But they may only do so by virtue of their being a girder in a Jewish house, a son or daughter, brother or sister, father or mother, husband or wife, either depending on it or supporting it:...*every man a lamb* —

according to their father's houses. Each household, then, is also like a lamb, the object of Divine Providence. And these houses constitute the infrastructure of God's nation, for first of all "He established their homes" (*Shemos* 1:21).

The fifth characteristic of the people of God is "he and his neighbor," as it says: "And if the household be too small for a lamb, then shall *he and his neighbor* who is near to his house take one according to the counting up of souls...." First of all, he and his family are to build a home, but if the lamb (the bounty God has bestowed upon the house) exceeds the needs of such a small family circle, if a household is too small to qualify alone to represent such a "lamb of His flock," then one family approaches the next, neighbors form a close relationship, two houses become one, and, so, before God, families join together and *society* is created.

Now, what are the factors that condition Jewish society, what is it that causes one household to approach its neighbor? One of the laws of the Pesach Sacrifice states that if the lamb exceeds the needs of a man's limited family, he is obliged to go and seek out his neighbor to share it with him. In other words, it is neither want nor the need for help, but superabundance and the necessity to distribute it which unlocks houses and families, binding them into a society and a nation. It is surplus on the one hand and insufficiency on the other which makes one family enter into a relationship with the next. However, this giving is not motivated by pity but by duty. The poor are not forced to approach the rich; it is the rich man who must seek out the poor. According to God's constitution, the wealthy man is obliged to make sure that not only is the portion needed by himself and his family put to Divinely sanctioned use, but he must also insure that the surplus which has been entrusted to him is put to its proper use, *i.e.*, the furtherance of human life and welfare.

Just as it was forbidden to leave over the mannah until the next day, and whatever had been selfishly hoarded became spoiled and worm-ridden, so, too, it was forbidden to leave over any part of the Paschal lamb until the next day, and whatever

16

did remain had to be burned. Consequently, he whose lamb exceeded the needs of his household was obliged to look for friends to share the surplus. Together, they constitute a social unit represented by the lamb.

According to every man's eating you shall make your count for the lamb. In Jewish society, every person is counted as an equal partner in the partaking of the lamb. In the community of God, no one is required to give up his individual identity. On the contrary, through coming together, each one will come into his own, and his individuality will only gain by it. We are taught:

"One can always join or withdraw from the group that slaughters the Paschal lamb together until it is actually slaughtered" (*Pesachim* 89a). When an individual joins the circle of his friend and is welcomed in the company of the latter's home, he does not thereby forfeit the freedom to make his own decisions and does not remain indebted to his host indefinitely. He is always permitted to change his mind, to withdraw and join the table of another. In the organizational structure of the Divine People, there is no such thing as servile dependence. Even the poorest man may hold his head high; even the person on the receiving end remains free. True, the poor may need the rich to survive, but the rich man equally needs the poor, for how else can he discharge his duty and make his regular declaration before God in the Temple: "I have removed that which is allowed from my house, and I have also given it to the Levite, to the stranger, to the orphan and to the widow, according to all Your commandments which You have commanded me; I have not transgressed any of Your commandments and have not forgotten anything" (*Devarim* 26:13). For if he has not complied with these commandments, how can he raise his head up to Heaven and ask: "Direct Your examining look, down from Your holy abode from Heaven, and bless Your People Yisrael and the ground which You have given us..." (*ibid.* 15).

This is the structure on which society in God's nation is based to this day. The obligation of being charitable pervades first, founding act of the Jewish nation — has shown us this through its precepts.

The individual, the family, the society, all of whose devotion and commitment to God is symbolized by the lamb, should be alive with a full, manly and youthful vigor, as it says: "Your lamb shall be complete, without blemish, a male of the first year...". These expressions of wholeness, masculinity and youthful vigor are further basic traits which characterize the Divine People.

Complete, without blemish. One cannot be a lamb before God in a limited sense. Rather, wholeness of devotion is always the first condition in our relationship to God. Just as the condition imposed on our first ancestor before his descendants could be consecrated to God was: "Conduct yourself before me and become complete" (*Bereishis* 17:1), so, too, are his descendants obliged from the very beginning of their relationship to God to be complete, to submit to God's Providence and to follow His lead with their entire being.

Following His lead involves not only the spirit, but also the body: heart, mind, speech and deed. It encompasses life in its every aspect, creative, remunerative, and pleasurable. Nothing without God and everything with God, to be "complete" in *all* of one's being and life — this is the first philosophical concept underlying Judaism.

A male. In other, man-made religions, fear of a deity is engendered by "female" characteristics — by susceptibility, weakness and infirmity, sorrow, pain, night, and death lead these peoples to religiosity and fanaticism. This is now how God wants to see His people. He wants them to be masculine, forceful in their actions, alert and clear-sighted, manly in their thinking. Straight, not cowed, free, not burdened — that is how a Jewish person is to walk with God through life and through history. "...I broke the bars of your yoke and taught you to walk upright" (*Vayikra* 26:13). God wants to see us raised upright and the harness of our yoke broken.

Moreover, *of the first year.* Youthful, always in the prime of life, always with youthful dedication and youthful vitality. Manliness, freedom, independence and vigor must never become old. In fact, as a result of our covenant with God, they are renewable from their Source: Every morning from the Hand of our Creator, our Redeemer, and daily by the Hand of our Lawgiver, we are alerted to fulfil our duty anew, as it is written:

> ...Hashem acted for *me* when *I* came forth from Egypt (*Shemos* 13:8). They are *new* every morning, great is Your faithfulness (*Eychah* 3:23).... Which I command you *this day*... (*Devarim* 6:6) — "They [the commandments] shall be as if *new* in your eyes each day" (*Sifri*). ...on *this day* they came to the wilderness of Sinai (*Shemos* 19:1) — "The words of Torah should be fresh as if they were given today" (*Midrash*).

Through the Korban Tamid, the daily offering in the Temple, Yisrael continues to renew, at the beginning and end of each day, what they learned through the Korban Pesach. Daily they stand before Hashem as an unblemished sheep, male, in its first year. Thus Yisrael remain the lamb of His flock who, in daily renewed awareness, faithfully follow their Shepherd over hills and dales, through centuries and millennia. *Complete* in body and soul, in noble *manliness* and never-aging *youthfulness*, they follow His secure lead to their eternal destiny — God's immortal people!

סדר אמירת קרבן פסח

After the Minchah Service it is customary to recite the order of the Pesach Sacrificial Service as a substitute for the actual sacrifice which we are unable to perform:

רבונו של עולם, אתה צויתנו להקריב קרבן הפסח במועדו באַרבעה עשר יום לחדש הראשון ולהיות כהנים בעבודתם ולוים בדוכנם וישראל במעמדם קוראים את־ההלל. ועתה בעונותינו חרב בית המקדש ובטל קרבן הפסח ואין לנו לא כהן בעבודתו ולא לוי בדוכנו ולא ישראל במעמדו, ואתה אמרת ונשלמה פרים שפתינו. לכן יהי רצון מלפניך יהוה אלהינו ואלהי אבותינו שיהא שיח שפתותינו חשוב לפניך כאילו הקרבנו את־ הפסח במועדו ועמדנו על־מעמדנו ודברו הלוים בשיר והלל להודות ליהוה. ואתה תכונן מקדשך על־מכונו ונעלה ונקריב לפניך את־הפסח במועדו כמו שכתבת עלינו בתורתך על־ידי משה עבדך כאמור:

20

The Order of the Pesach Sacrificial Service

After the Minchah Service it is customary to recite the
order of the Pesach Sacrificial Service as a substitute for
the actual sacrifice which we are unable
to perform:

Master of the universe, You have commanded us to offer the Pesach Sacrifice in its appointed time, on the fourteenth day of the first month. that the Kohanim perform their service, that the Levites be on their dais, and that the Israelites occupy their positions reciting the Hallel. But, now, because of our iniquities, our Holy Temple is destroyed and the Pesach Sacrifice is in abeyance; and we have no Kohen at his service, no Levite on his dais, and no Israelite standing in his position. You, however, have said: "...and we shall render for bullocks the offering of our lips" (*Hoshea* 14:3). Therefore, may it be Your will, Hashem, our God and God of our fathers, that the utterance of our lips be regarded before you as if we had offered the Paschal lamb in its appointed time and stood in our positions, and the Levites had spoken in song and praise to Hashem. And may You establish Your Holy Temple on its site, and then we shall ascend and offer the Pesach Sacrifice before You in its appointed time, as You have commanded us in Your Torah, by the hand of Moshe Your servant, as it says:

ויאמר יהוה אל־משה ואל־אהרן בארץ מצרים לאמר:
החדש הזה לכם ראש חדשים ראשון הוא לכם לחדשי השנה:
דברו אל־כל־עדת ישראל לאמר בעשר לחדש הזה ויקחו להם
איש שה לבית־אבת שה לבית: ואם־ימעט הבית מהיות משה
ולקח הוא ושכנו הקרב אל־ביתו במכסת נפשת איש לפי אכלו
תכסו על־השה: שה תמים זכר בן־שנה יהיה לכם מן־הכבשים
ומן־העזים תקחו: והיה לכם למשמרת עד ארבעה עשר יום
לחדש הזה ושחטו אתו כל קהל עדת־ישראל בין הערבים: ולקחו
מן־הדם ונתנו על־שתי המזוזת ועל־המשקוף על הבתים אשר־
יאכלו אתו בהם: ואכלו את־הבשר בלילה הזה צלי־אש ומצות
על־מררים יאכלהו: אל־תאכלו ממנו נא ובשל מבשל במים כי
אם־צלי־אש ראשו על־כרעיו ועל־קרבו: ולא־תותירו ממנו עד־
בקר והנתר ממנו עד־בקר באש תשרפו: וככה תאכלו אתו
מתניכם חגרים נעליכם ברגליכם ומקלכם בידכם ואכלתם אתו
בחפזון פסח הוא ליהוה:

ובכן כך היתה עבודת קרבן פסח בבית אלהינו ביום ארבעה עשר בניסן.

אין שוחטין אותו אלא אחר תמיד של בין־הערבים. ערב פסח בין בחול בין
בשבת היה התמיד נשחט בשבע ומחצה וקרב בשמונה ומחצה, ואם חל ע״פ
להיות בערב שבת היו שוחטין אותו בשש ומחצה וקרב בשבע ומחצה, והפסח
אחריו.

כל אדם מישראל, אחד האיש ואחד האשה, הגדולים והטהורים ונמולים
(וכשם שמילתו מעכבת מלעשות הפסח ומלאכול בו, כך מילת בניו הקטנים

"And Hashem spoke unto Moshe and unto Aharon in the land of Egypt, saying: 'This renewal of the moon shall be unto you the beginning of new moons; it shall be the first month of the year to you. Speak unto the whole of the congregation of Yisrael saying: "On the tenth day of this month they shall take unto them every man a lamb, according to their fathers' houses, a lamb for each household. And if the household be too small for a lamb, then shall he and his neighbor who is near to his house take one according to the counting up of souls; according to every man's eating you shall make your count for the lamb. Your lamb shall be complete, without blemish, a male of the first year; you may take it from the sheep or from the goats. And it shall be to you for a safekeeping until the fourteenth day of the same month; then the whole assembly of the congregation of Yisrael shall slaughter it between the two evenings. And they shall take of the blood and put it on the two door posts and on the lintel, upon the houses wherein they shall eat it. And they shall eat the flesh, that night, roasted with fire; with unleavened bread and bitter herbs shall they eat it. Eat not of it half-cooked nor cooked in water as usual, in no other way but roasted with fire; its head with its legs and with its innards. And you shall let nothing remain of it until morning; and that which does remain of it when morning comes you shall burn with fire. And thus shall you eat it; with your loins girded, your shoes on your feet, and your staff in your hand; and you shall eat it in haste — it is a Pesach directed to Hashem"'" (*Shemos* 12:1-11).

Thus was the service of the Pesach Sacrifice in the House of our God on the fourteenth of Nissan:

The Pesach Sacrifice is only slaughtered after the Daily Afternoon Sacrifice. On the day before Pesach, whether this was a weekday or a Shabbos, the Daily Sacrifice is slaughtered half an hour after the seventh hour and its offering is completed at half an hour after the eighth hour. If the day before Pesach falls on a Friday, however, the Daily Sacrifice is slaughtered half an hour after the sixth hour, its offering is completed one hour later, and the Pesach Sacrifice takes place immediately afterwards.

Every adult Jew, male or female, who is ritually pure, circumcised (just as an uncircumcised Jew may not offer or eat a Paschal lamb, so too, if his minor sons or adult or minor slaves have not undergone circumcision, or if his

ומילת עבדיו בין גדולים ובין קטנים וטבילת אמהותיו מעכבת) כל שיכול להגיע לירושלים בשעת שחיטת הפסח חייב בקרבן-פסח.

מביאו מן הכבשים או מן העזים זכר תמים בן-שנה, ואינו טעון סמיכה, ושוחטו בכל מקום בעזרה אחר גמר עבודת תמיד הערב ואחר הטבת הנרות. ואין שוחטין הפסח ולא זורקין הדם ולא מקטירין החלב על החמץ (אפילו היה כזית חמץ ברשותו של אחד מבני החבורה, בעת אחת מהעבודות של קרבן פסח, הוא לוקה והפסח כשר).

שחט השוחט (אפילו זר) וקבל דמו הכהן שבראש השורה ונותן לחברו, וחברו לחברו, כהן הקרוב אצל המזבח זורקו זריקה אחת כנגד היסוד, וחוזר הכלי ריקם לחברו, מקבל המלא ואח"כ מחזיר את הריקן. והיו הכהנים עומדים שורות שורות, ובידיהם בזיכים שכולם כסף או כולם זהב, ולא היו מעורבים, ולא היו לבזיכים שולים, שלא יניחום ויקרש הדם.

אח"כ תולין את הפסח באונקליות (או במקלות דקים, מניח על כתף ועל כתף חברו, ותולה), ומפשיט אותו כולו (ובשבת עד החזה, ומשם ולמטה בברזי), וקורעין בטנו ומוציאין אימורים, החלב שעל הכרס, ויותרת הכבד, ושתי הכליות, וחלב שעליהן, והאליה – אם היה ממין הכבשים – ולעומת העצה. נותן בכלי-שרת ומולחן ומקטירין הכהן על המערכה, חלבי כל זבח וזבח לבדו, בחול ביום, ולא בלילה שהוא יום-טוב, אבל אם חל ע"פ בשבת מקטירין והולכין כל הלילה, ומוציאו קרביו וממחה אותן עד שמסיר מהם הפרש (כדי שיהיו נקיים כשצלוהו עמם).

שחיטתו וזריקת דמו ומיחוי קרביו והקטר חלביו דוחין את השבת, שאר ענייניו אין דוחין.

בשלש כתות הפסח נשחט, ואין כת פחותה משלשים אנשים, נכנסה כת אחת נתמלאה העזרה נועלין אותה, ובעוד שהן שוחטין ומקריבין וכהנים תוקעין החליל מכה לפני המזבח והלויים קוראין את ההלל, אם גמרו קודם שיקריבו את

bondwomen have not undergone ritual immersion, he may not offer or eat the Paschal lamb), and able to reach Yerushalayim in time for the slaughtering is obliged to offer a Paschal lamb.

The Pesach Sacrifice is to consist of a male, unblemished sheep or goat in its first year. No Laying on of Hands is required. It may be slaughtered anywhere in the Temple court, after the completion of the Afternoon Sacrifice and the Setting in Order of the Lamps. It may not be slaughtered, its blood poured, or its fats burned together with the possession of chametz. (Even if there is an amount of chametz as small as an olive in the possession of any member of the group at the time any of the rituals involved in the Pesach Offering are performed, the guilty person incurs the penalty of lashes. The sacrifice nevertheless remains valid.)

Anyone (even a non-Kohen) may perform the slaughtering. The Kohen at the head of the column receives the blood and hands it to the Kohen next to him and that Kohen to the one next to him. The Kohen nearest to the altar pours the blood in a single action against the base and returns the empty basin to the Kohen next to him. First he receives the full basin, and then he returns the empty one. In any line there are gold or silver basins but never both. The bottoms of the basins are rounded to prevent their being set down and the blood from congealing.

The carcass is then suspended from hooks (or else from thin sticks held by the owner on his shoulder and that of his neighbor), and it is skinned in one piece. (On Shabbos, it is skinned down to the chest in one piece and thereafter in strips.) Its belly is then split open and the parts to be sacrificed extracted — that is, the fat on the innards, the diaphragm of the liver, the two kidneys, and the fat on them, and, in the case of a sheep, the fat tail is severed at the backbone. These parts are placed in utensils of service and salted. The Kohen burns the fats of each sacrifice separately on the pyre. On weekdays they burn during the day, but not at night, for by then it is yom tov. If the day before Pesach falls on Shabbos, however, the members will be burnt all night long. The innards are removed and cleansed of all dung (so that later the lamb may be roasted with them).

Slaughtering, pouring the blood, cleansing the innards and burning the fats override Shabbos. The other processes do not.

Three groups, one at a time, slaughter the Paschal lamb, no group consisting of less than thirty persons. The first group enter. When the Temple court is filled, it is locked. While the sacrifices are being slaughtered and offered up, the Kohanim blow the shofar, the flute is played before the altar, and the Levites read the Hallel. If they finish the Hallel before all has been offered, it is repeated; if the Hallel is read a second time and the sacrifices are

כולם שנו, אם שנו שלשו, על כל קריאה תקעו והריעו ותקעו. גמרה כת אחת להקריב פותחין העזרה, יצאה כת ראשונה נכנסה כת שניה, נעלו דלתות העזרה, גמרה, יצאה שניה נכנסה שלישית, כמעשה הראשונה כך מעשה השניה והשלישית.

אחר שיצאו כולן ורחצין העזרה מלכלוכי הדם, ואפילו בשבת, אמת־המים היתה עוברת בעזרה שכשרוצין להדיח הרצפה סותמין מקום יציאת המים והיא מתמלאת על כל גדותיה, עד שהמים עולין וצפין ומקבצין אליהם כל דם ולכלוך שבעזרה, אח"כ פותחין הסתימה ויוצאין המים עם הלכלוך, נמצאת הרצפה מנוקה, זהו כבוד הבית.

יצאו כל אחד עם פסחו (ועור שלו) וצלו אותם. כיצד צולין אותו, מביאין שפוד של רמון, תוחבו מתוך פיו עד בית נקובתו, ותולהו לתוך התנור והאש למטה, ותולה כרעיו ובני־מעיו חוצה לו, ואין מנקרין את הפסח כשאר בשר.

בשבת אין מוליכין את הפסח לביתם, אלא כת הראשונה יוצאין בפסחיהן ויושבין בהר־הבית, השניה יוצאין עם פסחיהן ויושבין בחיל, והשלישית במקומה עומדת. חשכה, יצאו וצלו את פסחיהן.

כשמקריבין את הפסח מקריבין עמו ביום ארבעה־עשר זבח שלמים, מן הבקר או מן הצאן, גדולים או קטנים, זכרים או נקבות, והיא נקראת חגיגת ארבעה־עשר, על זה נאמר בתורה וזבחת פסח ליי אלהיך צאן ובקר, ולא קבעה הכתוב חובה אלא רשות בלבד, מכל־מקום היא כחובה מדברי־סופרים, כדי שיהא הפסח נאכל על השובע.

אימתי מביאין עמו חגיגה, בזמן שהוא בא בחול, בטהרה, ובמועט, ונאכלת לשני־ימים ולילה אחד. ודינה ככל תורת זבחי שלמים, טעונה סמיכה ונסכים ומתן דמים שתים שהן ארבע ושפיכת שירים ליסוד.

זהו סדר עבודת קרבן פסח וחגיגה שעמו בבית אלהינו שיבנה במהרה בימינו אמן. אשרי העם שככה לו אשרי העם שיי אלהיו.

not yet completed, they recite it a third time. For every reading, a tekiah, teruah, tekiah is sounded. When the first group are finished, the court gates are opened, the second group enter, and the doors are locked again. When the second group are finished, they depart and the third enter. The order of service is the same for all three groups.

After all have left, the court is washed of refuse from the blood, even on Shabbos. How is this done? A channel of water passes through the court. To wash the floor, the opening through which the water flows out is closed, making the water overflow the sides, rise, and collect all the blood and refuse in the court. Then the stopper is opened, and the water with all its refuse flows out, leaving the floor clean. This lends dignity to the court.

Each person departs with his Paschal lamb (and its hide) and roasts it. How is it roasted? A spit of pomegranate wood is brought and inserted from the animal's mouth to its buttocks. Then the animal is suspended in an oven — the fire burning underneath — with its legs and innards hanging down outside the carcass. The Paschal lamb is not gouged like other meat.

The Paschal lamb is not taken home on Shabbos. Instead the first group leave with their Paschal lambs and remain on the Temple Mount. The second depart with theirs and stay within the rampart. The third remain where they are. When it becomes dark, they all go and roast their lambs.

When the Pesach Sacrifice is offered, a Peace Offering is offered with it on the fourteenth day of the month, either from the bullocks or the sheep, large or small, male or female. This is called the "Chagigah of the Fourteenth." Of it, the Torah states: "And you shall bring the Pesach as an offering of a meal to Hashem, your God; from the flock and the herd..." (*Devarim* 16:2). Scripture did not make this mandatory, but optional. Nevertheless, the Sages made the Chagigah obligatory to ensure that the Pesach Sacrifice be eaten when one is no longer very hungry.

When is the Chagigah brought together with the Pesach Sacrifice? They are offered together only in a state of ritual purity on weekdays when the Paschal lamb is too small for all those eating. It may be eaten for two days and one night. It is governed by the same regulations as all Peace Offerings: it requires Laying on of Hands, Drink Offerings, two Applications of Blood which add up to four, and the Pouring of the Remainder of the Blood against the base of the altar.

This is the order of the Pesach Sacrifice and its accompanying Peace Offering in the House of our God, may it be rebuilt speedily, in our days, Amen. To salvation strides that nation with whom it is so. To salvation that nation whose God is Hashem.

אלהינו ואלהי אבותינו מלך רחמן רחם עלינו טוב ומטיב
הדרש לנו שובה אלינו בהמון רחמיך בגלל אבות שעשו רצונך
בנה ביתך כבתחלה וכונן בית מקדשך על מכונו והראנו בבנינו
ושמחנו בתקונו והשב שכינתך לתוכו והשב כהנים לעבודתם
ולוים לשירם ולזמרם והשב ישראל לנויהם ושם נעלה ונראה
ונשתחוה לפניך בשלש פעמי רגלינו ונאכל שם מן הזבחים ומן
הפסחים אשר יגיע דמם על קיר מזבך לרצון. יהיו לרצון אמרי פי
והגיון לבי לפני יהוה צורי וגאלי.

Our God and God of our fathers, compassionate King, have compassion upon us, cause us to find You a good and beneficent Being. Return to us in the fullness of Your compassion, for the sake of the fathers who did Your will; build Your House as at the beginning and establish Your Sanctuary upon its site. And let us behold its rebuilding and gladden us by its restoration, return Your Presence within it, and restore the Priests to their service, and the Levites to their songs and praises. Lead Yisrael back to their dwelling places, and there we shall ascend and appear and cast ourselves down before You at the three seasons of our pilgrimage, and we shall eat there from the sacrifices and from the Pesach Offerings whose blood will be sprinkled on the sides of Your altar for gracious acceptance. May the words of my mouth and the meditation of my heart be pleasing before Your countenance, o' Hashem, my Rock and my Redeemer.

עֵרוּב תַּבְשִׁילִין

If the first day of Pesach falls on a Thursday, those who
live in chutz la'aretz must prepare an eruv tavshilin on
erev yom tov so that one may make preparations on yom
tov for Shabbos. A matzah is taken with some of the
food which was cooked on erev yom tov (usually an egg,
meat or fish) and the following
berachah is said:

בָּרוּךְ אַתָּה יהוה אֱלֹהֵינוּ מֶלֶךְ הָעוֹלָם אֲשֶׁר
קִדְּשָׁנוּ בְּמִצְוֹתָיו וְצִוָּנוּ עַל־מִצְוַת עֵרוּב:

Blessed be You, Hashem our God, King of
the universe, Who has sanctified us by His
commandments and commanded us concerning the
commandment of the eruv.

בְּדֵן עֵרוּבָא יְהֵא שְׁרֵא לָנָא לְמֵיפָא וּלְבַשָּׁלָא
וּלְאַטְמָנָא וּלְאַדְלָקָא שְׁרָגָא וּלְמֶעְבַּד כָּל צָרְכָּנָא
מִיּוֹמָא טָבָא לְשַׁבַּתָּא לָנוּ וּלְכָל הַדָּרִים בָּעִיר הַזֹּאת.

By means of this eruv may we be permitted to bake,
cook, keep food warm, kindle lights and prepare on
yom tov all that we require for the Shabbos, we and
all the inhabitants of this city.

30

Requirements for the Seder

"In every single generation, one is obligated to look upon himself as if he personally had gone forth out of Egypt" (*Haggadah text*).

In order to fulfill this obligation properly at the Seder, one must experience both the bondage and the servitude of the slaves and the freedom of the redeemed. The ritual is arranged into a definite pattern designed to help one achieve this experience. This is one of the reasons why the Seder is called the Seder, meaning order. Throughout the evening there are various requirements and customs, some symbolizing the state of bondage and some the state of freedom, some both and some either.

The leader of the Seder personifies the epitome of freedom, a king, and, consequently, ought to act and be treated accordingly. In many communities, he conducts the Seder clothed in a white kittel. Interestingly, among the reasons given for this custom, one says that it is to liken him to Heavenly angels, and, in contrast, another says that it is to remind him of the shroud of the dead, lest in the expression of so much honor and freedom he forget that he is still a servant of Hashem.

Twice during the Seder the leader washes his hands, and both times the washbasin and towel are brought to his seat. In some homes, another person even pours the water over his hands. His cup is always filled by someone else, just as a king is always served by others (in many homes the custom is that everyone's cup is filled by someone else).

At the start of the Seder, the Seder plate is brought and placed before the leader. With certain exceptions, he and the other participants in the Seder eat and drink in a reclining position (leaning to the left). In many homes, a cushion or pillow is placed at the left to recline upon.

MATZAH: The matzah represents both the bondage and the redemption (*Shelah*). It is a "poor man's bread," being unleavened and without eggs or additives, and it was the staple that the slaves in Egypt existed upon, since it was neither expensive nor time-consuming to prepare. Therefore, it is broken at the start of the Seder, when we begin to experience the feeling of slavery and poverty, and it is introduced as the "bread of dependence."

For the Jewish people, however, the matzah has a unique additional significance. Towards the end of the narration of maggid, the leader of the Seder again shows the matzah to all the participants, but this time he describes it as the bread of freedom. Our redemption came so quickly that we "had been driven out of Egypt and could not tarry," and so, we ate unleavened bread, matzah, instead of leavened bread. Therefore we recline when we eat the matzah as a sign of our independence.

The matzah of the Seder has a special meaning and must be shemurah, "guarded" for this specific purpose from any wetness or anything else which could cause it to become chametz from the time the wheat was cut until the matzah is finally baked. Some are particular that it be produced by hand, and some insist that it be round.

MAROR: The word means "bitterness" and the aim of the maror is to help us recall the bitterness we were forced to suffer in Egypt. For this reason, many use horseradish, whose sharp taste serves as an excellent reminder. However, because it is so very sharp, it is difficult to eat the minimum required amounts and to fulfill one's obligation on Pesach night. Therefore, romaine lettuce is commonly used, even though it does not taste bitter, since if left in the ground long enough it will develop a bitter taste. One must keep in mind that it is extremely difficult to clean its leaves, as they are usually heavily infested with tiny insects. The recommended solution is to cut away and discard the green leaves altogether and to use only the white center, which can (and must) be easily cleaned and inspected. Some use endives as another suitable alternative, since they have very little leafy green around a white center. Some even use iceberg lettuce. The required amounts differ, depending upon what is used, as will be explained below.

During the Seder, maror is eaten twice: once alone and again with matzah in korech. On some Seder plates (which will be described below), there is one place for maror and another for chazeres, the bitter herbs combined with the matzah and eaten together in korech. Some use the same type twice, some use one type the first time and another type the second time, and some mix types.

ZEROA AND BEYTZAH: At the time of the Beis Hamikdash, the roasted Pesach Sacrifice was the focal point of the Seder. A second sacrifice, known as the Chagigah, was also offered, on erev Pesach, to be eaten together with the Pesach. Unfortunately, due to our many sins, our Holy Temple no longer stands in Yerushalayim and the altar is no more, and we are forbidden to offer sacrifices anywhere else. Therefore, we prepare the zeroa as a remembrance of the Korban Pesach and the beytzah to commemorate the Chagigah.

The zeroa is any roasted bone with some meat on it, usually the shank bone of a lamb. However, it is important to keep in mind that today it is forbidden to designate anything to serve as a sacrifice or even to appear to do so. Therefore, some do not roast the zeroa at all but rather cook it, and some even prefer to use a part of a chicken. For this reason, too, one should be careful not to refer to the zeroa as the Pesach, and we do not lift it up or point to it when we describe, in the narration of maggid, the Pesach that our fathers used to eat...when the Holy Temple was still standing.

The beytzah, in remembrance of the Chagigah, is a hard-boiled egg. In some homes, the egg is also roasted a bit.

CHAROSES: This is a mixture of apples, (figs and pomegranates) walnuts, almonds, cinnamon sticks (and ginger), grated together to form a thick texture. The charoses symbolizes the mortar we were forced to mix and build with in

Egypt. Some red wine, symbolizing the blood, is then added to make it slightly liquidy. The maror and the korech are dipped into it. This serves to neutralize the sharp taste of the maror and protect us from any harmful effects it might have. However, in order not to lose the taste of the maror completely, it must not remain in the charoses too long, and one must shake off any excess charoses which may stick to it. (Those who wish to eat this delicious mixture may do so at the meal.)

KARPAS: Towards the beginning of the Seder, a small piece of the karpas is dipped into salt water or vinegar and eaten. Karpas must be a vegetable whose berachah is borei pri ha'adama but not any one of the aforementioned bitter herbs which may be used for maror. The karpas must be served in a manner in which most people would normally eat it, whether that be raw or cooked. Usually, parsley, celery or radishes are used (but they must first be thoroughly cleaned and inspected for insects). Some have a family custom to use potatoes, since in certain parts of Europe, no other vegetable was available (or affordable) at Pesach time.

There is an indication in the Hebrew letters of the word "karpas" that 60 (the letter "samech") times 10,000 *toiled* (the word *perech* formed from the remaining three letters) in bondage in Egypt. On the other hand, dipping an appetizer before a meal is a sign of luxury. Therefore, there are differing customs whether or not to recline while eating the karpas.

SALT WATER: A mixture of salt and water or a portion of vinegar should be prepared in a bowl in order to dip the karpas. In accordance with the first explanation given for the karpas, the salt water is to symbolize the bitterness of the bondage or the tears of the slaves.

WINE: During the course of the Seder, everyone will be required to drink four cups of wine (the required measurements and amounts are discussed below). Wine is a free man's beverage and, therefore, the four cups must be drunk while reclining.

34

Red wine is preferable, but children, women or one who finds it difficult to drink wine may use as a substitute pure grape juice or a mixture of both. (According to the opinion of Hagaon Harav Moshe Feinstein zt"l, unless one will become bedridden or will not be able to complete the Seder, he should force himself to use intoxicating wine, even though he will suffer extreme discomfort as a result.) Enough wine should be prepared for everyone attending the Seder, and all bottles should be opened before yom tov.

CUPS: Unlike the kiddush of Shabbos and other yom tov days, everyone must have his or her own cup from which to drink the required four cups of wine. The cups should be elegant (within one's means) and whole. An extra cup for Eliyahu Hanavi should be prepared as well.

TABLE SPREAD: The table should be covered with an elegant clean tablecloth and decorated with the finest dishes and silverware one possesses. Even utensils not usually used, owing to their value, should be used or at least displayed on Pesach Eve as a sign of our freedom and dignity. During the year, we refrain from putting out all of our finery as a remembrance of the destruction of the Beis Hamikdash. On the Seder night, however, it is a mitzvah to do so.

AFIKOMAN HOLDER: One should prepare a clean pillowcase or some other sort of cloth in which to wrap the afikoman which he will hide until after the meal.

SEDER PLATE: A large plate upon which will be placed samplings of the items to be used at the Seder should be prepared. The arrangement of these items on the plate is described below. However, one should note that some commercial "seder plates" sold in stores do not conform with any of the customs, and one should avoid using them.

TREATS: It is of utmost importance that the children remain awake throughout the Seder, so that the father can fulfill his obligation to relate to them the story of the Exodus from Egypt. A child who has the abilty to understand should not be put to sleep after he has successfully "asked" or, rather, recited the four questions. On the contrary, he should remain at the Seder until after his father has answered his questions by reading "We were slaves...". Preferably, he should remain at least until after the matzah, maror and korech have been eaten.

For this reason, one should endeavor to keep his child awake in spite of the late hour. There are several ways to accomplish this: 1) the child should take a nap in the afternoon before the Seder; 2) one should have everything prepared and the Seder table completely set before yom tov, so that one can begin the Seder immediately upon arriving home from shul, taking care to make kiddush after nightfall; 3) the order of the Seder, by its requiring that we do many things differently from the whole year, is designed to arouse the child's curiosity and hold his interest; 4) one should let the child "steal" the afikoman and hold it for a "ransom" at the end of the meal; 5) one should distribute nuts and candies and fruits to the children during the Seder.

CANDLES: The candles for the Seder should be big enough to burn until after the yom tov meal.

HAGGADOS: Enough haggados should be prepared for everyone attending the Seder (children will want one, too). Haggados should be stored all year round in a place free of chametz.

Women, as well as men, share in all of the required mitzvos of the Seder, including the recitation of the Haggadah and the Hallel. The only exception is the mitzvah of reclining about which they are not commanded, but they may do so if they wish to. If the wife or a helper must spend some time in the kitchen preparing the meal, she should not leave until after she drinks the first cup after the kiddush is said, and she should be called back before reading "Rabban Gamliel used to say...", whereupon she should remain until the maggid is completed with the drinking of the second cup. If possible, she should also be present when the ten plagues are read and explained.

Required Measurements (Shiurim) and Amounts

These measurements and amounts are based upon the decisions of Hagaon Harav Moshe Feinstein, zt"l in *Sefer Kol Dodi* (second edition) by Rabbi Dovid Feinstein, shlitah. Other opinions do exist.

All of these required measurements and amounts apply to women as well as to men. Regarding children, there are more lenient laws, depending upon their ages.

CUPS: The cup of every man and woman attending the Seder must hold at least a revi'is, which is 2.9 fluid ounces. If, however, it is Friday night, then the first cup over which the kiddush is recited must hold 4.42 fl. ozs. However, the cups of those who are hearing kiddush from the leader of the Seder need only hold 2.9 fluid ounces as usual.

WINE: One should preferably drink the entire contents of each of the four cups. However, if this is difficult, then one should drink more than half the wine in the cup.

MATZAH: One kezayis of matzah is the equivalent of enough thin matzah to cover an area of 7" x 4". When eating two kezaysim, however, the equivalent of enough thin matzah to cover an area of 7" x 6 1/4" is sufficient.

One who is old or, because of health reasons, cannot chew matzah may use shemurah matzah meal. For motzi-matzah he should consume an amount of meal that can be packed into a 1.5 fl. oz. cup. For korech he need only eat an amount of meal that can be packed into a 1.1 fl. oz. cup.

For motzi-matzah, one kezayis total of *both* the upper and

middle matzos is required. However, it is preferable to eat two kezaysim. Some are of the opinion that if the other participants in the Seder cannot obtain a full kezayis from *each* of the two matzos of the leader of the Seder, then they are not required to eat more than one kezayis. For korech, the requirement is for one kezayis of matzah to be combined with one kezayis of maror. For afikoman, only one kezayis of matzah is required but two are preferable.

MAROR: One kezayis of maror is required after reciting the berachah on maror, and another kezayis is needed for korech. The measurement of the kezayis depends upon what is being used for maror:

If using romaine lettuce stalks or endives: enough to cover an area of 3" x 5".

If using romaine or iceburg lettuce leaves: enough to cover an area of 8" x 10".

If using pure grated horseradish: for maror — 1.1 fl. ozs (if this is difficult, one may use only .7 fl. ozs.); for korech — .7 fl. ozs.

PLEASE NOTE: In order to be able to measure the matzah and the maror during the Seder, one should prepare a sheet of paper which has been marked off according to the proper dimensions. Likewise, if he uses grated horseradish or matzah meal, he should prepare a jigger of the required volume.

REQUIRED TIME PERIOD FOR EATING AND DRINKING: One has fulfilled his obligation only when he consumes the proper amount of matzah, maror and wine within the required period of time. There are many conflicting views concerning how long this time period actually is. Regarding a kezayis, opinions range from the most stringent of two minutes to the most lenient of nine. Therefore, since the eating of the matzah the first time is a Torah commandment, one should attempt to satisfy the stricter opinion. At other times when eating the matzah or the maror or both, one may rely on the more lenient opinions. Since the time for eating a kezayis does not begin until one has actually begun to *swallow*, one should attempt to chew the food as much as possible before swallowing so as to speed up the process of consumption.

If one is drinking the entire cup, he should preferably finish it in two quick swallows. If he only drinks most of the cup, it should preferably be done in one quick swallow. However, there are many authorities who allow the wine to be consumed within the time span of two to nine minutes.

IMPORTANT NOTE: Anyone who, for health reasons, is not able to comply with these amounts and measurements, should consult a competent rabbi.

Preparations before the Seder

As mentioned before, all preparations for the Seder should be finished early so that the Seder may begin immediately upon returning from shul. (However, contrary to other Shabbos and yom tov evenings, kiddush on Pesach Seder nights may not be said before dark, since all the mitzvos of this evening must be performed when it is night.)

Another reason to prepare early is to avoid the possibility of violating one or more of the yom tov laws relevant to these preparations. These include bereirah (selecting), techina (grinding), shechittah (drowning the bugs and worms) and ibud (tanning). Early preparation is even more important if Pesach begins on a Friday night.

One should prepare in advance enough matzos, maror, wine, Haggados and all other items necessary for all of his guests. This will save him precious time later and enable him to truly enjoy his Seder.

39

Arrangement of the Matzos and the Seder Plate

Three shemurah matzos are placed on the table, one above the other, in front of the leader of the Seder (according to the custom of the Gaon of Vilna, only two matzos are used). They are separated by napkins or the like. Some place the Seder plate over the matzos, while some put the matzos on the Seder plate.

A sampling of the items which will be used during the Seder should be arranged on the Seder plate.

In most homes, it is common to arrange the Seder plate according to the custom of the Arizal, Rabbi Yitzchak Luria. Some follow the custom of the Gaon of Vilna, while others follow the instructions of the Rama.

As mentioned previously, these are only samplings. The proper amount of matzah, maror, etc. for all assembled at the Seder must be prepared separately.

THE SEDER PLATE
ACCORDING TO:

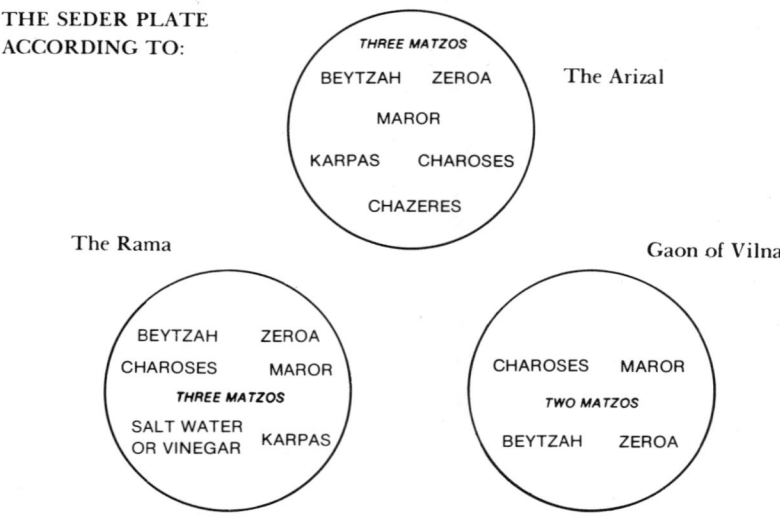

The Arizal

THREE MATZOS

BEYTZAH   ZEROA

MAROR

KARPAS   CHAROSES

CHAZERES

The Rama

BEYTZAH   ZEROA

CHAROSES   MAROR

THREE MATZOS

SALT WATER
OR VINEGAR   KARPAS

Gaon of Vilna

CHAROSES   MAROR

TWO MATZOS

BEYTZAH   ZEROA

40

הַדְלָקַת הַנֵּרוֹת

Kindling of the Candles

The lady of the house kindles the yom tov lights. She then extends her hands, placing them between her eyes and the lights, and recites the following berachah:

בָּרוּךְ אַתָּה יהוה אֱלֹהֵינוּ מֶלֶךְ הָעוֹלָם אֲשֶׁר קִדְּשָׁנוּ בְּמִצְוֹתָיו וְצִוָּנוּ לְהַדְלִיק נֵר שֶׁל (שַׁבָּת וְשֶׁל) יוֹם טוֹב:

Blessed be You, Hashem our God, King of the universe, Who has sanctified us by His commandments and commanded us to kindle the (Shabbos and) yom tov light.

In many communities the women also say:

בָּרוּךְ אַתָּה יהוה אֱלֹהֵינוּ מֶלֶךְ הָעוֹלָם שֶׁהֶחֱיָנוּ וְקִיְּמָנוּ וְהִגִּיעָנוּ לַזְּמַן הַזֶּה:

Blessed be You, Hashem our God, King of the universe, Who has kept us alive and preserved us, and enabled us to attain this season.

סֵדֶר לֵיל פֶּסַח

The Traditional Order of the Seder

This order is attributed to Rashi. Many announce each new step at its appropriate time throughout the Seder (but Motzi-Matzah must be announced before washing the hands since afterwards one should not speak unnecessarily).

1. קַדֵּשׁ   *Kaddesh*

Kiddush, the sanctification of the Festival

2. וּרְחַץ   *Urechatz*

Washing the hands in preparation for karpas

3. כַּרְפַּס   *Karpas*

Eating a bit of vegetable dipped in salt water or vinegar

4. יַחַץ   *Yachatz*

Dividing the middle matzah and hiding the larger part

5. מַגִּיד   *Maggid*

Reciting the Haggadah, the story of our Exodus and liberation

6. רָחְצָה   *Rochtzah*

Washing the hands before the meal

7. מוֹצִיא *Motzi*

Blessing over the matzah

8. מַצָּה *Matzah*

Special blessing before performing the mitzvah of
eating matzah at the Seder, and eating it

9. מָרוֹר *Maror*

Special blessing before performing the mitzvah of
eating the bitter herbs, and eating them

10. כּוֹרֵךְ *Korech*

Combining the maror with matzah and eating them
together

11. שֻׁלְחָן עוֹרֵךְ *Shulchan Orech*

Eating the yom tov meal

12. צָפוּן *Tzafun*

Eating the afikoman, that part of the matzah which
was hidden

13. בָּרֵךְ *Barech*

Birkas hamazon, grace after meals

14. הַלֵּל *Hallel*

Chanting psalms of praise and affirmation of faith in
God

15. נִרְצָה *Nirtzah*

Concluding the Seder with the hope and prayer that
it was properly observed and was acceptable to God

The matzos are covered and the first cup of wine is poured. Everyone should have in mind that, with this cup, it is his intention to fulfill the requirement of reciting kiddush on (Shabbos and on) yom tov over wine and also of drinking the first of the four cups of wine.

בלחש: וַיְהִי־עֶרֶב וַיְהִי־בֹקֶר

יוֹם הַשִּׁשִּׁי: וַיְכֻלּוּ הַשָּׁמַיִם וְהָאָרֶץ וְכָל צְבָאָם: וַיְכַל אֱלֹהִים בַּיּוֹם הַשְּׁבִיעִי מְלַאכְתּוֹ אֲשֶׁר עָשָׂה וַיִּשְׁבֹּת בַּיּוֹם הַשְּׁבִיעִי מִכָּל מְלַאכְתּוֹ אֲשֶׁר עָשָׂה: וַיְבָרֶךְ אֱלֹהִים אֶת יוֹם הַשְּׁבִיעִי וַיְקַדֵּשׁ אֹתוֹ כִּי בוֹ שָׁבַת מִכָּל מְלַאכְתּוֹ אֲשֶׁר בָּרָא אֱלֹהִים לַעֲשׂוֹת:

KADDESH. Although we mentioned the sanctity of the day in our Festival tefillah earlier, in the synagogue, we do so once more when reciting the kiddush at home, since the holiness of the day must, first and foremost, find its expression in the home. The fact that all work has ceased and that the sanctity of the Festival lives in our heart, is witnessed not only in our houses of worship and in the prayer service, but primarily in the rooms where our families live and conduct their activities. Our homes are testimony to the fact that we fulfill the precepts of the Festival not only conscientiously, but joyfully. The outward manifestation of this joy is the festive meal. The kiddush, which testifies to the sanctity of the day, must commence the festive meal. Kiddush must therefore be recited only in the place where the meal is eaten (*Pesachim* 101a).

AND IT WAS EVENING AND IT WAS MORNING: THE SIXTH DAY. "Resh Lakish said: Why is it written '…and it was evening and it was morning, *the* sixth day'? What is the purpose of the additional 'the'? This teaches that the Holy One, blessed be He, made an accord with the works of Creation, saying to them: 'If Yisrael accepts the Torah, you will exist, but if not — I shall make you revert to formlessness and void'" (*Shabbos* 88a). "R. Yudan said: This alludes to the extra time

44

Kaddesh

Quietly: And it was evening and it was morning,

The sixth day: Thus the heaven and the earth and their whole host were brought to their destined completion. Then God completed with the seventh day His work that He had made, and with the seventh day He ceased from all of His work that He had made. And God blessed the seventh day and made it holy, for with it He had ceased from all of His work which He, God, had created in order to continue shaping it.

that is added from the profane to the sacred" (*Bereishis Rabbah* 9).

These two passages may be understood to complement each other. In contrast to the preceding five days (identified as יום אחד, יום שני, וגו׳ — "one day," "a second day," and so forth), the sixth day is introduced by the definite article "ה." The definite article precedes a noun (one not modified by a relative clause) which has been anticipated. "This is *a* man" introduces the new, previously unknown concept, "man"; "here is *the* man" presents the concept "man" as one which was already known and anticipated.

Had the term "a sixth day" been used here, the day's relationship to its predecessors would have been no more than a consecutive one. There would have been no indication that this day was the one for which all the others had paved the way, the day which was known and anticipated. However, since the term יום הששי appears, "it was *the* sixth day," it should be understood to indicate the one day for which all the preceding days had served only as preliminaries and which was to signify the completion of all that had come before.

The sixth day presented the earth,"אדמה," with "אדם," Man, her master and governor, who would rule over her as the representative of

God. The "ה," then, might have been understood simply and literally: God made an accord with the works of Creation, stipulating that their continued existence hinged upon that which was created on the sixth day. Accordingly, everything depended on Man's acceptance of his exalted role and faithful fulfillment of it. But Man failed to recognize his status and misused the role assigned him, leaving his mission unfulfilled. The works of Creation should, then, have returned to "formlessness and void."

In truth, however, God's accord with the works of Creation was: "You (the Creation) will endure on condition that Yisrael accepts the Torah, and if not, I shall make you revert to formlessness and void." Only with the advent of Yisrael into the arena of world history was the first step taken in the return of mankind to ultimate recognition and fulfillment of his exalted mission. The sixth day was rehabilitated only on the day on which the Torah was given and Yisrael accepted it.

Thus the sixth day became the seal of the Creation, and thus that day itself was uplifted and brought into the realm of the Sabbath. For this is the goal of the seventh day, the Sabbath of the Creation: to remind Man (who was created on the sixth day) of his high calling, and of all the duties this calling imposes upon him. The sixth day is the precondition of the Sabbath; the Sabbath is the sixth day's direct consequence and its complement, the guarantee for the ultimate realization of man's exalted vocation in the Creation. Therefore, the sanctity of the Sabbath spills over onto the sixth day. This is the profound truth which Rabbi Yudan imparts to us: יום הששי — "this alludes to the extra time that is added from the profane (sixth day) to the sacred (Sabbath)." This too, is the reason that we begin the kiddush by mentioning the sixth day: יום הששי ויכלו השמים והארץ וכל צבאם.

AND THE HEAVEN AND THE EARTH AND THEIR WHOLE HOST WERE BROUGHT TO THEIR DESTINED COMPLETION. This verse proclaims the completion of the Creation and parallels the first verse of *Bereishis* which announces its beginning. Just as at the commencement of the Creation the Torah presents the heaven and the earth and proclaims that it was God Who created all that exists, so too when all is finally done, the Torah declares that everything was *brought to its destined completion.* Heaven and earth did not always exist — they *became.* However, even before they "became," they were present in the *thoughts* of their Creator, that is to say, the intent of their creation existed in His Mind. The actual Creation was the manifestation of this preconceived purpose. For the reason for the

46

heaven and the earth lies not within themselves; they are not their own cause for having come into existence — the most contradictory, unthinkable, completely unimaginable thought! The cause of their existence is external of them. But they are not the result of some force working blindly; rather their existence is the culmination of the planned purposeful doing of the One thinking Creator.

GOD BLESSED THE SEVENTH DAY AND MADE IT HOLY. He conferred upon it the power to accomplish the spiritual and moral education of mankind and established this ethical education as the absolute, ultimately prevailing value, not subject to disruption or the passage of time. The purpose of this instrument, the seventh day, is identical with the goal of the entire physical world which God made. Indeed God had created the world for the purpose of the spiritual and moral elevation of mankind from the very beginning. If so, God could cease from "all of His [creating] work" once He had granted the Sabbath the power of the purpose of the Creation.

If man, like all the other creatures on earth, had been created without a free will, then God's work would have been completed with the sixth day. However, because man was created with a free will and because this freedom, though it places him on a higher level than the angels, of necessity also entails the possibility of error and sin, man must be educated to recognize the truth and to do good of his own free will. Therefore, even though God's work in nature had been completed, His impact on the history of mankind and on the continued shaping of the physical world for the sake of man's spiritual and moral education had only begun with the seventh day. So the Sages said: "He rested from the work of creating His world, but not from the work of the wicked and the work of the righteous" (*Bereishis Rabbah* 11:10). To the Shabbos was given the task of educating man — raising him — to the spiritual and moral eminence of being "Adam." All the subsequent history of God's dispensations and revelations has no other purpose but to lead the Shabbos to victory and, as the Sages so felicitously put it, to create for the Shabbos an ever-growing number of "mates," or "partners," to act as its "bearers."

For this reason God blessed the Shabbos and made it holy. As it says: אשר ברא אלהים לעשות — "which He, God, had created in order to continue shaping it." The repetition of "which He had created" at the end of the Shabbos chapter and of the story of Creation is the granite rock upon which the whole is based. The same God who set the spiritual and moral goals that man is to attain of his own free will

בָּרוּךְ אַתָּה יהוה אֱלֹהֵינוּ מֶלֶךְ הָעוֹלָם בּוֹרֵא פְּרִי הַגָּפֶן:

בָּרוּךְ אַתָּה יהוה אֱלֹהֵינוּ מֶלֶךְ הָעוֹלָם אֲשֶׁר בָּחַר בָּנוּ מִכָּל־עָם וְרוֹמְמָנוּ מִכָּל־לָשׁוֹן וְקִדְּשָׁנוּ בְּמִצְוֹתָיו. וַתִּתֶּן לָנוּ יהוה אֱלֹהֵינוּ בְּאַהֲבָה (שַׁבָּתוֹת לִמְנוּחָה וּ)מוֹעֲדִים לְשִׂמְחָה חַגִּים וּזְמַנִּים לְשָׂשׂוֹן אֶת יוֹם

also created the entire physical, material and spiritual world for this very purpose out of *His* own free will. If so, nothing in this whole world can impede the attainment of these spiritual and moral goals; indeed, how can it be other than that everything should work toward the realization of these goals. Since the gradual winning of mankind for all that is good and true had been God's purpose from the very beginning, the realization of this goal is the one thing sure of ultimate triumph. Thus, the fact that God created the world *ex nihilo* and of His own free will is not only the cornerstone of all human verities but is, moreover, the cornerstone of all human morality.

BLESSED BE. There are some who object to interpreting this term in the same way when directed by man to God and when emanating from God to man. [They cannot fathom how man could possibly "bless God". Does God need man's blessing? What purpose could such a blessing fulfill?] They interpret ברוך as "blessed is...," an attribute of God denoting the "source of blessing" in the same way that חנון and רחום, for example, designate God as the source of grace and mercy. [For this reason, many translate ברוך אתה י׳: Blessed *are* you God.] But nothing much is gained by this interpretation of baruch in its passive form, because innumerable times, we find the expression לברך את י׳ — to bless *Hashem* [as in נשמת כל חי תברך את

48

By your leave, my masters and teachers:

❦ **BLESSED** be You, Hashem our God, King of the universe, Who creates the fruit of the vine.

Blessed be You, Hashem our God, King of the universe, Who has chosen us from among all peoples, exalted us above all tongues, and has sanctified us by His commandments. And You have given us, Hashem our Lord, in love, (Sabbaths for rest and) festivals of assembly for rejoicing, feasts of rallying and seasons for delight, (this Shabbos day and) the

שמך — The soul of every living thing shall bless Your Name]. Consequently, although it is correct to say that Hashem is blessed (passively) there is no escaping the fact that man blesses Hashem (actively). And, indeed, why should we even try to avoid interpreting baruch in its simple sense? The moment God made the fulfillment of His will on earth dependent on the free will of man, He in effect said to him: *Bless me! I have entrusted you with the implementation of My purpose on earth. By promoting My purpose, fulfilling my commandments, carrying out My will you bless My work and bless Me!*

Just as "His messengers... all His hosts, His servants who do His bidding... all His works in all the places of His dominion..." (*Tehillim* 103:20-22), being instrumental in the fulfillment of His great purpose in the world, not only praise and thank God but *bless* Him, so does every Jew sense and say to himself: "You, too, o' my soul, bless Hashem" (*ibid.*)!

In other words, to say "Blessed be You..." means to pledge oneself to fulfill Hashem's will. Understood in this way, the concept of berachah, blessing, is the theme underlying all of a Jew's thinking. It is the idea which every Jew should convert into a reality, and the entire Torah exists only to teach us the way in which we can and should bless Hashem. Indeed, the word baruch, from which the noun

49

berachah is derived, encompasses the entire mission of the life of the Jew. This understanding of blessing is what distinguishes Yisrael from the rest of the nations.

All other human beings approach their gods begging and beseeching them. Their prayer says: *Bless me!* Beginning with the savage kneeling in front of his idol and ending with the savant attempting to impart religion to the enlightened, what they call "religion" is the product of a feeling of dependence. Their sense of utter helplessness on the one hand, and their intuition of the existence of a higher being upon which all are dependent on the other — that is the faith on which their altars are built and which makes both savant and savage pray from their heart: *Bless me!*

But what leads the Jew to God is not the request: *Bless me*, for he understands that his blessing has already been granted. He realizes that everything — the forces of nature, the workings of history, and the highlights and pleasures, as well as the sorrows, of his personal life — are his blessing. He always considers himself blessed in both happiness and grief. What motivates him is not to *receive* blessing, but to *dispense* blessing, not בָּרֵךְ, "bless me," but ברוך אתה, *Be You blessed!* These are the words through which the Jew relates to God.

The Jew, in effect is saying: *You have entrusted the fulfillment of Your will, the granting of Your wishes, the promotion of Your Kingdom, the implementation of Your work, to man's free will. It is for this purpose that I am, that I exist. For this purpose You have created me a man and a Jew. For this purpose You have granted me, as a man, the energy to act and You have revealed to me, as a Jew, what You wish to see carried out by us on earth. Every event in nature and history that You are letting me experience, all that You allow me and whatever You deny me — it is all there to remind me of my mission, to revive the strength and resolve within me to fulfill it. My God, it is my wish to discharge my duty! Be Blessed in all that You give me and in all that You withhold from me.*

And the great power, serenity and joy with which this idea, *to bless Hashem*, infuses the heart of every Jew is beyond compare, impossible to describe!

Those who say "bless me" — can they ever find the fulfillment of their prayer? Standing alone, in impotent isolation, they seek to defy the hostile forest of nature and a destructive society and achieve their own aims and pleasures, even if these be for the good. They expect that simply mouthing "bless me" will enable them to do all this, that they will then gain the courage and strength to pursue these aims. But will this prayer on their lips ensure that they attain what is denied others [who may be beseeching God at the same time for the opposite result.]? Will this prayer make them succeed where thousands have failed?

However, to say "may God be Blessed through me" means that one's work is no longer his own doing; at the same time one is not trying to gain his own ends. His status may be ever so humble, his beginnings may well be ridiculed by others, but he has been assigned to his post by God, the Master of heaven and earth, the King of the universe. God knows a man's strength, God's spirit animates him and He has placed him within the particular context of his occupation so that he may perform His will there and then. Man is His worker and, consequently, he has God at his side always. He fights the struggle against nature and society for him. God is man's Shield and Protector. Before *Him*, not man, will the entire hostile world retreat. "Renounce your will for the sake of His will, so that He may nullify the will of others before your will" (*Pirkei Avos* 2:4). "Blessed be You, Hashem." *May Your work be implemented through me!* This is the Jewish call to arms in the ceaseless struggle of life.

May God be Blessed through me! means that one has reached the goal of his desire and remains there at every moment. Every moment — provided one has done his share in fulfilling of His will, provided that he has made use of it with all the strength granted him, in the service of his Master — every such moment, then, represents the summit of man's aspirations. Whether one has much or little is immaterial. That does not determine the measure of his blessing, nor even whether his exertions have been successful, for success, too, is God's, not his. As long as one can say to himself that he has dedicated himself with all his might to fulfilling His will, if to do so is his only and exclusive wish, then, surely, even when God gathers You to Him in the last moment of your life, He will leave you fulfilled and serenely contented in the knowledge that you have lived, not in order to receive blessing, but to give blessing. In this is found the only peace and the only happiness one can hope to obtain.

When the Almighty implanted the first Jew among mankind, He uprooted him from everything that is generally considered a source of blessing. He said to him: *Leave it to Me to bless you! And, you, for your part* "become a blessing" (*Bereishis* 12:2)! By this single expression He isolated Avram from among the rest of mankind who *sought blessing* and made him into a *source* of blessing. By this single expression, God showed Avram his mission for the rest of his life and the heritage he was to bequeath to his children and the generations after them.

51

(הַשַּׁבָּת הַזֶּה וְאֶת־יוֹם) חַג הַמַּצּוֹת הַזֶּה זְמַן חֵרוּתֵנוּ
(בְּאַהֲבָה) מִקְרָא קֹדֶשׁ זֵכֶר לִיצִיאַת מִצְרָיִם. כִּי בָנוּ
בָחַרְתָּ וְאוֹתָנוּ קִדַּשְׁתָּ מִכָּל־הָעַמִּים (וְשַׁבָּת) וּמוֹעֲדֵי
קָדְשֶׁךָ (בְּאַהֲבָה וּבְרָצוֹן) בְּשִׂמְחָה וּבְשָׂשׂוֹן
הִנְחַלְתָּנוּ. בָּרוּךְ אַתָּה יהוה מְקַדֵּשׁ (הַשַּׁבָּת וְ)יִשְׂרָאֵל
וְהַזְּמַנִּים:

At the close of Shabbos add the following two berachos:

בָּרוּךְ אַתָּה יהוה אֱלֹהֵינוּ מֶלֶךְ הָעוֹלָם בּוֹרֵא מְאוֹרֵי הָאֵשׁ:

בָּרוּךְ אַתָּה יהוה אֱלֹהֵינוּ מֶלֶךְ הָעוֹלָם הַמַּבְדִּיל בֵּין קֹדֶשׁ לְחוֹל
בֵּין אוֹר לְחֹשֶׁךְ בֵּין יִשְׂרָאֵל לָעַמִּים בֵּין יוֹם הַשְּׁבִיעִי לְשֵׁשֶׁת יְמֵי
הַמַּעֲשֶׂה. בֵּין קְדֻשַּׁת שַׁבָּת לִקְדֻשַּׁת יוֹם טוֹב הִבְדַּלְתָּ וְאֶת יוֹם
הַשְּׁבִיעִי מִשֵּׁשֶׁת יְמֵי הַמַּעֲשֶׂה קִדַּשְׁתָּ. הִבְדַּלְתָּ וְקִדַּשְׁתָּ אֶת עַמְּךָ
יִשְׂרָאֵל בִּקְדֻשָּׁתֶךָ. בָּרוּךְ אַתָּה יהוה הַמַּבְדִּיל בֵּין קֹדֶשׁ לְקֹדֶשׁ:

WHO CREATES THE FLAMES OF THE FIRE. Praise and blessing to
God, Who imbued man with the diligence and drive to subdue the
world by his strength and spirit in order that he might serve his
Creator!

God gave Man the artificial element of fire, thereby enabling Man
to subdue nature. Fire gives Man dominion over the world and over
his own fate. God has set the world at our feet "to work and guard it"
and to conquer our portion (see *Bereishis* 2:15) in His Name. Through
what we master, we are to fulfill His goal on earth!

Praise and blessing to God. He has aroused in our hearts the vigor
and impetus to be creative, each of us in his chosen occupation. And
He waits expectantly for our genuine and dynamic creativity in order
that He may bless the work of our hands! While the Havdalah wine
pours strength into our hearts, and the fragrance of the spices
refreshes our souls, the flaming torch encourages us to be energetic
and diligent. It teaches us the Divine sanctity of labor, and enjoins us

day of this Festival of Unleavened Bread, the season of our freedom, (in love), a convocation to the Sanctuary, a remembrance of the departure from Egypt. For You have chosen us and You have sanctified us from among all peoples; and (Shabbos and) Your holy festivals of assembly (in love and in favor) in joy and delight have You given us as an inheritance. Blessed be You, Hashem, who sanctifies (Shabbos,) Yisrael and the festive seasons.

At the close of Shabbos add the following two berachos:

Blessed be You, Hashem our God, King of the universe, Who creates the flames of the fire.

Blessed be You, Hashem our God, King of the universe, Who has made a distinction between holy and profane, between light and darkness, between Yisrael and the nations, between the seventh day and the six days of toil. You have made a distinction between the sanctity of Shabbos and the sanctity of the festival, and You have sanctified the seventh day above the six working days. You have set apart Your people Yisrael and sanctified them by Your holiness. Blessed be You, Hashem, Who has made a distinction between holy and holy.

to work, to be industrious, to do our share towards achieving all goals, for the success of which we pray to God. The flaming torch reminds us that God awaits our deeds, and only after we have done our share are we entitled to raise our eyes on high and say: "We have done our share — look down and bless us!" (see *Devarim* 26:14-15). We have done our share in supporting and maintaining our household. We have done our share in raising and educating our children. We have done our share towards the preservation and progress of society. We have done our share in upholding the sanctity of Judaism. We have done our share towards subduing the world and towards establishing the Kingdom of God within it. We have done what is our share, now look down and bless us!

Blessed be you, Hashem, Who creates the flames of the fire.

*One should have in mind that the following berachah
pertains to the yom tov as well as
all the mitzvos of the evening.*

בָּרוּךְ אַתָּה יהוה אֱלֹהֵינוּ מֶלֶךְ הָעוֹלָם שֶׁהֶחֱיָנוּ
וְקִיְּמָנוּ וְהִגִּיעָנוּ לַזְּמַן הַזֶּה:

*The required amount of the first cup should be drunk
(see Required Measurements and Amounts, page 37),
within the required period of time, while
reclining to the left.*

וּרְחַץ

*A washbasin is brought to the leader of the Seder who
proceeds to wash his hands without reciting a berachah.
In some communities, the one who brings the water
also pours it over the leader's hands, and in many
homes, all the participants of the Seder
wash their hands, too.*

כַּרְפַּס

*The leader of the Seder takes a piece of karpas (less than
a kezayis so as not to incur the obligation of saying a
berachah acharonah), dips it in vinegar or salt water,
and distributes similar pieces to all assembled at the
Seder. Then the following berachah is recited with the
intention that it refers also to the maror which
will be eaten later on:*

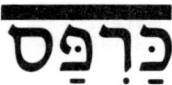 בָּרוּךְ אַתָּה יהוה אֱלֹהֵינוּ מֶלֶךְ
הָעוֹלָם בּוֹרֵא פְּרִי הָאֲדָמָה:

*In some communities, the custom is to eat the karpas
while reclining, while in some communities
they do not recline.*

54

One should have in mind that the following berachah
pertains to the yom tov as well as
all the mitzvos of the evening.

Blessed be You, Hashem our God, King of the universe, Who has kept us alive and preserved us, and enabled us to attain this season.

The required amount of the first cup should be drunk
(see Required Measurements and Amounts, page 37),
within the required period of time, while
reclining to the left.

Urechatz

A washbasin is brought to the leader of the Seder who proceeds to wash his hands without reciting a berachah. In some communities, the one who brings the water also pours it over the leader's hands, and in many homes, all the participants of the Seder wash their hands, too.

Karpas

The leader of the Seder takes a piece of karpas (less than a kezayis so as not to incur the obligation of saying a berachah acharonah), dips it in vinegar or salt water, and distributes similar pieces to all assembled at the Seder. Then the following berachah is recited with the intention that it refers also to the maror which will be eaten later on:

❧ **BLESSED** be You, Hashem our God, King of the universe, Who creates the fruit of the earth.

In some communities, the custom is to eat the karpas while reclining, while in some communities they do not recline.

יַחַץ

The leader of the Seder then takes the middle matzah
and breaks it in two. The larger portion is hidden away
for the afikoman, while the smaller portion is to
be replaced between the two whole matzos.

מַגִּיד

Before beginning the narrative part of the Haggadah,
everyone should have in mind that it is his intention to
fulfill his obligation to recount the Exodus from Egypt.
The narrative should be read or explained in a language
that is understood by all those assembled at the
Seder, including the women and the children.
Upon beginning the narrative, the leader of the Seder
displays the broken piece of matzah to those assembled
and recites the following (many lift the entire Seder
plate in order to display the uncovered matzos thereon
and some first remove the zeroa and the egg):

הָא לַחְמָא עַנְיָא דִּי אֲכָלוּ אַבְהָתָנָא
בְּאַרְעָא דְמִצְרָיִם. כָּל דִּכְפִין יֵיתֵי
וְיֵכֻל. כָּל דִּצְרִיךְ יֵיתֵי וְיִפְסַח. הָשַׁתָּא הָכָא
לְשָׁנָה הַבָּאָה בְּאַרְעָא דְיִשְׂרָאֵל. הָשַׁתָּא עַבְדֵי
לְשָׁנָה הַבָּאָה בְּנֵי חוֹרִין:

MAGGID. Each year on Pesach one must not only give expression to
the content and significance of the event of redemption by
performing the symbolic observances — such as chametz and matzah
— but also revive in one's heart the memory of the event of liberation
by word of mouth. By the power of the living, spoken word, we take to

56

Yachatz

*The leader of the Seder then takes the middle matzah
and breaks it in two. The larger portion is hidden away
for the afikoman, while the smaller portion is to
be replaced between the two whole matzos.*

Maggid

*Before beginning the narrative part of the Haggadah,
everyone should have in mind that it is his intention to
fulfill his obligation to recount the Exodus from Egypt.
The narrative should be read or explained in a language
that is understood by all those assembled at the
Seder, including the women and the children.
Upon beginning the narrative, the leader of the Seder
displays the broken piece of matzah to those assembled
and recites the following (many lift the entire Seder
plate in order to display the uncovered matzos thereon
and some first remove the zeroa and the egg):*

THIS is the bread of dependence which our fathers ate in the land of Egypt. Whoever is hungry, let him come and eat; whoever is in need, let him come and celebrate the Pesach. This year we are here; next year may we be in the Land of Yisrael. This year we are in bondage; next year may we be free men.

heart the full import of the event of the Exodus, wherein God's might was revealed and which forms the basis for the existence of Yisrael. Most importantly, we make it penetrate the hearts of the members of our family — and especially our little children — as the foundation for the knowledge of God and the basis for all their lives.

The Holy One, blessed be He, requires us, as Jewish parents, to always infuse our young children with the Torah of Yisrael and its spirit. We are to bring them at a tender age to God and to imbue them with a Jewish soul, which shall be aflame with Jewish living and be a part of the Jewish destiny. This night, however, the night on which we celebrate our birthday in history and the commencement of our role as Jews, has been especially designated by God for the dedication of our little children. The survival of our people, as well as the continuation and flowering of the relationship which began at the time of the Exodus, depend on their sanctification. And now, when we share the unleavened bread with them, thereby taking part in the mission of Jewish dedication, let there be no dearth of words emanating from our hearts. Let our hearts be permeated with the consciousness of our noble role as Jewish parents. We must teach the meaning of this unleavened bread, the spirit of this Festival and the significance of this great event, so that our children thereby become aware of the mission of Yisrael.

The Torah is by no means satisfied that we should educate our children by wordless rote alone, by mere external acts, lacking inner spiritual meaning. We will only have fulfilled half our duty if the Divine commandments become a mere matter of routine to our children. We must draw from the wellsprings of the Torah and allow our children to absorb it.

Our Sages instituted the execution of this duty on the night of Pesach, in its entire scope. They even prepared for us the Order of the Pesach Eve, and provided us with a Haggadah, to guide us in the fulfillment of this mitzvah.

BREAD OF DEPENDENCE. This term accurately expresses the significance of matzah, for matzah is the bread of the slave, entirely dependent upon and subjugated by others.

Our oppressors denied us even the time for our dough to rise. Because of the heavy burden the taskmaster placed upon us, we were unable to prepare our bread properly; for fear of the lash, we were compelled to bake it hurriedly. Therefore we still refer to the matzah as "the bread of dependence which our fathers ate in the land of Egypt." This, then, is the meaning of the Torah commandment, "...seven days shall you eat unleavened bread, the bread of dependence..." (*Devarim* 16:3).

The Torah continues: "...for in haste did you come forth out of the land of Egypt, so that you may remember the day when you came forth out of the land of Egypt all the days of your life" (*ibid.*). It was in a hurry too that we left Egypt, and our entire departure therefrom bore the mark of חפזון, "being hurried on." The hand of God bore down heavily on the Egyptians. In the past, they had refused us a respite of even three days; now they *chased* us out to freedom. But still they denied us the time to bake our bread properly, just as they had during the days of our slavery. In truth, even at the moment of redemption, we remained slaves. Liberation was not achieved through our own efforts — we received it from God *through our oppressors.* Our oppressors were being hurried, and so were we: they were pressed on by God, and we, in turn, were pressed on by them. "And the Egyptians were forcible with the people to send them out of the land urgently, for they said: 'We be all dead men.'" "...because they were driven out of Egypt and could not tarry, neither had they prepared any provisions for themselves" (*Shemos* 12:33,39). On this fateful day in human history, only God acted freely.

This fact, that even at the moment of liberation we were subject to the will of others and *forced* to depart, stamps the Exodus with the seal of the Almighty and defines it as purely an act of God. This is what transforms the prohibition of chametz and the commandment to eat matzah into a symbol of such compelling scope. Were it not for this symbol, Yisrael's descendents might have regarded the event as no more than a human occurrence similar to so many events in world history, merely a victorious revolt of our forefathers. We know that 600,000 armed men went out of Egypt. Surely, then, the liberation could hardly be deemed so miraculous; what was miraculous was that they had tolerated such cruel oppression for so long! The matzah, however, serves as a reminder that our forefathers were *driven* from Egypt, *chased* out in such haste that they were unable to bake proper bread. Had they been truly "liberated," truly independent, they would certainly have chosen to delay their departure long enough for their dough to rise, so that during the difficult journey ahead they could partake of "rich man's bread." But freedom of choice was beyond them. Even at the moment of their departure, they were subject to the will of their taskmasters.

And presiding over both — as over a mother and child at the time of birth — stood God alone, commanding in His Omnipotence.

*The second cup is then poured. Some have the custom
to cover the matzos, some move the Seder plate to the
other end of the table, and some remove it from the table
completely, while others do none of these. And now the
youngest child (or, if there are no children present, the
wife or some other adult present) asks
the Four Questions:*

מַה נִּשְׁתַּנָּה הַלַּיְלָה הַזֶּה מִכָּל־
הַלֵּילוֹת. שֶׁבְּכָל הַלֵּילוֹת אָנוּ
אוֹכְלִין חָמֵץ וּמַצָּה הַלַּיְלָה הַזֶּה כֻּלּוֹ מַצָּה.

**THE SECOND CUP IS THEN POURED... AND NOW THE
YOUNGEST CHILD ASKS.** In what way is man's superiority over beast
manifest? It would not be wrong to say: "Man questions."
Undoubtedly, the very first reaction of a newborn child to the sight of
the world is: "What is this?" The human spirit seeks to understand
what is happening around it and the question, "What is this?" arises
in the child's heart even before his mouth can articulate the words. If
only we could read the expression in his eyes, we could understand the
query in his mind. Questioning sums up the entire nature of the
child's soul, and only because his soul continues to ask incessantly,
does the child learn so much in his first years.

Later, when the child's mouth can serve his soul and he continues
to ask and ask untiringly, "What is this?" we must not tire of
answering. We must look upon this thirst for knowledge as a healthy
sign and devote the same willingness and painstaking care with
which we satisfy our children's hunger for food, to quenching their
thirst for knowledge, thus providing them with mental nourishment.
Should we not, then, exert ourselves to satisfy their inquiring souls?
Should we not examine, not recognize all that our children come in

*The second cup is then poured. Some have the custom
to cover the matzos, some move the Seder plate to the
other end of the table, and some remove it from the table
completely, while others do none of these. And now the
youngest child (or, if there are no children present, the
wife or some other adult present) asks
the Four Questions:*

❦ **WHY** is this night different from all other nights? On all other nights, we may eat leavened or unleavened bread; tonight we must eat only matzah.

contact with so that we will be able to teach them and supply adequate answers to their questions?

Let us not imagine that when the child begins to attend school, answering his questions will become the province of the teacher, not the parent. Let us, rather, enter the school, where the child's soul is nurtured. It is easy to identify those children who received answers at home to their childish questions, who did not raise the question: "What is this?" in vain, whose fathers and especially whose mothers chatted with their children, satisfied their thirst for knowledge and properly cultivated their minds. These are the fortunate ones! While other women delighted in idle gossip, or wasted time at the theater and at parties, the mothers of these children derived satisfaction from the company of their children, and occupied the time being their teachers and educators. Whatever their sons and daughters are destined to be as adults, the best and noblest in them will not have been acquired through their school, but through the pre-school education received in their mother's company.

It is also easy to identify those children whose parents lacked the patience or desire or sufficient understanding to spend time with their

שֶׁבְּכָל הַלֵּילוֹת אָנוּ אוֹכְלִין שְׁאָר יְרָקוֹת הַלַּיְלָה הַזֶּה מָרוֹר. שֶׁבְּכָל הַלֵּילוֹת אֵין אָנוּ מַטְבִּילִין אֲפִילוּ פַּעַם אֶחָת הַלַּיְלָה הַזֶּה שְׁתֵּי פְעָמִים. שֶׁבְּכָל הַלֵּילוֹת אָנוּ אוֹכְלִין בֵּין יוֹשְׁבִין וּבֵין מְסֻבִּין הַלַּיְלָה הַזֶּה כֻּלָּנוּ מְסֻבִּין:

In some communities, the leader of the Seder repeats the Four Questions.

children. These children, too, asked questions in their infancy, but when they received no answers, they stopped asking, and became indifferent to objects and events. And so they developed other tendencies, very different from the desire to know. They will attend school for years and years, but they will never acquire that which their parents, through neglect, failed to provide.

Accordingly, we should not feel annoyed when a child asks questions, even when he asks the same questions repeatedly and frequently. We must not answer him reprovingly and we must take care to answer him correctly, not to distort reality with fairy tales and foolish fantasies. He may ask a question to which we do not know the answer, or the answer is one which he is unable to grasp, should not know or is not generally known. Through the reply we give him he should realize that there are limits to his childish understanding and limitations to the human intellect in general. It is important for him to realize this, too: that there are things we do not know. But we must not nourish his soul with folly, nor let others do so. We should allow the child to stay near to us, and wherever we may be, create there a healthy atmosphere for his soul.

On all other nights, we may eat all kinds of vegetables; tonight we must eat bitter herbs. On all other nights, we are not required to dip even once; tonight we are required to dip twice. On all other nights, we may eat either sitting or reclining; tonight we must all recline.

In some communities, the leader of the Seder repeats the Four Questions.

This is especially valid and important in the area of our children's Jewish education. For after all, God is the legislator of our lives; he has communicated to us the truths and facts on which we build our lives. But He did not entrust these truths and facts to our rational understanding and verbal acknowledgement alone. For every truth that He impressed upon our rational consciousness, for every fact that He commanded us to embody in our lives, He instituted acts perceptible to our senses. These, indeed, will arouse and revive in our hearts recognition of the truths and reminders of the facts. From these acts, too, we learn of the nature of these truths and facts. They are not the mere repetition of some catechism, but the very basis of our entire lives and actions. The spirit of Yisrael and its actions will only be transmitted from generation to generation through these acts. Here, at this point in the Seder, the father performs them in the presence of his son. The son, in turn, approaches and asks: "What is this?" At that moment, he will hear the answers from his father, who is joyfully performing the deeds. At that moment, the son will learn the truths and facts to which these commandments testify.

עֲבָדִים הָיִינוּ לְפַרְעֹה בְּמִצְרָיִם. וַיּוֹצִיאֵנוּ יהוה אֱלֹהֵינוּ מִשָּׁם בְּיָד חֲזָקָה וּבִזְרוֹעַ נְטוּיָה. וְאִלּוּ לֹא

WE WERE SLAVES UNTO PHARAOH IN EGYPT. God foretold our slavery in Egypt to our patriarch, Avraham, long before it was actually to occur. In the vision of the "Covenant between the Portions," He detailed three characteristics of our future bondage.*

"And He said unto Avram: 'Know for sure that your seed shall be a *stranger* in a land that is not theirs, and they will *enslave* them and *afflict* them four hundred years'" (*Bereishis* 15:13). Our bondage was to be characterized by:

1) גרות — alienage: we were dispossessed strangers, stateless, owning nothing and without rights.
2) עבדות — enslavement: we were powerless to utilize our energy and capabilities.
3) עני — affliction: our bodies were physically afflicted and we were deprived of the joy of living.

Throughout the story of the Exodus from Egypt and upon in-depth study of the mitzvos which God commanded us

---

* See page 88 for a more detailed explanation.

64

*If the matzos were covered or removed, they are now
returned and/or uncovered and are to remain so
throughout the narration of the Hagaddah,
except when the cups of wine are lifted.*

*The narration of the Hagaddah is not said reclining,
but rather in a spirit of awe and fear of
the Almighty.*

WE were slaves unto Pharaoh in Egypt, and Hashem our God took us out from there with a strong hand and an outstretched arm. And if the Holy One, Blessed be

in commemoration of our liberation from bondage, we find demonstrated these three basic aspects of our slavery. Egypt to us was the "house of bondage," because there we were born into a slave caste. The fact that, once upon a time, we had been free men and that this freedom had been taken away had long been forgotten. Slavery was now considered our natural state — socially, we were at the point of extinction. At this moment of impending ruin, God called us out to freedom and independence.

This fact alone attests to our unique, complete "belonging" to God. More than any other nation, we owe to God whatever we possess — head, heart and hand. All that the Egyptians had denied us was restored to us by God Himself: our personal individuality (עִנּוּי), the right to acquire possessions (עֲבֹדוֹת), and the possessions themselves (גֵּרוּת). Consequently, we are beholden exclusively to Him. To His service we totally dedicate our bodies, capabilities and possessions, and we acknowledge Him as the Guide for all of our actions.

It was only this total subservience to God which freed us from human servitude. Only on this condition were we liberated and granted our independence. Whereas all other persons and nations are indebted to God for their creation and their physical existence, we are

65

הוֹצִיא הַקָּדוֹשׁ בָּרוּךְ הוּא אֶת אֲבוֹתֵינוּ
מִמִּצְרַיִם. הֲרֵי אָנוּ וּבָנֵינוּ וּבְנֵי בָנֵינוּ.
מְשֻׁעְבָּדִים הָיִינוּ לְפַרְעֹה בְּמִצְרָיִם. וַאֲפִילוּ
כֻּלָּנוּ חֲכָמִים. כֻּלָּנוּ נְבוֹנִים. כֻּלָּנוּ זְקֵנִים. כֻּלָּנוּ
יוֹדְעִים אֶת הַתּוֹרָה. מִצְוָה עָלֵינוּ לְסַפֵּר
בִּיצִיאַת מִצְרָיִם. וְכָל הַמַּרְבֶּה לְסַפֵּר בִּיצִיאַת
מִצְרַיִם הֲרֵי זֶה מְשֻׁבָּח:

מַעֲשֶׂה בְּרַבִּי אֱלִיעֶזֶר וְרַבִּי יְהוֹשֻׁעַ וְרַבִּי
אֶלְעָזָר בֶּן־עֲזַרְיָה וְרַבִּי עֲקִיבָא וְרַבִּי טַרְפוֹן שֶׁהָיוּ
מְסֻבִּין בִּבְנֵי־בְרַק וְהָיוּ מְסַפְּרִים בִּיצִיאַת מִצְרָיִם

indebted to Him for our historical and social existence, too. We
experienced an Exodus from servitude to Pharaoh only to become
slaves of the Almighty; only thus have we truly become masters. In
our National Anthem of Hallel we chant: "...I am Your servant, only
as the son of Your handmaid, o' You Who has now loosened my
bonds" (*Tehillim* 116:16). The meaning of this passage is: The reason
I am Your servant from birth is because You have freed me from my
previous bonds.

On Pesach, when we commemorate our freedom and independence
from the yoke of man, we symbolize the "yoke of the Heavenly
Kingdom" which we accepted in its place. The Torah commands us
to remember the day we left Egypt by not eating chametz — any

He, had not taken our fathers out of Egypt, then we, our children, and our children's children would still have been enslaved to Pharaoh in Egypt. Therefore, even if we were all wise, all understanding, all experienced, and all versed in the Torah, we would nevertheless be obligated to recount the story of the departure from Egypt; and he who elaborates upon the story of the departure from Egypt is worthy of praise.

It happened that Rabbi Eliezer, Rabbi Yehoshua, Rabbi Elazar ben Azaryah, Rabbi Akiva and Rabbi Tarfon were reclining [at the Seder table] in Bnei Berak, and were recounting the story of the departure from Egypt. They continued the entire

leavened products.* Actually, there are three parts to this prohibition: 1) we may not eat leavened products; 2) we may not derive any use from them; and 3) we may not have them in our possession. These three divisions relate directly to the three aspects of slavery from which God freed us. We do not *eat* chametz to indicate that our bodily needs are dedicated to God. We derive no *use* from chametz to show that it was through Him that we acheived the opportunity to use our capabilities. Finally, we do not keep any chametz in our *possession* to make it clear that all that we own comes from God and, thus, belongs only to Him.

---

* See page 3 for an in-depth explanation.

כָּל־אוֹתוֹ הַלַּיְלָה עַד שֶׁבָּאוּ תַלְמִידֵיהֶם וְאָמְרוּ לָהֶם.
רַבּוֹתֵינוּ הִגִּיעַ זְמַן קְרִיאַת שְׁמַע שֶׁל שַׁחֲרִית:

THE RECITAL OF THE MORNING SHEMA. Our knowledge of God's existence is based not on hearing, but on seeing — the actual visual perception experienced by our national community, as Moshe said to Yisrael: "You have been brought to know by seeing that Hashem alone is God; there is none else beside Him" (*Devarim* 4:35). This open revelation, such visible interference in earthly matters, was wrought by God only once — at the time that He laid the foundation for the creation of His People — so that they might relay testimony of this revelation from one generation to the next, from community to community, as the incontestable premise, the tradition on which every son of Yisrael bases the structure of his thinking and his actions.

Henceforth we are not told: "See, o' Yisrael," but "Hear, o' Yisrael." Neither natural occurrences nor personal experiences are to bring the individual to form his own conclusions of the existence of God. Far beyond any theory based upon speculative inferences and deductions, God manifested His existence and his Providence here on Earth, beyond the possibility of a doubt, to the sensory perceptions of the community of our fathers in its entirety, so that they should transmit — so that they should *tell* — to their children the evidence of what they had witnessed. They *saw* God affecting nature and history when He broke their bonds in Egypt and led them through the desert to the Promised Land. They *heard* His voice when He spoke to them on Mount Sinai. This testimony, which lies in the hands of the entire community of Yisrael, is the basis for our *knowledge* of God. Not from nature and history are we to deduce a *belief* in God; rather, on the basis of the *knowledge* which was transmitted to us, we are to night until their pupils came and said to them: "Our teachers! The time for the recital of the morning Shema has arrived."

examine nature and history and, thus, to understand natural phenomena and historical events. Then, our eyes will be opened by God to observe Him in nature, and our ears will be attuned to hear His voice in history. We will realize that everything in nature, be it minute or immense, and all events of history, be they incidental or momentous, proclaim God's rule. And, as our fathers did once, we too will perceive God's Providence in our own world; as our fathers did once, we shall walk with God in our own present time, and the Scriptural verse "For they have seen Your ways, o' God, the ways of my God, my King in holiness" (*Tehillim* 68:25) will become applicable to us. Therefore: "Hear, o' Yisrael!"

THE TIME FOR THE RECITAL OF THE MORNING SHEMA. The time for reading the evening Shema is all night, beginning with the appearance of the stars, until dawn. The time for the morning Shema is from the beginning of the day "when one is able to recognize his friend at a distance of four cubits away" and lasts until the first half of the morning, that is to say, until three-twelfths of the daytime (*Berachos* 2a, 8b, 9a). We are commanded to renew our affirmation of the Oneness of God at night, during the time when people sleep, and in the morning when people rise to begin the day's activities. In addition to affirming his Oneness, we must at these times consider how this Oneness affects our lives. The Shema at night inspires us with trust in the One Who directs our *fate*, the Shema in the morning with joy in obeying the One Who directs our *deeds*.

אָמַר רַבִּי אֶלְעָזָר בֶּן־עֲזַרְיָה. הֲרֵי אֲנִי כְּבֶן שִׁבְעִים שָׁנָה. וְלֹא זָכִיתִי שֶׁתֵּאָמֵר יְצִיאַת מִצְרַיִם בַּלֵּילוֹת. עַד שֶׁדְּרָשָׁהּ בֶּן זוֹמָא. שֶׁנֶּאֱמַר לְמַעַן תִּזְכֹּר אֶת יוֹם צֵאתְךָ מֵאֶרֶץ מִצְרַיִם כֹּל יְמֵי חַיֶּיךָ. יְמֵי חַיֶּיךָ הַיָּמִים. כֹּל יְמֵי חַיֶּיךָ הַלֵּילוֹת. וַחֲכָמִים אוֹמְרִים. יְמֵי חַיֶּיךָ הָעוֹלָם הַזֶּה. כֹּל יְמֵי חַיֶּיךָ לְהָבִיא לִימוֹת הַמָּשִׁיחַ:

AND I DID NOT SUCCEED IN PROVING THAT THE DEPARTURE MUST BE MENTIONED AT NIGHT. In *Devarim*, we are given the commandment for the daily remembrance of yetzias Mitzrayim:

"...so that you may remember the day when you came forth out of the land of Egypt all the *days* of your life..." (16:3). The Mishnah teaches us that this verse includes mention of the Exodus at night as well (*Berachos* 12b), this duty being implied by the added word "all" in "all the days of your life."

Earlier we are told expressly that Hashem "brought you out from Egypt in the night" (*Devarim* 16:1), and while the actual Exodus took place in the daytime (see *Bemidbar* 33:3), the redemption itself had already been accomplished the preceding night (*Berachos* 9a). Why then should it be necessary to provide special Scriptural proof for mentioning the Exodus at night? The necessity for providing such proof would imply that the recalling of yetzias Mitzrayim applies primarily to the daytime. This implication may well afford us valuable insight into the significance of this mitzvah.

Both the passive and the active aspects of our lives — our destiny and our deeds — have their basis in yetzias Mitzrayim. From that event, we derive our trust in Hashem regarding our fate and the awareness of our obligations to Him regarding our deeds. Our trust in Hashem, in His direction of our fate, expresses itself mainly during the dark periods of the nights of our lives; the submission of our actions to His discipline, must be proven during the working hours of the daytime.

Superficial reflection might lead us to conclude that, from the Exodus, we are mainly to learn trust in Hashem's Providence, and apply the commandment of remembering the departure from Egypt

Said Rabbi Elazar ben Azaryah: "Behold! I am like a man of seventy years old, and I did not succeed in proving that the Departure must be mentioned at night, until ben Zoma explained that the Torah states... 'so that you may remember the day when you came forth out of the land of Egypt *all* the days of your life' (*Devarim* 16:3). 'The days of your life' refers to the daytime. '*All* the days of your life' — includes nighttime as well. But the Sages say 'the days of your life' indicates your life in the present; '*all* the days of your life' refers to the time of the Mashiach as well."

primarily during the night. Jewish thinking, however, realizes that it is far easier to trust in Hashem during the darkness of our fate than it is to remain faithful to our obligations in the bright sunlight of our active daily work. It follows that the constant renewal of our awareness of our duties as Jews is of infinitely greater importance and that the primary emphasis of the reciting of the Shema must be on the day. Rabbi Elazar had no doubt on this point. He was simply looking for an allusion in the text to make this command applicable also for the nighttime, and he found it in the additional word "all."

The other Sages interpret this phrase as including the Messianic era as well; that is to say, the obligation to mention the Exodus will never be rescinded, even in the time of the Mashiach. True, it is stated of the Messianic redemption: "Therefore, behold the days come, says Hashem, that they shall no more say, 'As Hashem lives, Who brought the Children of Yisrael up out of the land of Egypt,' but 'As Hashem lives, Who brought up and Who led the seed of the House of Yisrael, out of the north country and out of all the countries where I had driven them'..." (*Yirmeyahu* 23:7-8). These words, however, do not mean that the mention of the Exodus will altogether be abolished, but that "the subjugation of the other kingdoms will have primacy and the Exodus will become subordinate" (*Berachos* 12b). That is, the ingathering of the exiles and the cessation of Yisrael's subjugation by other kingdoms will now furnish the primary basis for our obligations. For, indeed, the Messianic era merely represents the completion of the edifice, the foundation of which was laid in Egypt. Only in the days of the Mashiach will Yisrael rise to the culmination of the mission it undertook at the time of the going out from Egypt.

בָּרוּךְ הַמָּקוֹם. בָּרוּךְ הוּא. בָּרוּךְ שֶׁנָּתַן תּוֹרָה לְעַמּוֹ יִשְׂרָאֵל.

בָּרוּךְ הוּא.

כְּנֶגֶד אַרְבָּעָה בָנִים דִּבְּרָה תוֹרָה. אֶחָד חָכָם. וְאֶחָד רָשָׁע. וְאֶחָד תָּם. וְאֶחָד שֶׁאֵינוֹ יוֹדֵעַ לִשְׁאוֹל:
חָכָם מַה הוּא אוֹמֵר. מָה הָעֵדוֹת וְהַחֻקִּים וְהַמִּשְׁפָּטִים אֲשֶׁר צִוָּה יְהוָה אֱלֹהֵינוּ אֶתְכֶם. וְאַף אַתָּה אֱמָר־לוֹ כְּהִלְכוֹת הַפֶּסַח. אֵין מַפְטִירִין אַחַר הַפֶּסַח אֲפִיקוֹמָן:
רָשָׁע מַה הוּא אוֹמֵר. מָה הָעֲבוֹדָה הַזֹּאת לָכֶם. לָכֶם וְלֹא לוֹ. וּלְפִי שֶׁהוֹצִיא אֶת־עַצְמוֹ מִן הַכְּלָל כָּפַר בְּעִקָּר. וְאַף אַתָּה הַקְהֵה אֶת־שִׁנָּיו וֶאֱמָר־ לוֹ בַּעֲבוּר זֶה עָשָׂה יְהוָה לִי בְּצֵאתִי מִמִּצְרָיִם. לִי וְלֹא לוֹ. אִלּוּ הָיָה שָׁם לֹא הָיָה נִגְאָל:

BLESSED BE THE OMNIPRESENT, BLESSED BE HE! ... THE TORAH SPOKE CONCERNING FOUR SONS:* The Torah takes into account the wise, inquisitive son as well as the son who has forsaken and scorns his faith. It considers the guileless son, simply inquiring, and the one who merely gazes in astonishment. It knows the discerning youth as well as the one who has gone astray; it considers adolescence

* In Rabbi Hirsch's original essay, "The Four Sons," the order of the sons reflects the child's development: the son who does not know how to ask, the simple son, the wise son, and, finally, the wicked son whose educational training was not successful. This order is in accordance with Hirsch's educational method: first one must train the child to perform the mitzvos as unquestionable dictates of God, and only afterwards may the child ask, "What is this?" Then the father can proceed to explain to him the significance of the mitzvos.

72

§ **BLESSED** be the Omnipresent, Blessed be He! Blessed be He Who has given the Torah to His people Yisrael, Blessed be He.

The Torah spoke about four sons: one wise, one wicked, one simple, and one who does not know how to ask.

The wise son — what does he say? "What are the testimonies, the statutes, and the social ordinances which Hashem our God has commanded you?" (see *Devarim* 6:20). As for you, instruct him regarding the laws of the Pesach: "After the Pesach offering, no dessert is to be eaten!"

The wicked son — what does he say? "What is this service to you?" (see *Shemos* 12:26) To *you* — but not to *him*! Since he has excluded himself from the community, he has denied the essentials of our faith. Therefore, you should blunt his teeth, and say to him: "It is because of this [service] that Hashem acted for me when I came forth out of Egypt" (see *Shemos* 13:8). For *me* — but not for *him*! Had he been there, he would not have been redeemed.

and childhood. Blessed be He: He has foreseen everything and prepared His Law for every eventuality. And precisely for this reason, His Law is eternal, as is His people. It accompanies Yisrael in all stages of its development.

Times may come when youngsters will mock their elders, saying: "What is this service to you?" Yet this, too, shall pass, and youth will again seek knowledge and eagerly ask about "the testimonies, the statutes, and the social ordinances which Hashem, our God has commanded you" to transmit to us. It will be a time when young and old will rally around the *one* principle: "And it will remain a righteous duty to us that we scrupulously perform this entire commandment before Hashem our God, as He has commanded us" (*Devarim* 6:25).

תָּם מַה הוּא אוֹמֵר. מַה זֹּאת. וְאָמַרְתָּ אֵלָיו
בְּחֹזֶק יָד הוֹצִיאָנוּ יהוה מִמִּצְרַיִם מִבֵּית־עֲבָדִים.
וְשֶׁאֵינוֹ יוֹדֵעַ לִשְׁאוֹל אַתְּ פְּתַח לוֹ. שֶׁנֶּאֱמַר
וְהִגַּדְתָּ לְבִנְךָ בַּיּוֹם הַהוּא לֵאמֹר בַּעֲבוּר זֶה עָשָׂה
יהוה לִי בְּצֵאתִי מִמִּצְרָיִם:

THE WISE SON — WHAT DOES HE SAY. The query of the wise son is mentioned in the Torah as follows: "When your son asks you in time to come: 'What are the testimonies, the statutes and the social ordinances which Hashem our God has commanded you?' Then you shall say to your son: 'We were slaves unto Pharaoh in Egypt, and Hashem brought us out of Egypt with a mighty Hand. And Hashem gave signs and great and painful convincing deeds on Egypt, on Pharaoh and on all his household before our eyes. And us He has brought out from there that He might bring us home to give to us the land which he had sworn to our fathers. And Hashem commanded us to fulfill all these statutes, to fear Hashem our God, for our happiness all the days, to preserve us living as we are today. And it will remain a righteous duty to us that we scrupulously perform this entire commandment, before Hashem our God, as He has commanded us" (*Devarim* 6:20-25).

It is our mature son who is presented to us here. He has recognized that Hashem is his God and understands the rapport between God and Yisrael. He calls Him *our* God. This son is already familiar with the Divine laws from daily practice: he knows that he must distinguish among edos, chukim, and mishpatim; those laws which serve as a solemn reminder and instruct in the practices which accompany us on our journey through life, those which serve to keep our strivings and our senses within the boundaries of purity and sanctity, and those which regulate our social life according to the requirements of justice.

Moreover, he knows the source which can supply him with comprehensive information about these laws. He turns not only to manuscripts or books for his answers, but to his elders for their tradition. He asks his father about the precepts that God — his God as

74

The simple son — what does he say? "What is this?" (see *Shemos* 13:14). And you shall say to him: "By strength of Hand did Hashem bring us out from Egypt, from the house of bondage" (*ibid.*).

As for the son who does not know how to ask — you must begin the conversation with him, as it is stated in the Torah: "And you shall relate to your child on that day, saying: 'It is because of this that Hashem acted for me when I came forth out of Egypt'" (*Shemos* 13:8).

well as his father's — has commanded to be transmitted to him and to all future generations.

His question, however, includes no reference whatsoever to the Festival of Pesach and its commandments. The word "Pesach" is not mentioned once, either in his question or in the sentences preceding it. He is asking to learn. He would like to know the testimonies, statutes and social ordinances which God gave to the fathers to pass on to their sons. He simply wants to learn Torah. But the answer he receives is: "We were slaves unto Pharaoh in Egypt...".

By this reply, the Torah provides the key to the correct attitude to the study of Mishnah and Talmud. There is no point in sitting at the feet of one's father and teachers unless one shares with them the common premise, the experience of yetzias Mitzrayim. This reply means that it is useless to pore over volumes unless one is infused with the spirit requisite for the study and understanding of the laws: reverence for God. "The fear of God precedes wisdom" (see *Avos* 3:9) reads the motto over the portals of the sanctuary of Torah learning. Fear of God is one's passport to knowledge.

If one is a Jew, if he considers himself the son of those whom Hashem took out of Egypt with a mighty Hand, *elevating* them to *His* service and revealing to them His work on earth then, for this soul, all of His edos, chukim, and mishpatim will essentially become chukim. Indeed, this is the only term of the three used in the father's answer. All are chukim to him — immutable laws, unalterable because they are securely anchored in the Will of God, his Master. And then, too, it will become obvious that remaining "a righteous duty to us" means that one must scrupulously perform His "entire commandment" *exactly* as He has commanded it to us.

Only under these conditions may one enter His sanctuary, learn, study, think, investigate and pray to Him to teach one the wonders of His law — All of one's learning, studying, thinking, investigating, and penetrating into the secrets of His Law will only serve to make the devotion of one's practice more complete. It will only serve to increase the blessedness of one's service and to cement the bond of his obedience more firmly. — The deeper one penetrates, the higher he will set his aims: the more one investigates, the humbler he will become, and the more reverently he will bow before the sublimity of God's Torah. Whether one comprehends a particular mitzvah or whether it remains a riddle to him — he will fulfill all of them with the same reverence and the same joy. This is the meaning of: "And it will remain a righteous duty to us that we scrupulously perform this entire commandment...as He has commanded us."

The prerequisite, then, for limud haTorah is yetzias Mitzrayim, with all that it implies. Yetzias Mitzrayim led to נעשה ונשמע, the ancient Jewish devotion which, in the eyes of the cynical apikoris branded us as "a rash people, whose mouth preceded [their] ears" (*Shabbos* 88a). No matter — let us remain "rash"; they do not understand that the precedence given to *we shall do* over *we shall listen* is based on the experience of yetzias Mitzrayim. Little do they realize the rocklike basis for our uncritical acceptance of all the mitzvos: the unique, momentous, earth shattering experience which transformed our whole existence and raised us up "on eagles' wings" (see *Shemos* 19:4) to an entirely different level of perception.

Our Rabbis, too, interpret the reply to the wise son in this sense. The *Mechilta* (the Tannaic halachic explanation on *Shemos*) states: "What does the wise son say? 'What are the testimonies, the statutes, and the social ordinances which Hashem our God has commanded you?' As for you, instruct him regarding the laws of the Pesach (variant reading: like the laws of Pesach): 'After the Pesach offering, no dessert is to be eaten.'" Although his question does not refer to Pesach at all, his instruction begins with the laws of the Festival.

Let his study of the Torah begin with the laws of Pesach (or, according to the variant reading: begin speaking to him as on the Seder evening "We were slaves...") and tell him: "No dessert after the Pesach! The very last of the Pesach laws teaches you this: We must eat the Pesach lamb until we are satiated. We must use it to fulfill all our needs and to find our satisfaction. After being satiated by the Pesach, let us not negate its meaning; rather, let us take the idea of Pesach, of yetzias Mitzrayim, into our lives and, thus, illuminate all our paths by its light."

THE WICKED SON — WHAT DOES HE SAY. The question of the wicked son is mentioned as follows: "And then, when your children say to you: 'What is this service to you?' You shall say: 'It is a meal of a salvation performed through a hesitating pass-over, dedicated to Hashem Who hesitated as He passed over the houses of the Children of Yisrael in Egypt when He mortally smote the Egyptians and our houses He saved…" (*Shemos* 12:26-27).

God's message was not intended only for the innocent, wondering child, the inquiring boy, the searching young man. The Torah is not prepared only for those times when children grow up harmoniously following their parents' example, prepared to enter the portals of Torah learning with the instruction received at their father's table. It also foresees times when the bond between the generations will be severed, times when the younger generation not only will refrain from participating in the festive celebration and observances of their parents and refuse to accept from them that which is holy, but will regard it as their function to criticize their elders for living according to these observances and to undermine with biting sarcasm their parents' loyalty to their religion. The Torah foresees these times, when the father will be seated at the Seder in solemn joy while the "progressive" son will pass by, mocking, with the heartrending challenge: "What is this service to you?", which the Talmud Yerushalmi interprets as: "What is this bother with which you burden us every year!" (*Pesachim* 10:4).

The Sages in one opinion exclaim on this: "Evil tidings were brought to our forefathers at that time, namely that the Torah is destined to be forgotten." Others say: "Happy tidings were given to Yisrael at that time, namely that they were destined to see their children and grandchildren" (*Mechilta, Bo* 12:26). These very tidings may be considered good, for they point beyond the defecting children to the returning grandchildren and teach us not to despair in times of apostasy since such periods have also been foreseen by the Torah. The very fact that we are prepared for such times assures us that they will pass and that, in spite of them, the Torah will continue to be transmitted with undiminished vigor.

But how, according to the Torah, should one answer these wayward sons who believe that their apostasy is progressive and who call the loyalty of their fathers "outmoded." To them nothing should be said! The Torah teaches us to answer the bewildered child, the inquiring boy and the searching youth, respectively: "Tell your son," "and you shall say to him," "and you shall say to your son." But concerning the generation of mockers, it does not state: "you shall say *to them.*" It says merely: "You shall say"!

To such a generation there is nothing one can say, for they expect no instruction from anyone. After all, they have "progressed" far beyond their elders, they have advanced sufficiently to be able to teach *them!* They would like to rescue their elders from their antiquated outlook which they think to be burdensome encumbrances and, in their arrogant derision, initiate them into the wantonness and facility of their "progress." What can one tell this son? After all, he does not speak to receive instruction. He is not quite sure enough of himself to be able to listen to a different point of view with impartial tolerance. He still feels so ill at ease that he sees in his father's loyalty to the Torah a personal reproof. He still loves his father too much to be able to witness him caught up in "foolish prejudices."

What can one say to him? One cannot expect him to change his mind as a result of one's words, be they the most brilliant arguments for the Torah, because in his heart of hearts he has lost his belief in the Divine origin of the Torah. One must continue to devote oneself to the belief in the Divine origin of the Law. One will find the profound happiness of his life in this belief. But as for that generation — it might long ago have carried this entire belief to the grave.

The key to unlocking the hearts of this estranged generation rests in the Hands of God. Only experience can bring them back — the experience of emptiness, futility and frustration, the disillusionment with the frivolous things to which they had turned. This experience will ultimately fill their hearts with longing for the lost happiness which the ancient truth had given them and it will lead them to confess: "I will go and return to my first husband for then it was better with me than now" (*Hoshea* 2:9). One will have to wait for that time to arrive.* Till then, one is not to tell them anything; not even to reply to their foolish jeering.

On the other hand, one is not to remain completely silent. The Torah instructs the father not to answer *him* but it most decidedly enjoins him: "You shall say"! The less one has to say to

---

* Today, one hundred years after Rabbi Hirsch's petirah, "that time" has ב"ה arrived.

78

him, the more should one state in general, with great conviction, what the Divine precepts are to *himself*. All the more firmly and decidedly is one to show the joy and satisfaction he finds in fulfilling the mitzvos, all the more firmly and clearly is he to state his certainty in the face of his son's skepticism, his faith in the face of his son's disbelief, his resolve in the face of his son's hesitancy, his vitality in the face of his son's decadence, his serene happiness in the face of his son's vapid and raucous delights.

The more this generation importunes its elders, asking "What is this service to you?", all the more clearly and more emphatically shall their parents' declaration sound: "It is a meal of a salvation performed through a hesitating pass-over, dedicated to Hashem Who hesitated as He passed over the houses of the Children of Yisrael in Egypt when He mortally smote the Egyptians and our houses He saved..." One should state it clearly and forcefully, describing the firm historic basis on which his entire existence as a Jew and his devoted, joyous service to God rests. This foundation will not be shaken by doubt or contradiction and, to this day, the existence of every Jew and every Jewish home attests to it.

One is to speak up, even when all around him remain silent, or when all around him suggest that he should be ashamed of being a Jew. If they try to imply that one should not make his observance of the mitzvos too obvious, that one should not raise his voice on behalf of Torah observance, then one must not remain silent. One must speak up and proclaim aloud that the mitzvos which he fulfills are his most precious possessions, that they constitute the bond between God and himself. One must tell them that even today he dedicates himself and his household to God by performing these mitzvos; just as his fathers did in Egypt, that fulfillment of the mitzvos brings him before God Himself and that, therefore, the approval or disapproval of mortals leaves him totally unmoved.

One must say it loudly — that in his eyes *he* and the others like him are the progressive ones, that the performance of the mitzvos alone signifies progress in his eyes. One must say it aloud that God made His choice of Yisrael conditional upon its performance of the mitzvos. This obedience is what distinguished Yisrael from the Egyptians and set apart the houses of Yisrael from the Egyptian houses. Only because of this did Hashem pass over the houses of Yisrael when He smote the Egyptians. One must proclaim it loudly — that to observe the Divine commandments means to be carried aloft on "eagles' wings," while non-observance of the commandments means to sink back into Egyptian degeneracy, to regress into the Egyptian night from which we were rescued only by Divine mercy.

By making such a clearly proclaimed pronouncement, one can save himself and his children from the depravity of the generation that has gone astray. In addition, this statement will serve as a beacon of light which will enable this generation to find its way back when the time of their repentance arrives.

Our Sages in the *Mechilta* and in the Haggadah, did not construe the sentence "You shall say..." as an *answer* to the mocking son. It is a general statement of truth formulated in the same terms as the preliminary explanation to the bewildered child, the one who does not know how to ask. "It is because of this [service]," *which to you seems a wearisome, needless bother, for the sake of these commandments* "that Hashem acted for me when I came forth out of Egypt"!

The Sages show us that, in dealing with the apostate, one must readdress the fundamentals of faith, the *abc* which constitutes the basis of the Jewish child's first consciousness of Judaism. This is the foundation and its abnegation is tantamount to apostasy. As long as he does not accept this fundamental truth without equivocation or revision — the historical fact that yetzias Mitzrayim constitutes the Divine seal to all our mitzvos and that the fulfillment of these mitzvos is the sole condition for our having been chosen and saved from Egypt — there is no point in having any further discussion with him. Explanations of the mitzvos are only beneficial to the person who still abides by them. The person who has denied the fundamental tenets of Judaism, casts off the yoke of mitzvos and approaches the circle of observant Jews only to mock them, has, simply by virtue of his non-fulfillment of the mitzvos, turned his back on God and on the community of Yisrael.

"Had he been there, he would not have been redeemed." With principles such as his, Yisrael would not have been delivered. All that remains for us to do, is to show this son clearly what he has done — to tell him that, by having "emancipated" himself from the fulfillment of the mitzvos, he has severed the single bond connecting him to God and to the Jewish community and has destroyed the basic condition for our deliverance from Egypt and our election as God's People. Such a firm declaration may be the only thing that can still bring him to his senses.

THE SIMPLE SON — WHAT DOES HE SAY. The question of the simple son is mentioned as follows: "And it shall be when your son asks you in time to come, saying: 'What is this?' you shall say to him: 'By strength of Hand did Hashem bring us out from Egypt, from the house of bondage'" (*Shemos* 13:14).

Let one suppose that, in the education of his child, the father has already prepared in his son's heart the broad basis of a happy, sincere obedience to God's commandments. Let one suppose the son already shares with him the common ground of observing the mitzvos joyfully and respectfully, in the knowledge that they are a sign of our allegiance, a mark of our devotion and obedience to Him and that, in reward, God blesses us with the serenity and protection flowing from His sanctity. Now the child is becoming older and, wishing to obtain a deeper explanation, asks: "What is the significance of these commandments, and why are these particular mitzvos a sign of our homage, devotion and obedience to Hashem?" By all means, one must answer him! One must not avoid such questions. The fact that the very first mitzvos Hashem gave us at the time of the exodus from Egypt — Pesach, matzah, maror, tefillin, bechoros — are so laden with symbolism seems to indicate that Hashem *expects* us to inquire about the significance of His commandments.

True, the simple performance of these acts is the most convincing proof of our worshipful, devoted obedience to God, and obedience alone is sufficient motivation for us to perform the mitzvos at any age and on all levels of understanding. In fact, our closeness to God is contingent purely on the performance of these acts. Nevertheless, at the same time, Hashem did intend these mitzvos to speak to our hearts, to stimulate our thinking and to impress upon us the eternal truths. When we perform the mitzvos, we should be entirely occupied with the thought that we act in obedience to Him, our One and Only Master and Ruler. Nevertheless the act itself should bring us and our children to the searching question of "What is this?" and always give us fresh cause for reflection and investigation into the Divine commandments.

And now, when the performance of these precepts causes one's son to ask "What is this?", one's answer should be: "By strength of Hand did Hashem bring us out from Egypt, from the house of bondage." Hashem led us out of Egypt through *His* power! Our freedom was not achieved by a natural course of events.

Of course, all natural occurrences, too, are subject to God's ever-wakeful eyes and to the guidance of His almighty Hand. But this can only be recognized by someone whose spirit has already been illuminated by God. The unenlightened spirit, the soul which has not been touched by Divine revelation, will miss Hashem's direction in the normal course of events. He believes that everything can be reduced to the principle of causality. Shrugging his shoulders, he will claim, exactly as the Egyptian nature-worshipers did: "Who is Hashem that I should hearken to His voice?" *to release that which, by nature, is mine and which, by the law of the strongest, belongs to me?*

Man sees that the laws of nature operate today exactly as they did yesterday and because of this, it does not occur to him to look for the One Who established these laws. But the very immutability of these laws and their unfathomable depths — are they not the greatest of all wonders? However, because man can understand some of these laws, he conveniently closes his eyes to the many things which remain eternal riddles beyond his grasp.

Perhaps the term "by chance," which comes so readily to human lips, is yet the greatest tribute we unwittingly accord to God's omnipresent Providence, because by this very word "chance," we admit that our understanding is inadequate and our knowledge of natural laws insufficient to explain all phenomena and events.

For us to realize that the laws of nature are not eternal but were established by God their Master Who remained in control of them even after He established them, for us to know that the laws do not exist because He established them once upon a time but, rather, because He still perceives their existence as good, for us to know that "blind necessity" and "pure chance" have no control over us but rather, we are to revere God and only Him for His shaping of the "ordinary course of events" — in order to give man eternal evidence of this truth, God emerged from the boundaries of nature which conceal Him and His actions from the unperceiving eye.

It was for this purpose that He introduced a נס into the midst of the natural order of things, an historical phenomenon that, then and to this day, stands completely contrary to the normal course of events in the way it came about. It rises supremely aloft like a great banner on high (נס literally means banner) and proclaims to all generations: *Know that the earth is Hashem's* and that *Hashem is in the midst of the land* (see *Shemos* 8:18, 9:29). He is immanent in all phenomena and events on earth. He is the personal, living God, acting and causing everything to occur. And this historical miracle, this phenomenon which testifies to God's might, is none other than the existence of the Jewish People — from that first moment when God saw us on the point of death and called out: *Arise and live* — unto this very day.

Where would the "natural course of events" in Egypt have

led us? We would have perished in slavery and abject misery. There, proud concepts of man's moral freedom — the freedom that makes him in a small way resemble God — had been done away with long ago to be replaced by nature-worship, worship which denied man's freedom to act. There, the Egyptians attempted to transform us into a slave caste. When we did go out to freedom, our odds were slim, according to the natural order of things.

We were faced with the arrogant refusal of an absolute despot. The oppression of slavery was intensified to the point of dehumanization, and in our personalities the very last glimmer of self-confidence and courage had been extinguished so that even after our liberation, the mere sight of our former masters was sufficient to impel us to return to our former servitude. As for Moshe — our "liberator," as many would have him — the text indicates that he was the man least suited for this task. He lacked every quality necessary for a national leader, this shy and modest man. "Who am I, that I should approach Pharaoh and lead Yisrael out from Egypt?" "Because I shall be with you!" came the Divine response. "...And just this..." *your very lack of courage and power to fulfill this mission, is the best proof that "I have sent you..."* (see *Shemos* 3:11-12).

So, in every respect, our freedom, our coming into existence is entirely due to the directly intervening Hand of God, which overthrew the entire pattern of cause and effect that would otherwise have brought about our inevitable ruin. This "strength of Hand," the fact that God, by His power, wrested us away from the Egyptians, is the fundamental basis of both our existence as a nation and our service. This "strength of Hand," the miraculous way in which Hashem forcibly took us out of Egypt, proclaims God not only as the Creator, but also as the Ruler of the universe and its Judge, Father and Redeemer in the midst of history. This alone is what makes yetzias Mitzrayim the "finger of God" (see *Shemos* 8:15), pointing over and beyond natural phenomena — to the Almighty; over and beyond blind determinism — to the ever independent Lawgiver; over and beyond wanton obliteration of human potential — to the God Who reigns in love and justice. It is the exodus from Egypt, over and beyond the multitude of forces and powers in nature and history, which guarantees to humanity the One and Only, personal, independent and living God.

Hashem raised us to freedom with His strong Hand. By this act, God, as it is written, "acquired" us (see *Shemos* 15:16), made us belong to Him. This fact is the basis of our special calling. We belong to God in every step we take and every task He assigns us. Everything in us and around us is His. The blood in our veins, every fiber in our nerves, every muscle in our flesh and every sensation in our hearts, the thoughts in our minds, the ground beneath our feet, the air we breathe, every ray of light and every fruit of the soil, every animal and every child — there is nothing we can call our own.

We had lost everything, but He restored it to us for use in His service. We were slaves to mortal beings, but He broke our chains so that we could become *His* servants. For us, there is no other option: Either we remain in His service and are the one people on earth possessing the greatest freedom, or we quit His service and once again fall prey to the vicissitudes of human history. So reads Hashem's answer to Moshe: "When you bring the people out of Egypt, you [and they] shall become the servants of God on this mountain" (*Shemos* 3:12). Yisrael will exchange human chains for the freedom of service to God.

Thus, at the time of the exodus from Egypt, the Almighty gave us mitzvos which express our allegiance, devotion and obedience to Him. Throughout the ages we were always to reaffirm this loyalty. Therefore, He assigned to us the performance of those actions which remind us most emphatically not only of the Exodus itself but of the character of the Exodus, that is, the "strength of Hand," the overwhelming, thoroughly Divine nature of our deliverance. In every one of these mitzvos — chametz and matzah, tefillin, and bechoros — the word "strength of Hand" or "strong Hand" is expressly mentioned. All of these commandments proclaim the fact that our historical origin is exclusively of Divine nature and that, consequently, we belong to God with all our lives and being.

AS FOR THE SON WHO DOES NOT KNOW HOW TO ASK. The answer to the son who does not know how to ask is as follows: "And you shall relate to your child on that day, saying 'It is because of this that Hashem acted for me when I came forth out of Egypt'" (*Shemos* 13:8). The Haggadah continues: "One might think that the obligation to recount the story of the departure from Egypt begins from the first day of the month of Nissan. However, the Torah states: 'on that day.' 'On that *day*' might be understood to mean *while it is still day*. Therefore, the text specifies 'it is because of *this*.' I can say 'it is because of this' only at such time when the matzah and the maror are in front of you."

Jewish education does not begin with speeches about religion.

Preaching will not win over the heart of one's child. Let one lead his son to the table set with matzah and maror. Let him observe how his father fulfills the Divine commandments cheerfully and diligently and, then, though the child is still unable to pose questions and merely looks at his father's actions in vague wonder, his father should begin to explain it to him.

One should "begin the conversation with him" and tell him the reasons for one's rejoicing and the meaning of one's earnestness. One should teach him the significance of the acts which he sees being performed.

Because of this: In other words, the father tells his son, "Not through my courage and might was I redeemed! In fact, I had been toiling for generations, laden with burdens. Powerless, I saw my infants being snatched from their mothers and thrown into the Nile. It was the nation which had enslaved me that excelled in *its* prowess and war-making capability. It was *they* who drove their chariots deep into bordering continents.

"Not through my treasures and riches was I redeemed! In fact, I had remained a stranger for centuries in a foreign land. I had sunk to the most abject level of slavery. There was nothing I could call my own, and when driven out of Egypt, I had to beg for clothing and utensils from my oppressors. The nation which had enslaved me was far wealthier, had thriving agriculture and flourishing trade, and led a life of pleasurable excess.

"Not through my knowledge of the arts and sciences was I redeemed! My sons and daughters had to gather straw and burn bricks under the lash of their tormentors. They had no time to think about culture, they had no leisure time, no spirit or mind to devote to contemplation of the arts and sciences. Alas, they were not even able to listen to the tidings of redemption because of "impatience and cruel bondage" (*Shemos* 6:9). Surely the nation which I slavishly served was far and away more outstanding in every respect, in scholarship and the arts, science and technology. To this very day, the monuments of their civilization, the monuments to my debasement and unspeakable agony, line the banks of the Nile.

"But I was saved 'because of this.' God acted for me because of the mitzvos which I found the courage to fulfill and the spirit to understand and exalt in defiance of my oppressors. These mitzvos raised me up into the realm of the One God Whom their wise men and magicians did not know. Through these mitzvos, I entrusted myself to the One Who thwarted the Egyptians. Through the mitzvos I entered into the service of Hashem. God saw that I fulfilled them in good faith and He descended to save me."

Hashem acted for me: "The mitzvos stood by me during that fateful hour when the Angel of Death passed over my home and went on to the oppressor's palace. With deathlike dread, Pharaoh came to my door and thrust me out into freedom. My hut had been transformed into a temple of the Holy One because I had gathered my children around these precepts, because God had seen the evidence of our devotion to His commands, and He caused death and enslavement to pass over us."

"They *were* my mitzvos — and they *remain* my mitzvos. They are still my way of communicating with God, they are still my pledge of allegiance and the expression of my devotion and obedience. Through them I consecrate myself and all I possess to the service of God, and He still sees my signs, understands my language and takes me and my home into the sphere of His protective peace.

"This is the reason for my joy and my solemnity. I know what the mitzvos mean: they are the eternal bond tying me to God, they are what makes God *my* God. My actions are His; my fate is in His hands. And this is no mere promise, no undefined hope, no mere assurance and consolation.

"I have experienced what these mitzvos mean: God has already acted on my behalf; my own past testifies to their great significance. When God first gave me His mitzvos, He staked my entire deliverance and redemption, life and liberation on their fulfillment."

Now, finally, we come to the eternal significance of *When I came forth out of Egypt*, for "in every single generation one is obligated to look upon himself as if he personally had gone forth out of Egypt..." This is the basic requirement of a child's education. We do not say: "it is because of this that Hashem acted for our nation" or "for our forefathers." We say: "it is because of this that Hashem acted for *me* when *I* came forth out of Egypt."

This is not a story, to be told in the way a father tells his child memories of the past. A father must speak to his child as the representative of the Jewish People and, by thus causing him to identify with his people he will lead him into the covenant of God. One must ensure that his enthusiasm for God is always fresh, never jaded. Then one's child will realize that his father has experienced liberation just as *his* fathers did, that his father is so sure of the tradition which *his* fathers transmitted to *him* that it is as if he had received it himself. The child then realizes that it was his *father's* head the angel of death passed over, his *father's* hand that had been fettered by the slaves' shackles, and it was his *father* whom God liberated in His great redemption. If one celebrates Pesach and performs its mitzvos, not simply as a memorial to an event in history, but as the foundation of one's own existence, then his child will accept from him this ever-renewed heritage of our redemption and consecration and he too will be experiencing the exodus from Egypt and will be receiving God's commandments. And so, the redemption and consecration of Pesach will be renewed from one year to the next, continuing the living bond of His mitzvos to all generations.

In Judaism, education is called חינוך — consecration. In Tanach the same term is used for the education of our children as for the consecration of other sacred possessions to the service of God. The consecration of our altar was concluded by the korban; the consecration of the Kohen by the avodah, the temple service; and the consecration of houses of prayer by the prayer service. In exactly the same way, the education of our children is not accomplished by speeches and invocations but by observance. The education of our children demands the actual performance of the mitzvos. "We shall do" precedes "we shall listen" in all aspects of Judaism, including education.

The mitzvah of education devolves upon the father, whom God has endowed with the necessary abilities. Where a father neglects this duty, no other means can compensate. All the textbooks, all the teaching aids that had been invented as surrogates for the consecration of our youth in the home, will be of no avail. Not even the best teachers and schools can take the place of the Pesach table at which the child observes him in solemn, joyful fulfillment of the mitzvos, at which he allows him to perform these mitzvos with his own hands, saying to him: *Look!* "It is because of this [service] that Hashem acted for me when I came forth out of Egypt."

If one seriously wishes to raise his children as Jews, he will first endeavor to become a truly accomplished Jew himself. It is not his scholarship that will win the heart of his son for God, but rather his sincere, faithful and honest example. One must remember that only "because of this" did God become his God. If one does so, he will indeed attain the joy and solemnity which sanctify every Jew as a priest of God and enable him by virtue of his example to bequeath this sanctity to his children.

יָכוֹל מֵרֹאשׁ חֹדֶשׁ. תַּלְמוּד לוֹמַר בַּיּוֹם הַהוּא. אִי בַּיּוֹם הַהוּא יָכוֹל מִבְּעוֹד יוֹם. תַּלְמוּד לוֹמַר בַּעֲבוּר זֶה. בַּעֲבוּר זֶה לֹא אָמַרְתִּי אֶלָּא בְּשָׁעָה שֶׁיֵּשׁ מַצָּה וּמָרוֹר מֻנָּחִים לְפָנֶיךָ:

מִתְּחִלָּה עוֹבְדֵי עֲבוֹדָה זָרָה הָיוּ אֲבוֹתֵינוּ. וְעַכְשָׁו קֵרְבָנוּ הַמָּקוֹם לַעֲבוֹדָתוֹ. שֶׁנֶּאֱמַר וַיֹּאמֶר יְהוֹשֻׁעַ אֶל־כָּל־הָעָם כֹּה־אָמַר יהוה אֱלֹהֵי יִשְׂרָאֵל בְּעֵבֶר הַנָּהָר יָשְׁבוּ אֲבוֹתֵיכֶם מֵעוֹלָם תֶּרַח אֲבִי אַבְרָהָם וַאֲבִי נָחוֹר וַיַּעַבְדוּ אֱלֹהִים אֲחֵרִים: וָאֶקַּח אֶת־אֲבִיכֶם אֶת־אַבְרָהָם מֵעֵבֶר הַנָּהָר וָאוֹלֵךְ אוֹתוֹ בְּכָל־אֶרֶץ כְּנָעַן וָאַרְבֶּה אֶת זַרְעוֹ וָאֶתֶּן לוֹ אֶת־

I TOOK YOUR FATHER AVRAHAM FROM THE OTHER SIDE OF THE RIVER...AND TO YITZCHAK I GAVE YAAKOV. "On the other side of the river," among hedonistic, polytheistic idol worshipers, Avraham recognized Hashem as being One and Alone. When God called, he abandoned his native land, his birthplace, and his father's house — all that which is most precious to a man's heart — because of his love only for Him. Following the One Who called him, he accepted the vocation to be progenitor of that People through whom "all the families of the earth shall be blessed" (*Bereishis* 12:3) if they, the people, kept the command "that they shall keep the way of Hashem to do benevolence as a duty and justice..." (*ibid.*, 18:19).

This ideal was actualized by Avraham in his own life. He expressed his love for the One and only God through love for His children, his fellow men who were created in the image of God. He cared for them, saved and instructed them whenever and wherever he could, and prayed on their behalf before the Judge of the whole world. And

One might think that the obligation to recount the story of the departure from Egypt begins from the first day of the month of Nissan. However, the Torah states: "on that day."* "On that *day*" might be understood to mean *while it is still day*. Therefore, the text specifies "it is because of *this*." I can say "it is because of this" only at such time when the matzah and the maror are in front of you.

At first our fathers were idol worshipers, but now the Omnipresent has brought us near to His service, as it is said: "And Yehoshua said to all the people: 'Thus said Hashem, the God of Yisrael: "On the other side of the river, your fathers dwelt of old, Terach, father of Avraham and father of Nachor, and they served other gods. And I took your father Avraham from the other side of the river and led him through the whole land of Canaan, and I multiplied

Hashem, for Whom Avraham had left everything and, by following His call, wandered to distant lands, protected him in his wanderings and blessed him. Henceforth, Avraham would receive sustenance and blessing from His Hands alone, and he would utilize these gifts solely for the salvation of the world.

Avraham's love was joined by that unwavering trust which sees everything in life as sustained by the One and Only God and which clings to His promise, no matter how little the present may seem to justify it. Added to these two was a reverent awe of God which allows one, at any time and without complaining, to surrender to the Most High that which is most precious to him, fully aware that it belongs to Him. This spirit and this way of life was bequeathed to Yitzchak his son and to Yaakov his grandson, the former manifesting more prominently in his life the quality of awe, and the latter, that of trust.

---

* See the immediately preceding quote.

יִצְחָק: וָאֶתֵּן לְיִצְחָק אֶת־יַעֲקֹב וְאֶת עֵשָׂו וָאֶתֵּן לְעֵשָׂו אֶת־הַר שֵׂעִיר לָרֶשֶׁת אוֹתוֹ וְיַעֲקֹב וּבָנָיו יָרְדוּ מִצְרָיִם:

בָּרוּךְ שׁוֹמֵר הַבְטָחָתוֹ לְיִשְׂרָאֵל. בָּרוּךְ הוּא. שֶׁהַקָּדוֹשׁ בָּרוּךְ הוּא חִשַּׁב אֶת הַקֵּץ לַעֲשׂוֹת כְּמָה שֶׁאָמַר לְאַבְרָהָם אָבִינוּ בִּבְרִית בֵּין הַבְּתָרִים. שֶׁנֶּאֱמַר וַיֹּאמֶר לְאַבְרָם יָדֹעַ תֵּדַע כִּי־גֵר יִהְיֶה זַרְעֲךָ בְּאֶרֶץ לֹא לָהֶם וַעֲבָדוּם וְעִנּוּ אֹתָם אַרְבַּע מֵאוֹת שָׁנָה: וְגַם אֶת־הַגּוֹי אֲשֶׁר יַעֲבֹדוּ דָּן אָנֹכִי וְאַחֲרֵי כֵן יֵצְאוּ בִּרְכֻשׁ גָּדוֹל:

TO ESAV I GAVE MOUNT SEIR FOR AN INHERITANCE; AND YAAKOV AND HIS CHILDREN WENT DOWN TO EGYPT. In the passage dealing with the kings of Edom it is stated: "And these are the kings that reigned in the land of Edom before there reigned any king over the children of Yisrael" (*Bereishis* 36:31). Esav's society rapidly developed in an entirely predictable pattern, consonant with exercising "the power of the sword." While Yaacov's descendants were still languishing in slavery in Egypt and their very first leader, Moshe, had not yet made his appearance, Edom had already become a flourishing kingdom with a succession of royal dynasties. This contrast is referred to by Yehoshua in the verse quoted here.

THE HOLY ONE, BLESSED BE HE, CALCULATED THE END [OF THEIR EXILE] TO DO AS HE HAD SAID TO OUR FATHER AVRAHAM AND IT IS THIS PROMISE WHICH STOOD BY OUR FATHERS AND BY US.

"And He said to him: 'Take unto Me three times a heifer and three times a goat, and three times a ram, and a turtledove and a young his descendants and gave him Yitzchak. And to Yitzchak I gave Yaakov and Esav; to Esav I gave Mount Seir for an inheritance, and Yaakov and his children went down to Egypt"'" (*Yehoshua* 24:2-4).

Blessed be He Who keeps His promise to Yisrael. Blessed be He. For the Holy One, Blessed be He, calculated the end [of their exile], to do as He had said to our father Avraham at the Covenant between the Portions, as it is written: "He said to Avram: 'Know for sure that your seed shall be a stranger in a land that is not theirs, and they will enslave them and afflict them four hundred years. But also that nation whom they shall serve, do I judge, and afterwards they shall go forth with great possessions.'" (*Bereishis* 15:13-14).

---

pigeon.' And he took all these unto Him, and He divided them in the center and laid each piece opposite its corresponding piece, but the birds He did not divide. Then the birds of prey came down upon the carcasses, and Avram drove them away. And when the sun was going down a deep sleep fell upon Avram and, lo, dread, a great darkness fell upon him. And He said to Avram: 'Know for sure that your seed shall be a stranger in a land that is not theirs, and they will enslave them and afflict them four hundred years'" (*Bereishis* 15:9-13).

"And in the fourth generation they shall come here again..." (*ibid.*, 16).

The Covenant was revealed to Avram with symbolic acts and signs. He was to experience for himself an endless night of dread and exultant awakening, so that the Covenant could be more surely understood and handed down with all the certainty of something already lived through.

The pronouncement which followed, "Know for sure, etc." is the translation of these symbolic acts and signs, into words. It remains for us to relate the symbolic acts to the subsequent verbal interpretation.

In other locations in Tanach, the word שָׁלֵשׁ means to perform an act for a third time (see *Melachim* I, 18:34), and חוּט הַמְשֻׁלָשׁ denotes a "threefold cord" (see *Koheles* 4:12). Similarly the use of מְשֻׁלֶּשֶׁת and מְשֻׁלָּשׁ here must refer to three — three heifers, three goats, three rams. However, the verse does not say עֲגָלוֹת שָׁלֹשׁ, "three heifers," and so forth. Rather, it says עֶגְלָה מְשֻׁלֶּשֶׁת and so forth, meaning "three times a heifer, three times a goat, three times a ram." There are two concepts of "three-ness" indicated here. We learn that three of each of these animals constitutes a group which belongs together and, also, that the bringing of these animals before God is an act to be repeated three times.

If we then link the symbolic acts with the subsequent, verbal part of this revelation, it is clear that the dismemberment of these living creatures, with the bird of prey greedily swooping down upon the carcasses, is intended to indicate the circumstances and the perils which the coming generations are to face.

Furthermore, as we are told, it is only the fourth generation that will be redeemed. If so, the symbolic meaning of a three-time presentation of these animals before God becomes clear: three of Avraham's future generations of descendants will have to give themselves up to God through the destruction of those qualities represented by the heifer, goat, and ram.

In each of the three generations those qualities represented by the three animals will be violently extirpated, as is indicated from the use of the word וַיְבַתֵּר, to divide. Only those qualities symbolized by the turtledove and young pigeon which were not divided will remain to survive. The other animals lay on the ground, welcome spoil to the birds of prey. It was only through Avram's merit that they, meaning his descendants, would not be consumed by these predators. It is quite clear that the subject of the verb "to divide" is God, not Avram, for it is not until verse 11 "... and Avram drove them away," that Avram occurs as the subject of that verb.

Now it remains for us to understand the meaning of heifer, goat, ram, turtledove, and young pigeon when used with reference to the personalities of individuals or to the character of nations.

The fact that these animal species should be considered as analogous to specific human personality types is readily apparent from a superficial glance at the sacrificial laws, under which only these particular animals are permitted as offerings, and which prescribe the species and sex of animals to be offered by various people under different circumstances.

Cattle, בקר , שור, are considered "working" animals, toiling in the service of their master (as distinct from חמור, which represents the beast of burden). The young offspring of cattle always appear in the Bible as animals that must be trained for work.

Accordingly, cattle in Tanach symbolize energy and usefulness. The fully developed member of the species is the bull. Therefore, the bull in the sacrificial offerings always symbolizes the "public" personality called upon to labor in the service of God and of the community and to set an example by his endeavors, while the עגלה, heifer, symbolizes energy still in its beginning or developing phases.

צאן, the species that includes sheep and goats, is the prototypic pasture animal. Hence it is so frequently used as a metaphor for the relationship of men and nations to God. Men and nations are the sheep, the flock, and God is the shepherd. In the sacrificial code, the lamb is the metaphor most generally used for Yisrael's national character (for example, the Paschal lamb and the daily offerings). In the same manner, the ewe lamb and the she-goat in the individual sin offering symbolize the "private" personality. Within the species of צאן, two animal types are characterized in a distinct manner: the goat and the ram.

The עז, goat, as indicated by its very name (derived from עז "hard," "firm," "strong") is tractable only with its master. It is obstinate with anyone else. Thus it is the most clear-cut characterization of resistance, particularly of that virile independence which, impervious to any temptation from without or within, heeds only the command of its master. For this reason the goat was the animal chosen for the sin offering which is intended to counteract levity, because it represents the power of resistance.

The איל, as indicated by its very name, is the mature ram, which, because of its vigor, leads the flock. For this reason the wealthy and prominent men in a nation, the men of property, are designated by this term (see *Melachim* II, 24:15; *Yechezkel* 17:13).

Consequently, it was the animal chosen for offerings intended as atonement for sins relating to property or privilege or to symbolize the installation of an individual into a position of greater privilege. Thus, the ram symbolizes a personage distinguished by property and privilege.

The צפור, the clean (i.e., "kosher") bird, is that creature which has neither strength nor power but which, nevertheless, by its ability to

וְהִיא שֶׁעָמְדָה לַאֲבוֹתֵינוּ וְלָנוּ.
שֶׁלֹּא אֶחָד בִּלְבַד עָמַד עָלֵינוּ
לְכַלּוֹתֵנוּ. אֶלָּא שֶׁבְּכָל דּוֹר וָדוֹר עוֹמְדִים עָלֵינוּ
לְכַלּוֹתֵנוּ. וְהַקָּדוֹשׁ בָּרוּךְ הוּא מַצִּילֵנוּ מִיָּדָם:

take wing, is able to escape man's sphere of power. Hence it
symbolizes a timid, ephemeral but free form of existence for which
snares are skillfully laid but which is able to avoid entrapment by
means of its wings. Specifically, the dove symbolizes the existence of
Yisrael, which are also weak and defenseless but nonetheless free,
happy and secure.

In certain sacrifices, the clean bird represents that personality
which has been divested of all property, power and privilege,
enjoying only a meager existence. Elsewhere in the sacrifices, it
symbolizes new life regained after deliverance from illness and
weakness.

The bird that symbolizes in even more striking terms a state of free
existence, borne upon its wings, is תור the turtledove, the bird of
passage whose return each year is the harbinger of spring (see *Shir
Hashirim* 2:12), as opposed to בני יונה (the young doves). The גוזל is
the baby bird, which is still in need of maternal care and protection
(see *Devarim* 32:11). The צפור therefore symbolizes a form of life that
is weak and defenseless but that is able to save itself and to survive by
"taking wing." תור וגוזל is the older generation, preserving and
protecting its young even as it saves itself by taking wing.

Translated into a verbal equivalent, the allegorical act of taking the
heifers, goats, rams, turtledoves and young pigeon means: *Place
yourself (Avram), as the Patriarch, at My (God's) service; in other
words, your descendants should do so — three times with their
energy, three times with their power of resistance, three times with
their property and privilege and with their momentum, their ability
to 'take wing,' which can raise both the old and the young generations
to renewed life.*

❧ **AND** it is this [promise] which stood by our fathers and by us, for not just one has risen up against us to destroy us, but in every single generation they rise up against us to destroy us, and the Holy One, Blessed be He, delivers us from their hand.

And so, he "took all these unto Him." Avram placed all these faculties at the service of God. Then God cut them up: He broke all the strength, all the resistance and all the authority of three generations of his children. God meant by all this to show Avram the future that lay in store for his descendants. Avram was to understand that his descendants would be *aliens* — without rights or privileges — in a land not of their own. This was symbolized by the dismembered ram. Moreover, they would become *slaves*, their energy broken, as symbolized by the dismemberment of the heifer. Finally they would be *afflicted* and have to endure all this without being able to offer resistance, as symbolized by the dismemberment of the goat. Slavery, alienage and affliction were to be the fate of the children of Avraham. "…but the birds He did not divide." This symbolized that God allowed only the inner strength to take wing and soar above misery to remain unbroken.

After the dismemberment, God "laid each piece opposite its corresponding piece," indicating by this juxtaposition that there would come a day when these powers would once again be joined together. The children of Avraham would not be lost to deliverance: the birds, symbolizing the power to overcome, "He did not divide."

"And it came to pass when the sun had gone down and it was dark, see, it was a smoking furnace and a torch of fire which had passed between these pieces" (*Bereishis* 15:17). Refinement and enlightenment was the reason for which the animals had been cut up. Now this process of education and purification was completed, just as the children of Avraham were to be refined into a nation through their travails, and the pieces could be joined together again.

95

Put down the cup and uncover the matzos:

צֵא וּלְמַד. מַה בִּקֵשׁ לָבָן הָאֲרַמִּי לַעֲשׂוֹת לְיַעֲקֹב אָבִינוּ. שֶׁפַּרְעֹה לֹא גָזַר אֶלָּא עַל הַזְּכָרִים וְלָבָן בִּקֵּשׁ לַעֲקוֹר אֶת הַכֹּל. שֶׁנֶּאֱמַר: **אֲרַמִּי אֹבֵד אָבִי וַיֵּרֶד מִצְרַיְמָה וַיָּגָר שָׁם בִּמְתֵי מְעָט וַיְהִי שָׁם לְגוֹי גָּדוֹל עָצוּם וָרָב:**

וַיֵּרֶד מִצְרַיְמָה. אָנוּס עַל פִּי הַדִּבּוּר:

AND HE WENT DOWN TO EGYPT — COMPELLED BY DIVINE DECREE. The Patriarchs had been promised the land of Canaan as the national heritage of their descendants. Yet, until the fulfillment of that promise, they remained without any right of residence — they were homeless — in the land which was to be their descendants' home. Indeed, it was Aram that Avraham called his cradle, "my country...my kindred" (*Bereishis* 24:4). But when Yaakov went back to Aram as a fugitive, the homeland of his forefathers rejected him: after years of rigorous service he was threatened with ruin by his scheming father-in-law Lavan. So, Yaakov, with his wives and children, returned to Canaan. But again he was not to find any peace there.

To escape a famine, he went down to Egypt. He was still the אֲרַמִּי, still homeless. And, now, in addition to that, due to the bitterest blows of his fate, he was also אֹבֵד, near ruin because of the famine. Without any hope of a future of independence, Yaakov went down to Egypt, where a strange language was spoken and where the moral and spiritual values were antithetical to those of the Patriarchs.

The above understanding is based on the grammar of the words אֲרַמִּי אֹבֵד אָבִי. אֹבֵד in the "kal" form is always intransitive, and means "to go to ruin," hence אֹבֵד, one going to ruin, one to whom ruin is

96

🌿 **GO** and learn what Lavan the Aramean planned to do to our father Yaakov. For while Pharaoh's decree applied only to the male children, Lavan sought to uproot all, as it says: **"...an Aramean near to ruin was my father, and he went down to Egypt and sojourned there as a stranger, few in number; and there he became a nation, great, strong and numerous"** (*Devarim* 26:5).

And he went down to Egypt — compelled by Divine decree.

near. ארמי and אבד are together the predicate of אבי, and the separating accent on ארמי requires one's thoughts to rest first on it and then add ארמי as a second predicate: "An Aramean — near to ruin was my father."

Yaakov and his children descended into Egypt a family without a future. Indeed, it was a "descent," a ירידה, in the fullest sense of the word, despite the temporary honors awaiting them upon arrival. By human reckoning, one would see this move as only further removing them from their destiny. A national future had been promised to their fathers only on Canaan's soil, while their native rights were only in Aram. Migration to Egypt could only lead them further from either. Therefore, Yaakov was in great need of the encouragement he received from Hashem on the way to Egypt: "...fear not to go down into Egypt, for there will I make of you a great nation" (*Bereishis* 46:3). Yosef, too, in spite of his lofty position there, indicated that only by means of an extraordinary intervention of Divine Providence, a special פקידה, would the Children of Yisrael be brought up from the land of Egypt, and returned to the promised land at the proper time (see *Bereishis* 50:24).

In spite of all this they did go down, apparently אבד, doomed, but אנוס, forced by the circumstances and על פי הדבור, in obedience to the Divine word.

וַיָּגָר שָׁם. מְלַמֵּד שֶׁלֹּא יָרַד יַעֲקֹב אָבִינוּ
לְהִשְׁתַּקֵעַ בְּמִצְרַיִם אֶלָּא לָגוּר שָׁם. שֶׁנֶּאֱמַר וַיֹּאמְרוּ
אֶל פַּרְעֹה לָגוּר בָּאָרֶץ בָּאנוּ כִּי אֵין מִרְעֶה לַצֹּאן
אֲשֶׁר לַעֲבָדֶיךָ כִּי־כָבֵד הָרָעָב בְּאֶרֶץ כְּנַעַן וְעַתָּה יֵשְׁבוּ
נָא עֲבָדֶיךָ בְּאֶרֶץ גֹּשֶׁן:

בִּמְתֵי מְעָט. כְּמָה שֶׁנֶּאֱמַר בְּשִׁבְעִים נֶפֶשׁ יָרְדוּ
אֲבֹתֶיךָ מִצְרָיְמָה וְעַתָּה שָׂמְךָ יהוה אֱלֹהֶיךָ כְּכוֹכְבֵי
הַשָּׁמַיִם לָרֹב:

AND SOJOURNED THERE AS A STRANGER... THIS TEACHES THAT OUR FATHER YAAKOV DID NOT GO DOWN TO SETTLE PERMANENTLY IN EGYPT, BUT TO STAY THERE TEMPORARILY. From the first the children of Yaakov did not intend to settle in Egypt permanently. They merely sought asylum there as strangers — and as strangers were they treated! Indeed, "the Egyptians ill-treated us, and they afflicted us and laid upon us hard bondage" (*Devarim* 26:6). All this oppression was the result of our being aliens, our condition of גרות. Thus, the three aspects of the Egyptian exile, alienage, enslavement, and affliction, predicted to Avram in the Covenant Between the Portions were fulfilled.*

It is the condition of גרות, i.e., the denial of justice to aliens, which lies at the root of enslavement and affliction. That is why the Torah's laws governing גרים, converts, are a striking contrast to every other nation's legislation regarding non-citizens — to this day. In each of the twenty-four instances where the legal status of persons and property is mentioned in the Torah, the "stranger in the land" is expressly mentioned and placed under the special protection of the Law. Whether a country is to be considered just depends less on what rights it accords its citizens, who are in any case secure and well-represented, and more on what rights it confers upon defenseless

---

* See pages 61 and 90.

And sojourned there as a stranger — this teaches that our father Yaakov did not go down to settle permanently in Egypt, but to stay there temporarily, as it says: "And they [the sons of Yaakov] said to Pharaoh: 'We have come to sojourn in the land, as there is no pasture for your servants' sheep, because the famine is severe in the land of Canaan; and now, please, let your servants dwell in the land of Goshen'" (*Bereishis* 47:4).

Few in number — as it says: "With seventy souls, your forefathers went down to Egypt, and now Hashem your God has made you as the stars of the heavens for multitude" (*Devarim* 10:22).

---

strangers. In Jewish law, the complete equality before the law of the stranger and the indigenous citizen is axiomatic.

It is not nationality which entitles a man to rights, but the acknowledgement of human rights which grants nationality. Jewish law knows no distinction between human rights and citizens' rights. Anyone was entitled to dwell in Eretz Yisrael provided he acknowledged basic moral standards, that is, the seven Noachide Laws. Equal respect for everyone, by the very fact of his being human, regardless of origin and means, is a principle proclaimed throughout the Torah. And wherever this principle is mentioned in the Torah, we are reminded of *our* experience of alienage in Egypt, for there, the preliminary measures taken against the Hebrew foreigners were carefully manipulated infringements on their rights. Harshness and cruelty followed automatically, as they always do and will, once the basic concept of human rights and justice is perverted.

AND NOW HASHEM YOUR GOD HAS MADE YOU AS THE STARS OF THE HEAVENS FOR MULTITUDE. Seeing the starry heavens, one is mainly impressed by their countless number. It never occurs to anyone to count them singly, one by one. Yisrael give rise to the same impression when anyone looks at them collectively. Indeed, there have been few opportunities in history to count an entire nation —

600,000 men, some three-and one-half million souls — located in one place. At the same time, however, comparison with the stars prevents the misconception that the nation in its totality is a numberless mass in which the individual counts for nothing. Just as each star retains its own importance within the vast galaxies, so, too, every individual is a "world unto himself." He has been assigned his personal mission by God, and is guided by His Providence.

This idea is emphasized even more clearly in God's promise to our forefather Avraham when he was still known as Avram: "And He led him forth outside and said: 'Look, please, to the heavens and count the stars, if you be able to count them.' And He said to him: 'So shall be your seed'" (*Bereishis* 15:5).

It would hardly have been necessary to lead Avram outside to make him realize the impossibility of counting the stars. Earlier, when Hashem promised him that his seed would be "as the dust of the earth," he was not asked to look at the dust.

The expression "so shall be your seed" indicates not principally the quantity but mainly the character, the quality of the children of Avram. Whenever in Scripture the hearer is shown something as well as told or wherever perceptible signs, experiences, and symbols occur in addition to the spoken word of God, it means that we have to look for a deeper and more lasting interpretation of those words. It follows that through the contemplation of the stars, Hashem intended to represent to Avram some basic concept which was to make a deep impression upon his soul.

Let us now examine this verse more closely. הבט נא, "Look, please." Wherever the word נא, please, occurs, it is intended to counteract some existing attitude, opinion, or mood. Hence, Avram at this moment was apparently in a frame of mind which needed to be countered by this Divine word. We can easily guess this mood from his earlier statement: "...what will You give me, seeing I go childless..." (*ibid.*, 2).

Avram had despaired of having a child and indeed, in the natural way of things, could no longer expect to experience the blessing of fatherhood. Under the sway of this emotion, he had said: *Whatever You might give me, of what value would it be, seeing I depart from this world childless?* At this moment, God took him outside, saying: "Look, please, to the heavens." *There you see a different governance of the world.* On earth, we no longer see things or beings created directly by God — whatever we see here is generated or produced by

100

something else. It is not the direct handiwork of God without intermediary but is contingent upon other existing beings or causes. Within the causality of earthly circumstances, Avram was right: any reason to hope for children was non-existent. In the heavens, however, matters are different. What we see there, just as they were at the time of the Creation, are bodies that were called into existence directly by God (as our planet, seen from afar, would present us with a similar sight). So if anyone wishes to see something created directly by God, let him look up at the stars, from whence countless other worlds, God's direct creation, radiate out to us. *Well, then, are you able to count them?* The stars are much more numerous than anything being generated through an intermediary in the limited space of earth. Therefore the Sages revealed to us the hidden message in God's words as being: צא מאצטגנינות שלך. *Let go of your nature-based, earthly calculations and base your conceptions on the world of stars. "So shall be your seed." For the creation of your people will be a direct act of God, overriding any and all earthly premises, like a second work of Creation which was brought into being* ex nihilo.

For the next thirty years, Avram and Sarai would remain childless until not even the remotest natural possibility of parenthood remained. In spite of themselves, they were to laugh; the whole world would laugh: "...all that hear will laugh at me" (*ibid.*, 21:6). Only then, when any thought of having children would be "ludicrous," was the first child of the Divinely-promised nation to be born!

The Psalmist, too, teaches the significance of contemplating the stars in order to illustrate Yisrael's direct dependence upon God:

> The Builder of Yerushalayim, Hashem,
>> gathers together the banished ones of Yisrael.
>
> He Who is a Healer to the broken-hearted
>> will also bind up their wounds,
>
> He Who fixes the number of the stars,
>> calls them all by name.
>
> Great is our Master and abundant in strength,
>> and no number counts before His insight.
>> (*Tehillim* 147:2-5)

As long as one is a Jew, even if he be as wretched and miserable as the "banished ones of Yisrael," he remains under the personal supervision of God — the same God who calls each star by name. For indeed חֵרוּת עַל הַלּוּחוֹת, the freedom which was granted with the

101

וַיְהִי שָׁם לְגוֹי. מְלַמֵּד שֶׁהָיוּ יִשְׂרָאֵל מְצֻיָּנִים
שָׁם:

גָּדוֹל עָצוּם. כְּמָה שֶׁנֶּאֱמַר וּבְנֵי יִשְׂרָאֵל פָּרוּ
וַיִּשְׁרְצוּ וַיִּרְבּוּ וַיַּעַצְמוּ בִּמְאֹד מְאֹד וַתִּמָּלֵא הָאָרֶץ
אֹתָם:

וָרָב. כְּמָה שֶׁנֶּאֱמַר רְבָבָה כְּצֶמַח הַשָּׂדֶה נְתַתִּיךְ
וַתִּרְבִּי וַתִּגְדְּלִי וַתָּבֹאִי בַּעֲדִי עֲדָיִים שָׁדַיִם נָכֹנוּ
וּשְׂעָרֵךְ צִמֵּחַ וְאַתְּ עֵרֹם וְעֶרְיָה: וָאֶעֱבֹר עָלַיִךְ
וָאֶרְאֵךְ מִתְבּוֹסֶסֶת בְּדָמָיִךְ וָאֹמַר לָךְ בְּדָמַיִךְ חֲיִי
וָאֹמַר לָךְ בְּדָמַיִךְ חֲיִי:

Tablets of the Law, (see *Eruvin* 54a) guarantees that walking in the ways of God is tantamount to being free, since one is raised above the causality of natural forces and lives directly under God's Providence.

AND THE CHILDREN OF YISRAEL WERE FRUITFUL BY MULTIPLE BIRTHS, AND THEY INCREASED ABUNDANTLY AND BECAME EXCEEDINGLY STRONG... The children of Yisrael were as prolific as insects. The smaller and lower the creature is, the greater the number at each birth. Among human beings, however, twins and triplets are normally weak and are often unable to survive. Hence, such births do not generally lead to any substantial increase in population or else they produce an increase of weaklings and feeble offspring. The Torah teaches us that in Egypt, the opposite was the case. Although they were fruitful by multiple births, yet *they increased abundantly*, meaning that their offspring survived and added to the population, and, furthermore, that they were not weaklings but *became exceedingly strong*.

AND I PASSED OVER YOU AND SAW YOU WALLOWING IN YOUR BLOOD; AND I SAID TO YOU: 'IN YOUR BLOOD LIVE!' AND I SAID TO YOU: 'IN YOUR BLOOD LIVE!' And Yisrael did arise, and it lived — it lives still, born out of mortal agony, never to die again, as an

There he became a nation — this teaches that Yisrael were distinctive people there.

Great, strong — as it says: "And the Children of Yisrael were fruitful by multiple births, and they increased abundantly and became exceedingly strong and the land was filled with them" (*Shemos* 1:7).

And numerous — as it says: "I let you become as myriads, like the plants of the field, and you increased and grew big; and you came of age to wear jewelry of outstanding beauty, your breasts properly formed and your hair grown, but you were naked and bare" (*Yechezkel* 16:7). "And I passed over you and saw you wallowing in your blood; and I said to you: 'In your blood, live!' and I said to you: 'In your blood, live!'" (*ibid.*, 6).

everlasting witness to mankind's resurrection. Yisrael goes about in the midsts of the other nations being born and dying out as the one eternal People which has no need to fear death. Death stood by its cradle and was vanquished, all the sickness and deterioration that accompany decadent peoples to their grave were overcome at its birth. For He, Who not only quickens the earth by His perennial call for revival but also smites nations and brings them to life again, "leads into the grave and brings up" (*Shemuel* I 2:6). He, Who alone lives forever, had spoken: *Arise and live.* He chose this People, stillborn upon earth but resurrected by Him to everlasting life, to be His witness in the midst of the nations.

And every year, when new life stirs in the dark folds of the earth, in slumbering germs, in dormant fibers and sleeping chrysalises, when the earth is wresting free from the icy embrace of winter, and nature celebrates its spring-revival — then this People, too, celebrates the festival of its revival. It is the People of the Spring of Nations heralding the revival of mankind. It recalls the time it lay stillborn on the earth and the Living One passed over it and spoke to it: "In your blood, live, in your blood, live!"

In that hour of resurrection, the Living One set His mark upon His people. He implanted in them the ideas to re-illuminate their minds

103

וַיָּרֵעוּ אֹתָנוּ הַמִּצְרִים וַיְעַנּוּנוּ וַיִּתְּנוּ עָלֵינוּ
עֲבֹדָה קָשָׁה:

וַיָּרֵעוּ אֹתָנוּ הַמִּצְרִים. כְּמָה שֶׁנֶּאֱמַר הָבָה
נִתְחַכְּמָה לוֹ פֶּן יִרְבֶּה וְהָיָה כִּי תִקְרֶאנָה מִלְחָמָה
וְנוֹסַף גַּם הוּא עַל שֹׂנְאֵינוּ וְנִלְחַם בָּנוּ וְעָלָה מִן
הָאָרֶץ:

וַיְעַנּוּנוּ. כְּמָה שֶׁנֶּאֱמַר וַיָּשִׂימוּ עָלָיו שָׂרֵי מִסִּים
לְמַעַן עַנֹּתוֹ בְּסִבְלֹתָם וַיִּבֶן עָרֵי מִסְכְּנוֹת לְפַרְעֹה אֶת
פִּתֹם וְאֶת רַעַמְסֵס:

וַיִּתְּנוּ עָלֵינוּ עֲבֹדָה קָשָׁה. כְּמָה שֶׁנֶּאֱמַר וַיַּעֲבִדוּ
מִצְרַיִם אֶת בְּנֵי יִשְׂרָאֵל בְּפָרֶךְ:

וַנִּצְעַק אֶל יהוה אֱלֹהֵי אֲבֹתֵינוּ וַיִּשְׁמַע יהוה
אֶת־קֹלֵנוּ וַיַּרְא אֶת־עָנְיֵנוּ וְאֶת עֲמָלֵנוּ וְאֶת־לַחֲצֵנוּ:

וַנִּצְעַק אֶל־יהוה אֱלֹהֵי אֲבֹתֵינוּ. כְּמָה שֶׁנֶּאֱמַר
וַיְהִי בַיָּמִים הָרַבִּים הָהֵם וַיָּמָת מֶלֶךְ מִצְרַיִם וַיֵּאָנְחוּ
בְנֵי־יִשְׂרָאֵל מִן־הָעֲבֹדָה וַיִּזְעָקוּ וַתַּעַל שַׁוְעָתָם אֶל־
הָאֱלֹהִים מִן־הָעֲבֹדָה:

and fortified their hearts for new endeavors. He gave them tasks to test their new strength and enriched them with new possessions. And these very ideas, tasks and possessions remain the basic conditions on which life for this resurrected People depends. It is these treasures which they are called upon to appreciate with renewed enthusiasm at every recurrence of their festival of rebirth. They are to guard them through history as God's tidings until they finally will have become the *common property* of the whole family of man. At such a time the

104

"And the Egyptians ill-treated us, and they afflicted us and laid upon us hard bondage" (*Devarim* 26:6).

And the Egyptians ill-treated us — as it says: "Come, let us deal wisely with them, lest they multiply, and then, when circumstances bring about war, they too will join our enemies, or they will also fight against us, and move up out of their land" (*Shemos* 1:10).

And they afflicted us — as it says: "And they set over them fiscal officers in order to afflict them with their burdens, and they built storage cities for Pharaoh, Pisom and Raamses" (*Shemos* 1:11).

And laid upon us hard bondage — as it says: "And the Egyptians made slaves of the Children of Yisrael, with crushing harshness" (*Shemos* 1:13).

"And we cried out to Hashem, the God of our fathers, and Hashem heard our voice and saw our affliction and our misery and our oppression" (*Devarim* 26:7).

And we cried out to Hashem, the God of our fathers — as it says: "And it came to pass in the course of those many days that the king of Egypt died and the Children of Yisrael sighed from the slavery, and they cried, and their cry for help rose up to God from the slavery" (*Shemos* 2:23).

Living One in His majesty of love will pass over all of humanity, wallowing in its blood, and will call out to it: *In your blood, revive and live!*

THE KING OF EGYPT DIED AND THE CHILDREN OF YISRAEL SIGHED FROM THE SLAVERY, AND THEY CRIED. The connection between the death of the king and the sighs and cries of the people is obvious. As long as the individual responsible for this grievous

וַיִּשְׁמַע יהוה אֶת־קֹלֵנוּ. כְּמָה שֶׁנֶּאֱמַר וַיִּשְׁמַע
אֱלֹהִים אֶת־נַאֲקָתָם וַיִּזְכֹּר אֱלֹהִים אֶת־בְּרִיתוֹ אֶת־
אַבְרָהָם אֶת־יִצְחָק וְאֶת־יַעֲקֹב:
וַיַּרְא אֶת־עָנְיֵנוּ. זוֹ פְּרִישׁוּת דֶּרֶךְ אֶרֶץ. כְּמָה
שֶׁנֶּאֱמַר וַיַּרְא אֱלֹהִים אֶת־בְּנֵי יִשְׂרָאֵל וַיֵּדַע אֱלֹהִים:

injustice, the one who had passed the edict enslaving an entire free
and innocent people, is still alive, there is hope that his conscience
will be aroused and cause him to abolish the wrong which resulted
from his tyranny. But once a state institution, no matter how
obviously unjust its founding, passes into other hands with all the
power of the state, it is recognized as an established fact, perhaps of
unknown origin, and is considered as being the norm. It is something
which the new government believes it has not the right to tamper
with. It will assume the legality and force of the law of the land, and
the free people who had been enslaved with such satanic cruelty are
doomed to be pariahs for eternity. This is the curse inherent in the
vestigial development of states. The past cultivates a field with blood
and tears, while the present reaps the harvest in gladness, with a clear
conscience, on the grounds of a *fait accompli*, unaware of the curse
upon each and every sheaf.

As long as the king of Egypt lived, the Children of Yisrael still
hoped for a change in their fortunes. Once he died, they looked upon
themselves as slaves in perpetuity, and they sighed and cried for
deliverance from this slavery.

It is twice emphasized that they sighed and cried from *the slavery*.
Their groans and cries for help were not on account of their physical
burdens and their toil. They were strong and able to endure much,
and had lived in the hope that their bad situation might be changed
for the better. But now, as a result of the death of the king, they cried
from the slavery to which they felt themselves condemned forever. A
great injustice had been done to them, and so they cried out to God,
the Judge.

**AND GOD HEARD THEIR GROANING, AND GOD REMEMBERED
HIS COVENANT WITH AVRAHAM, WITH YITZCHAK AND WITH**

And Hashem heard our voice — as it says: "And God heard their groaning, and God remembered His covenant with Avraham, with Yitzchak and with Yaakov" (*ibid.*, 24).

And saw our affliction — this refers to the enforced disruption of normal family relations, as it says: "And God saw the Children of Yisrael, and God took note of it" (*ibid.*, 25).

YAAKOV. AND GOD SAW THE CHILDREN OF YISRAEL AND GOD TOOK NOTE OF IT. All elements of human consciousness are here attributed to God: He heard, He remembered, He saw, He took note. The Torah does not tell us that He heard "their sighs" or their "cry for help" but rather, He heard "their groaning." The root נאק — to groan — occurs rarely in Tanach: "...and he shall groan before him with the groanings of a deadly wounded man" (*Yechezkel* 30:24); "Men groan from out of the city..." (*Iyyov* 24:12). It denotes a last despairing cry, intimating to everyone who hears that this man is lost unless help is immediately forthcoming.

The Children of Yisrael cried out solely against the injustice done to them, not comprehending the real danger they faced. God, however, did realize it. In their groaning He *heard* unconsciously expressed the threat of a complete moral degeneration. The very future of the Children of Yisrael was in danger and so, He *remembered* the covenant of the past. Had they degenerated totally and irrevocably, God's unconditional promise to the Patriarchs that their children would have a moral future would have been broken. It was because of this covenant that Hashem intervened on their behalf — and not because of the wrong being done to them in the present.

Such an understanding finds support in that which Yechezkel elaborates upon (see chapter 20). The Children of Yisrael had *not* cast aside the abominations of Egypt. Based on their own merits, they were not worthy of redemption. It was the threat of extinction and the consequent violation of the existing covenant which God heard and remembered. Hence, "*God saw,*" and "*God took note of it.*" He saw their present condition and understood the effects it would have on their future and therefore, He directed His Providence upon them. The time about which Yosef had assured his brothers a few centuries

וְאֶת **עֲמָלֵנוּ.** אֵלּוּ הַבָּנִים. כְּמָה שֶׁנֶּאֱמַר כָּל־
הַבֵּן הַיִּלּוֹד הַיְאֹרָה תַּשְׁלִיכֻהוּ וְכָל־הַבַּת תְּחַיּוּן:
וְאֶת **לַחֲצֵנוּ.** זֶה הַדְּחַק. כְּמָה שֶׁנֶּאֱמַר וְגַם־
רָאִיתִי אֶת־הַלַּחַץ אֲשֶׁר מִצְרַיִם לֹחֲצִים אֹתָם:

וַיּוֹצִאֵנוּ יהוה מִמִּצְרַיִם בְּיָד חֲזָקָה וּבִזְרֹעַ
נְטוּיָה וּבְמֹרָא גָּדֹל וּבְאֹתוֹת וּבְמֹפְתִים:

וַיּוֹצִאֵנוּ יהוה מִמִּצְרַיִם. לֹא עַל־יְדֵי מַלְאָךְ
וְלֹא עַל־יְדֵי שָׂרָף וְלֹא עַל־יְדֵי שָׁלִיחַ. אֶלָּא הַקָּדוֹשׁ
בָּרוּךְ הוּא בִּכְבוֹדוֹ וּבְעַצְמוֹ. שֶׁנֶּאֱמַר:

וְעָבַרְתִּי בְאֶרֶץ־מִצְרַיִם בַּלַּיְלָה הַזֶּה וְהִכֵּיתִי כָל־בְּכוֹר בְּאֶרֶץ
מִצְרַיִם מֵאָדָם וְעַד בְּהֵמָה וּבְכָל אֱלֹהֵי מִצְרַיִם אֶעֱשֶׂה
שְׁפָטִים אֲנִי יהוה:

ago had arrived: "God will surely consider you again..." (*Bereishis* 50:24). Until now, God had not specially intervened, but had allowed events to take their natural course. What they had suffered until now was the direct consequence of being a homeless, stateless people in a country of degeneration and low morality. Now God intervened, and their redemption was assured.

I, HASHEM. אלוהים denotes the God Who hides Himself from view while governing the visible world (אלה). Until this point, the world had been governed by God in His attribute of Elohim. The despair and derision, all the trouble and sorrow the children of Yisrael had endured, had been the outcome of the natural course of events, permitted by God to develop unhampered by His will. Their suffering stemmed from the depravity and might of Egypt and from their own helplessness. *From now on, however, It is I, Hashem — I*

And our misery — these are the children, as it says: "...every son that is born, you shall throw into the river, and every daughter you shall let live" (*Shemos* 1:22).

And our oppression — this is the pressure, as it says: "...and I have also seen the oppression with which the Egyptians oppress them" (*ibid.* 3:9).

"And Hashem brought us out from Egypt with a mighty hand and with an outstretched arm and with great awesomeness, and with instructive signs and with punishing miracles" (*Devarim* 26:8).

And Hashem brought us out from Egypt — not through an angel, not through a seraph, and not through a messenger. But it was the Holy One, Blessed be He, Himself in all His glory, as it says:

"And I will pass through the land of Egypt in this night, and I will smite every firstborn in the land of Egypt, from man to beast, and against all the gods of Egypt I will execute judgment, I, Hashem" (*Shemos* 12:12).

---

have chosen to set My will in motion without paying heed to things as they should be, even completely counteracting what ought to be. At this moment, a new world was revealed to mankind, one no longer bound by the factors that had determined human history hitherto.

Even if one could understand the entire world, with all its matter and forces, its laws and phenomena, even if one were to succeed in gaining mastery over the entire world, through knowledge of its laws, he would still be unable to predict with certainty what will happen the next moment. All one's calculations and predictions might be rendered worthless because "I am Hashem." This implies: "Not only am I the God of the past and present, but first and foremost, I am the God of *the future.* I rule in complete freedom over everything that is about to happen, freely shaping it. I am not only the One 'Who will be,' but as My Name indicates, I am He Who shapes every future moment.

וְעָבַרְתִּי בְאֶרֶץ־מִצְרַיִם בַּלַּיְלָה הַזֶּה. אֲנִי וְלֹא מַלְאָךְ.
וְהִכֵּיתִי כָל־בְּכוֹר בְּאֶרֶץ מִצְרַיִם. אֲנִי וְלֹא שָׂרָף.
וּבְכָל־אֱלֹהֵי מִצְרַיִם אֶעֱשֶׂה שְׁפָטִים. אֲנִי וְלֹא הַשָּׁלִיחַ.
אֲנִי יהוה. אֲנִי הוּא וְלֹא אַחֵר:

בְּיָד חֲזָקָה. זוֹ הַדֶּבֶר. כְּמָה שֶׁנֶּאֱמַר הִנֵּה יַד
יהוה הוֹיָה בְּמִקְנְךָ אֲשֶׁר בַּשָּׂדֶה בַּסּוּסִים בַּחֲמֹרִים
בַּגְּמַלִּים בַּבָּקָר וּבַצֹּאן דֶּבֶר כָּבֵד מְאֹד:

וּבִזְרֹעַ נְטוּיָה. זוֹ הַחֶרֶב. כְּמָה שֶׁנֶּאֱמַר וְחַרְבּוֹ
שְׁלוּפָה בְּיָדוֹ נְטוּיָה עַל־יְרוּשָׁלָיִם:

וּבְמֹרָא גָּדֹל. זֶה גִּלּוּי שְׁכִינָה. כְּמָה שֶׁנֶּאֱמַר אוֹ
הֲנִסָּה אֱלֹהִים לָבוֹא לָקַחַת לוֹ גוֹי מִקֶּרֶב גּוֹי בְּמַסֹּת
בְּאֹתֹת וּבְמוֹפְתִים וּבְמִלְחָמָה וּבְיָד חֲזָקָה וּבִזְרוֹעַ
נְטוּיָה וּבְמוֹרָאִים גְּדֹלִים כְּכֹל אֲשֶׁר־עָשָׂה לָכֶם יהוה
אֱלֹהֵיכֶם בְּמִצְרַיִם לְעֵינֶיךָ:

"With all its substance and forces, with every one of its laws, the
world is still My handiwork. I exist in freedom over and above all My
Works, and man's calculations remain correct only as long as I keep
My Laws in operation and only under the specific conditions which
I have set. His calculations will go wrong at any time that I
choose to intervene in the course of the world for the sake of men,
nations, and humanity. At such times, I change the laws of the world
and obstruct their consequences.

"I create anew in the heavens and the earth and in the heart of man,
according to My Will and My attributes of compassion and

And I will pass through the land of Egypt in this night — I, and no angel.

And I will smite every firstborn in the land of Egypt — I, and no seraph.

And against all the gods of Egypt I will execute judgments — I, and no messenger.

I, Hashem — it is I, and no other.

With a mighty hand — this refers to the pestilence, as it says: "Behold, the hand of Hashem will be upon your property which you have in the fields, on the horses, on the asses, on the camels, on the cattle, and on the sheep, a very severe pestilence" (*Shemos* 9:3).

And with an outstretched arm — this is the sword, as it says: "...and his drawn sword in his hand, outstretched over Yerushalayim" (*Divrei Hayamim* I, 21:16).

And with great awesomeness — this is the revelation of the Divine Presence, as it says: "Or has a god proved himself, to come to take a nation unto himself from out of the midst of another nation, with proofs of might, with signs and with instructive miracles, and with war and with a strong hand and with an outstretched arm and with great awesomeness, comparable to all that Hashem your God did for you in Egypt before your eyes?" (*Devarim* 4:34).

---

lovingkindness, I create for the good of man a new heaven and a new earth, a new human spirit and a new heart in man. One can only understand with difficulty what I have already set before him, but the future lies completely beyond the grasp of man's intellect. Indeed, *you may look at Me as I move away from you, but My face shall not be seen by any man* (see *Shemos* 33:23).

וּבְאֹתֹות. זֶה הַמַּטֶּה. כְּמָה שֶׁנֶּאֱמַר וְאֶת־הַמַּטֶּה הַזֶּה תִּקַּח בְּיָדֶךָ אֲשֶׁר תַּעֲשֶׂה בּוֹ אֶת־הָאֹתֹת: **וּבְמֹפְתִים** זֶה הַדָּם. כְּמָה שֶׁנֶּאֱמַר וְנָתַתִּי מֹופְתִים בַּשָּׁמַיִם וּבָאָרֶץ.

One dips his finger into the cup and dabs a bit of wine onto his plate when saying each of the words "blood and fire and pillars of smoke," as well as when reciting each of the ten plagues and pronouncing "detzach, adash beachav," for a total of 16 times. Some have the custom of pouring from the cup rather than dabbing their finger. The cups are then refilled.

דָּם וָאֵשׁ וְתִמְרֹות עָשָׁן:

דָּבָר אַחֵר. **בְּיָד חֲזָקָה** שְׁתַּיִם. **וּבִזְרֹעַ נְטוּיָה** שְׁתַּיִם. **וּבְמֹרָא גָּדֹל** שְׁתַּיִם. **וּבְאֹתֹות** שְׁתַּיִם. **וּבְמֹפְתִים** שְׁתַּיִם: אֵלּוּ עֶשֶׂר מַכֹּות שֶׁהֵבִיא הַקָּדֹושׁ בָּרוּךְ הוּא עַל־הַמִּצְרִים בְּמִצְרַיִם וְאֵלּוּ הֵן:

AND THIS STAFF SHALL YOU TAKE IN YOUR HAND, WITH WHICH YOU SHOULD PERFORM THE SIGNS. The staff has a dual connotation corresponding to the two meanings of the root נטה; (1) to lean, to bend over; (2) to stretch out (one's hand). The staff serves firstly as an extension of the human hand, permitting man to lean on the ground for support and secondly, as an extension of the area of his control, the sign and symbol of his mastery over nature. The staff turning into a snake demonstrated to the Children of Yisrael that what supports man and facilitates his mastery can, when God so wishes, become converted into its exact opposite, a snake. All animals will to some extent come to terms with man, the sole exception being the snake which will hate man forever and which man will always fear. When God wills it, He can cause even man's support and his tool of mastery to rebel against him. Similarly, even man's enemy may become his support and obedient tool when God so wills.

112

And with instructive signs — this is the staff, as it says: "and this staff shall you take in your hand, with which you should perform the signs" (*Shemos* 4:17).

And with punishing miracles — this is the blood, as it says: "I will do miracles in heaven and on earth:

One dips his finger into the cup and dabs a bit of wine onto his plate when saying each of the words "blood and fire and pillars of smoke," as well as when reciting each of the ten plagues and pronouncing "detzach, adash beachav," for a total of 16 times. Some have the custom of pouring from the cup rather than dabbing their finger. The cups are then refilled.

blood and fire and pillars of smoke" (*Yoel* 3:3).

An alternative explanation: **with a MIGHTY HAND** — two (Hebrew words imply two plagues); **and with an OUTSTRETCHED ARM** — two; **and with GREAT AWESOMENESS** — two; **and with instructive SIGNS** — two (plural); **and with punishing MIRACLES** — two (plural). These, then, are the ten plagues which the Holy One, Blessed be He, brought upon the Egyptians in Egypt, and they are as follows:

AN ALTERNATIVE EXPLANATION. The "mighty hand" became manifest in God's mastery over the Nile, Egypt's lifeline. Its waves were now transformed into *blood* and, from it, *frogs* swarmed onto the land.

The "outstretched arm" intervened in Egypt's national life by taking away the land from the Egyptians. The very dust under their feet was turned into *vermin*, and *wild beasts* of the forest invaded their dwellings.

"Great awesomeness" affected the bodies of living beings, man and beast. God smote the beasts with *pestilence* and plagued man with *boils*.

"Instructive signs" came from above and revealed the Master and Judge to the Egyptians. *Hail* and *locusts* descended from the air upon

113

דָם. צְפַרְדֵּעַ. כִּנִּים. עָרוֹב.
דֶּבֶר. שְׁחִין. בָּרָד. אַרְבֶּה. חֹשֶׁךְ.
מַכַּת בְּכוֹרוֹת:
רַבִּי יְהוּדָה הָיָה נוֹתֵן בָּהֶם סִמָּנִים:
דְּצַ"ךְ עַדַ"שׁ בְּאַחַ"ב:
רַבִּי יוֹסֵי הַגְּלִילִי אוֹמֵר. מִנַּיִן אַתָּה אוֹמֵר
שֶׁלָּקוּ הַמִּצְרִים בְּמִצְרַיִם עֶשֶׂר מַכּוֹת וְעַל הַיָּם לָקוּ
חֲמִשִּׁים מַכּוֹת. בְּמִצְרַיִם מַה הוּא אוֹמֵר. וַיֹּאמְרוּ

agricultural produce and destroyed the pride and wealth of Egypt.

Finally came the "punishing miracles," which struck at the source of all life and being. *Darkness* extinguished the sun's light, and the *slaying of the firstborn* blotted out life itself. Thus the plagues are divided into five groups of two each. Rabbi Yehudah, however, arranged them differently.

RABBI YEHUDAH MADE A MNEMONIC OF THEIR HEBREW INITIALS AS FOLLOWS: DETZACH, ADASH, BEACHAV. That the plagues are divided into three groups is clearly evident from the Scriptural narrative. In each group, the first two plagues are preceded by warnings, while the third comes without prior notice. Thus, the third plague in each group seems to have come as a punishment for not heeding the previous two.

On closer inspection, we can see that the nature of the three groups of plagues bears a close relationship to the galus suffering which the Egyptians inflicted upon the Children of Yisrael and from which God finally delivered them, namely: alienage, enslavement, and affliction (see page 64). The Egyptians were made to suffer parallel afflictions in order to strip them of their sense of superiority and to let them feel for themselves the misery they had brought upon others.

Upon examing the three groupings of Rabbi Yehudah, we notice that the first plague of each group — Blood, Wild Beasts, and Hail — impressed upon the Egyptians that they themselves were no more than aliens in their own land. In turn, they had no right to treat the Children of Yisrael as strangers, depriving them of their rights. The second plagues in the groups — Frogs, Pestilence, and Locusts —

114

Blood, Frogs, Vermin, Wild Beasts, Pestilence, Boils, Hail, Locusts, Darkness, Slaying of the Firstborn.

Rabbi Yehudah made a mnemonic of their Hebrew initials, as follows:

DETZACH, ADASH, BEACHAV

Rabbi Yose the Galilean said: From what passage can you infer that the Egyptians were smitten with ten plagues in Egypt and with fifty plagues at the Sea? Of the plagues in Egypt, it says: "And those knowledgeable of the writings said to Pharaoh: 'It is a

showed the Egyptians the foolishness of their undue pride and haughtiness. It was this feeling of superiority which caused them to think they were entitled to be masters over slaves. Finally, the last plague of each of the three groups — Vermin, Boils, and Darkness — exercised upon the Egyptians' own bodies a torment similar to that which they had caused the innocent Children of Yisrael. The Slaying of the Firstborn brought the whole series of plagues to a climax and accomplished the redemption.

These, then, are the plagues, schematically grouped:

גרות	עבדות	ענוי
דם	צפרדע	כנים
ערוב	דבר	שחין
ברד	ארבה	חשך

מכת בכורות

Affliction	Enslavement	Alienage
Vermin	Frogs	Blood
Boils	Pestilence	Wild beasts
Darkness	Locusts	Hail

Slaying of the Firstborn

"Detzach" was intended to disabuse the Egyptians of their erroneous conceptions of alienage, enslavement and affliction by

הַחַרְטֻמִּם אֶל־פַּרְעֹה אֶצְבַּע אֱלֹהִים הִוא. וְעַל־הַיָּם
מַה הוּא אוֹמֵר. וַיַּרְא יִשְׂרָאֵל אֶת־הַיָּד הַגְּדֹלָה אֲשֶׁר
עָשָׂה יהוה בְּמִצְרַיִם וַיִּירְאוּ הָעָם אֶת־יהוה וַיַּאֲמִינוּ
בַּיהוה וּבְמֹשֶׁה עַבְדּוֹ. כַּמָּה לָקוּ בְּאֶצְבַּע עֶשֶׂר מַכּוֹת.
אֱמֹר מֵעַתָּה בְּמִצְרַיִם לָקוּ עֶשֶׂר מַכּוֹת וְעַל־הַיָּם לָקוּ
חֲמִשִּׁים מַכּוֹת:

revealing to them God's power over water and land. "Adash" was meant to do the same by showing God's might over the living inhabitants of the land. Finally, "Beachav" would teach the lesson by exhibiting God's command over the climate, affecting the entire world and its creatures.

To fully understand the meaning of these groupings, we must study each plague in depth. As mentioned above, the plagues of Blood, Wild Beasts, and Hail were meant to counteract the state of alienage forced upon us by the Egyptians.

An alien is one who lives in a land not his own only by the grace and sufferance of others. If so, what was it that caused the Egyptians to be so completely sure of their singular bond to their land that they, more than any other nation, could deem themselves free even of the grace of heaven? It was the Nile — *their* river — which granted the Egyptians this self-assurance. They claimed: "My Nile is mine, and I have made (it) myself" (*Yechezkel* 29:3). Through the plague of Blood, God impressed upon the Egyptians: *Your Nile is Mine. If I will it,* He was demonstrating, *your river will dry up and spread pollution rather than serve as a source of blessing and fertility. It will drive you from the land, and you will see that you yourselves are merely aliens, abiding here only so long as I permit it.*

The plague of Wild Beasts emphasized this point. Wild beasts give up territory to human habitation only as long as God banishes them. Let Him annul His decree, and the wild animals will come to invade the land. Man will no longer be secure even in his own home. So it was that only the area of those whom the Egyptians considered dispossessed aliens remained safe. Finally, by means of the Hail, God showed the Egyptians — to their complete horror — that at will He could alter the weather. Ordinarily, precipitation is very scant in Egypt. Therefore, the first hailstorm ever seen in Egypt presented a finger of God'..." (*Shemos* 8:15), while at the Sea, it is said: "And Yisrael saw the great Hand which Hashem had used upon Egypt; and the people feared Hashem and trusted in Hashem and in Moshe, His servant" (*ibid.* 14:31). How many plagues were visited on them by a *finger*? Ten plagues. Thus, in Egypt the Egyptians were smitten with ten plagues, while at the Sea they were smitten [by the *hand*], with fifty plagues.

threat to the climate and very nature of the country — and, so, to the Egyptians' attachment to it. (That explains why the hail was announced with the words "for this time, I will send all my plagues upon your heart..." [*Shemos* 9:14]).

The second plague of each group served to reveal to the Egyptians the self-deception underlying their enslavement of the Children of Yisrael. The slavemaster believes that his tyranny over the slave has a justification, firstly, because of the illusion that he is a superior being, and secondly, because of the illusion of grandeur resulting from too much power and wealth. As a counterpoint to this arrogant self-delusion, the frog, an extremely shy animal which ordinarily scurries into the swamps and reeds as soon as it sees human beings, now boldly entered human habitations and even dared to hop onto the sacred person of His Majesty himself. This plague showed the Egyptians that even the smallest, most insignificant animal was not intimidated by them — a sobering rebuke indeed to their sense of self-importance.

With the onset of the plague of Pestilence, the Egyptians witnessed the destruction of their pride and glory — their horses, their beasts of burden — their asses and camels, and their source of wealth — their cattle and flocks. Following on this came the locusts to glean whatever rich agricultural produce still remained after the hail.

Finally, the last plague of each group worked to make visceral the pain and torment of affliction. The plagues of Vermin and Boils tormented the Egyptians just as they had afflicted the Children of Yisrael with the harsh stroke of the taskmaster's whip. God needs neither chains nor cages to imprison men, and so the plague of Darkness visited upon the Egyptians a gloom so thick they were literally imprisoned wherever they happened to be when the plague occurred and were forced to go hungry for days. And so they

רַבִּי אֱלִיעֶזֶר אוֹמֵר. מִנַּיִן שֶׁכָּל מַכָּה וּמַכָּה
שֶׁהֵבִיא הַקָּדוֹשׁ בָּרוּךְ הוּא עַל הַמִּצְרִים בְּמִצְרַיִם
הָיְתָה שֶׁל אַרְבַּע מַכּוֹת. שֶׁנֶּאֱמַר יְשַׁלַּח־בָּם חֲרוֹן
אַפּוֹ עֶבְרָה וָזַעַם וְצָרָה מִשְׁלַחַת מַלְאֲכֵי רָעִים.
עֶבְרָה אַחַת. וָזַעַם שְׁתַּיִם. וְצָרָה שָׁלֹשׁ. מִשְׁלַחַת
מַלְאֲכֵי רָעִים אַרְבַּע. אֱמֹר מֵעַתָּה בְּמִצְרַיִם לָקוּ
אַרְבָּעִים מַכּוֹת וְעַל־הַיָּם לָקוּ מָאתַיִם מַכּוֹת:

רַבִּי עֲקִיבָא אוֹמֵר. מִנַּיִן שֶׁכָּל מַכָּה וּמַכָּה
שֶׁהֵבִיא הַקָּדוֹשׁ בָּרוּךְ הוּא עַל הַמִּצְרִים בְּמִצְרַיִם
הָיְתָה שֶׁל חָמֵשׁ מַכּוֹת. שֶׁנֶּאֱמַר יְשַׁלַּח־בָּם חֲרוֹן אַפּוֹ
עֶבְרָה וָזַעַם וְצָרָה מִשְׁלַחַת מַלְאֲכֵי רָעִים. חֲרוֹן אַפּוֹ
אַחַת. עֶבְרָה שְׁתַּיִם. וָזַעַם שָׁלֹשׁ. וְצָרָה אַרְבַּע.
מִשְׁלַחַת מַלְאֲכֵי רָעִים חָמֵשׁ: אֱמֹר מֵעַתָּה בְּמִצְרַיִם
לָקוּ חֲמִשִּׁים מַכּוֹת וְעַל הַיָּם לָקוּ חֲמִשִּׁים וּמָאתַיִם
מַכּוֹת:

remained, hungry and frightened — until the light of God was
restored to them.

**HE LETS BREAK FORTH AGAINST THEM THE GLOW OF HIS
ANGER...A MISSION OF MESSENGERS OF EVIL.** The ten plagues
were not merely physical occurrences whose causes have remained
obscure since no explanations were found for them in the physical
world. The moral motive behind each and every plague was easily
evident and pointed to its obvious provocation: the immoral conduct
of the Egyptians. Each plague, then, was the revelation of a Divine
decree of He Who watches the acts of men and the deeds of nations.
Consequently, the Egyptians' acts aroused "the glow of His anger"
(חרון אפו). Once His anger had been aroused, He intervened: He
emerged and crossed through (עבר) the veil of His concealment

118

Rabbi Eliezer said: From what passage can it be inferred that each plague which the Holy One, Blessed be He, brought upon the Egyptians in Egypt was actually a fourfold one? For it says: "He lets break forth against them the glow of His anger: excess of wrath, and condemnation, and distress; a mission of messengers of evil" (*Tehillim* 78:49). [Excess of] wrath — one, condemnation — two, distress — three, a mission of messengers of evil — four. Thus, in Egypt the Egyptians were smitten with forty plagues, while at the Sea they were smitten with two hundred plagues (see above).

Rabbi Akiva said: From what passage can it be inferred that each plague which the Holy One, Blessed be He, brought upon the Egyptians in Egypt was actually a fivefold one? For it says: "He lets break forth against them the glow of His anger, excess of wrath, and condemnation, and distress; a mission of messengers of evil" (*ibid.*). [The glow of His] anger — one, [excess of] wrath — two, condemnation — three, distress — four, a mission of messengers of evil — five. Thus, in Egypt the Egyptians were smitten with fifty plagues, while at the Sea they were smitten with two-hundred-and-fifty plagues.

producing "excess of wrath" (עברה). His "condemnation" (זעם) rose against their depravity and through "distress" (צרה), He demonstrated their impotence. These fateful events were His "mission of messengers of evil" (משלחת מלאכי רעים) to human beings.

The supernatural origin and moral purpose of the plagues can be clearly seen from the fact that they were preceded by warnings, that they ceased at a Divinely ordained time, and that the sinful Egyptians were clearly distinguished from the Hebrew slaves, who remained unscathed throughout the entire upheaval. All this was emphasized with fivefold clarity at the time of the ultimate cataclysm: the entire armed might of Egypt was buried in the very floods which formed a passageway to eternal freedom and redemption for the Jewish people.

כַּמָּה מַעֲלוֹת טוֹבוֹת לַמָּקוֹם עָלֵינוּ:

אִלּוּ הוֹצִיאָנוּ מִמִּצְרַיִם
וְלֹא־עָשָׂה בָהֶם שְׁפָטִים דַּיֵּנוּ:
אִלּוּ עָשָׂה בָהֶם שְׁפָטִים
וְלֹא־עָשָׂה בֵאלֹהֵיהֶם דַּיֵּנוּ:
אִלּוּ עָשָׂה בֵאלֹהֵיהֶם
וְלֹא־הָרַג אֶת־בְּכוֹרֵיהֶם דַּיֵּנוּ:
אִלּוּ הָרַג אֶת־בְּכוֹרֵיהֶם
וְלֹא־נָתַן לָנוּ אֶת־מָמוֹנָם דַּיֵּנוּ:
אִלּוּ נָתַן לָנוּ אֶת־מָמוֹנָם
וְלֹא־קָרַע לָנוּ אֶת־הַיָּם דַּיֵּנוּ:
אִלּוּ קָרַע לָנוּ אֶת־הַיָּם
וְלֹא־הֶעֱבִירָנוּ בְתוֹכוֹ בֶּחָרָבָה דַּיֵּנוּ:
אִלּוּ הֶעֱבִירָנוּ בְתוֹכוֹ בֶּחָרָבָה
וְלֹא־שִׁקַּע צָרֵינוּ בְּתוֹכוֹ דַּיֵּנוּ:
אִלּוּ שִׁקַּע צָרֵינוּ בְּתוֹכוֹ
וְלֹא־סִפֵּק צָרְכֵּנוּ בַּמִּדְבָּר אַרְבָּעִים שָׁנָה דַּיֵּנוּ:
אִלּוּ סִפֵּק צָרְכֵּנוּ בַּמִּדְבָּר אַרְבָּעִים שָׁנָה
וְלֹא־הֶאֱכִילָנוּ אֶת־הַמָּן דַּיֵּנוּ:
אִלּוּ הֶאֱכִילָנוּ אֶת־הַמָּן
וְלֹא־נָתַן לָנוּ אֶת־הַשַּׁבָּת דַּיֵּנוּ:
אִלּוּ נָתַן לָנוּ אֶת־הַשַּׁבָּת
וְלֹא־קֵרְבָנוּ לִפְנֵי הַר־סִינַי דַּיֵּנוּ:
אִלּוּ קֵרְבָנוּ לִפְנֵי הַר־סִינַי
וְלֹא־נָתַן לָנוּ אֶת־הַתּוֹרָה דַּיֵּנוּ:
אִלּוּ נָתַן לָנוּ אֶת הַתּוֹרָה
וְלֹא הִכְנִיסָנוּ לְאֶרֶץ יִשְׂרָאֵל דַּיֵּנוּ:
אִלּוּ הִכְנִיסָנוּ לְאֶרֶץ יִשְׂרָאֵל
וְלֹא בָנָה לָנוּ אֶת בֵּית הַבְּחִירָה דַּיֵּנוּ:

How Many Stages of Benevolence Did the Omnipresent Grant Us!

Had He brought us out of Egypt and
    not executed judgment on the Egyptians   Dayenu.*

Had He executed judgment on
    them and not upon their idols   Dayenu.

Had He destroyed their idols
    and not slain their firstborn   Dayenu.

Had He slain their firstborn
    and not given us their wealth   Dayenu.

Had He given us their wealth
    and not split the Sea for us   Dayenu.

Had He split the Sea for us
    and not led us through it on dry land   Dayenu.

Had He led us through it on dry land
    and not drowned our tormentors in it   Dayenu.

Had He drowned our tormentors in it
    and not provided our needs in the
    desert for forty years   Dayenu.

Had He provided our needs in the desert
    for forty years and not fed us with mannah   Dayenu.

Had He fed us with mannah
    and not given us Shabbos   Dayenu.

Had He given us Shabbos
    and not brought us near to Mount Sinai   Dayenu.

Had He brought us near to Mount Sinai
    and not given us the Torah   Dayenu.

Had He given us the Torah
    and not brought us into Eretz Yisrael   Dayenu.

Had He brought us into Eretz Yisrael
    and not built the Holy Temple for us   Dayenu.

---

* Dayenu — it would have sufficed for us

עַל אַחַת כַּמָּה וְכַמָּה טוֹבָה כְפוּלָה וּמְכֻפֶּלֶת לַמָּקוֹם עָלֵינוּ. שֶׁהוֹצִיאָנוּ מִמִּצְרַיִם. וְעָשָׂה בָהֶם שְׁפָטִים. וְעָשָׂה בֵאלֹהֵיהֶם. וְהָרַג אֶת־בְּכוֹרֵיהֶם. וְנָתַן לָנוּ אֶת־מָמוֹנָם. וְקָרַע לָנוּ אֶת־הַיָּם. וְהֶעֱבִירָנוּ

HE BROUGHT US OUT OF EGYPT...AND DESTROYED THEIR IDOLS. What is it that makes yetzias Mitzrayim so much more than a mere occurrence of the past, more than just the founding event of our national history to which our yearly spring festival is dedicated? What is it that makes it the basis for every moment of our life and for our every aspiration? How is it that we "go out" from Egypt every day, daily see God's judgments pass over our dwellings, and each day once again stand together with our fathers and mothers at the Red Sea? The key to understanding these questions can be found in the verse: "...and against all the gods of Egypt I will execute judgments, I, Hashem" (*Shemos* 12:12).

The idea of God, Judaism's acknowledgment of Hashem, an idea which diverges sharply from all other definitions of divinity whether they be idolatrous, speculatively philosophical, naturalistic or otherwise, is based on the departure from Egypt. It was then, at that time, that God dethroned with one blow "*all* the gods of Egypt," whether they be the chained god of Spinoza, the evolutionary god of Hegel or the god of atheistic materialism. Every other understanding of the term "god" was refuted. For in yetzias Mitzrayim, He revealed Himself as *Hashem* Who reversed the processes of nature: He laid low immensely powerful nature-worshipers and raised up abysmally abject slaves who had been reduced to the lowest political, social and spiritual level. In fulfillment of His promise, which he made 430 years earlier to Avraham, *Hashem*, in Whose Hands the future lies, lifted the Children of Yisrael to ethical and spiritual freedom on the highest human and national level.

It follows that any human being or any nation which dedicates itself to the fulfillment of His holy Will will thereby elevate itself to the realm of Divine freedom which transcends the purely material world and puts to shame the "clever calculations" of those who rationalize the future as the sum total of the consequences of given causes.

Thus, we owe the Omnipresent a debt of gratitude, not for one, but for many and repeated benefits. For He brought us out of Egypt. And executed judgment on them. And destroyed their idols. And slew their firstborn. And gave us their wealth. And split the Sea for us. And led us through it on dry land. And

AND SLEW THEIR FIRSTBORN … AND SPLIT THE SEA FOR US AND LED US THROUGH IT ON DRY LAND, AND DROWNED OUR TORMENTORS IN IT. And so it says, too, in the Great Hallel:

> "To Him Who slays Egypt through their firstborn, that His lovingkindness endures forever.
> And brought Yisrael out from their midst, that His lovingkindness endures forever…
> To Him Who divides the Sea of Reeds into parts, that His lovingkindness endures forever.
> And made Yisrael pass through the midst of it, that His lovingkindness endures forever.
> And poured out Pharaoh and his host into the Sea of Reeds, that His lovingkindness endures forever" (*Tehillim* 136:10-11, 13-15).

God disciplines men and nations with lovingkindness. He does not immediately decree the actual destruction of those who would rebel against His will. Divine discipline first strikes by depriving such people of that which they love best; it "slays Egypt through their firstborn." Next, it strikes by leading those who came under the heels of these tyrants "from their midst" to freedom. Thus, too, His might has shown the "strong Hand" which refuses to permit anything or anyone to snatch away His children, and the "outstretched arm" which commands the mightiest forces and most powerful despots and knows how to reach everything they call "theirs." But when even the most grievous chastisement and the most obvious display of Divine power are not sufficient to crush spite permanently, to bring about a change of heart in the rebellious and cause them to acknowledge Hashem, then and only then will He, with the lovingkindness of His rule, proceed to the destruction of those who, attempting to revolt against His will, would enslave other men. In this manner, He brings about the permanent liberation of those human beings who would

בְּתוֹכוֹ בֶּחָרָבָה. וְשִׁקַּע צָרֵינוּ בְּתוֹכוֹ. וְסִפֵּק צָרְכֵּנוּ
בַּמִּדְבָּר אַרְבָּעִים שָׁנָה. וְהֶאֱכִילָנוּ אֶת הַמָּן. וְנָתַן לָנוּ
אֶת הַשַּׁבָּת. וְקֵרְבָנוּ לִפְנֵי הַר־סִינַי. וְנָתַן לָנוּ אֶת־
הַתּוֹרָה. וְהִכְנִיסָנוּ לְאֶרֶץ יִשְׂרָאֵל. וּבָנָה לָנוּ אֶת בֵּית
הַבְּחִירָה לְכַפֵּר עַל־כָּל־עֲוֹנוֹתֵינוּ:

otherwise be menaced again and again by these powers of violence.
Hence, at first God only "...slays Egypt through their firstborn," but
finally He "...poured out Pharaoh and his host into the Sea of
Reeds."

AND PROVIDED OUR NEEDS IN THE DESERT FOR FORTY YEARS.
The Exodus and the dividing of the Sea of Reeds had demonstrated to
Yisrael that God was near them in times of extraordinary crisis. But
the journey through the desert would show them that they could
place their trust in God at all times, even for the provision of everyday
necessities. Even the most trifling day-to-day human needs are the
concern of His Providence, and He takes account of every single
breath of those who fear Him. Therefore, one can always rely upon
Him confidently for all one's needs.

Indeed, all the miracles of the redemption in Egypt and at the Sea of
Reeds, together with all the primary lessons at Marah, all dwindled to
insignificance when the Children of Yisrael confronted the specter of
hunger threatening their wives and children. This too may be the
point of the Rabbinic dictum: "It is more difficult to provide man's
daily sustenance than it is to split the Sea of Reeds." Whether real or
imagined, the threat of hunger undermines every principle and
reverses every resolution. As long as man cannot disengage himself,
not from the responsibility to provide for his family, but from
the overwhelming anxiety resulting from that care, he is unable
to completely realize the Divine Torah. Freedom from this
overwhelming anxiety, however, is possible only when one is
convinced that concern for man's material sustenance, does not rest
on man alone, nor even primarily on him. One must realize that one
can but do his part; indeed, God expects him to do this much. But
ultimately he must depend on Him for the success of his endeavors.

drowned our tormentors in it. And provided our needs in the desert for forty years. And fed us with mannah. And gave us Shabbos. And brought us near to Mount Sinai. And gave us the Torah. And brought us into Eretz Yisrael. And built for us the Holy Temple to atone for all our sins.

Man must realize that his efforts for his sustenance are not his privilege, but his duty, and he must be convinced that the soul of every single human being and every household with all its hungry members, be their number great or small, are all the object of God's constant, ever-watching, almighty, caring love.

But until one has accomplished this feat, as long as he believes that it is he and he alone who, with all his limited powers, is bound to the yolk of toil to ensure the necessities of life for himself and his dependents, there will be no end to his anxiety. Indeed, this anxiety will turn any man's world into a wilderness, even in the midst of a society abundant with wealth. His will be a wilderness of social competition. His endless fears will convince him that he must secure and protect not only the morrow but his whole future and the future of his children, grandchildren and even great-grandchildren. He will come to believe that he must ruthlessly acquire ever-increasing portions of the world's wealth, for himself and his dependents. Consequently, he will find himself with almost no time at all for the pursuit of other goals.

Therefore, God led the future people of His Torah out into the actual desert, bare of all the necessities of life. There, He made them feel all the anxiety of a place where the requirements of the present were completely unobtainable and the prospects for the future seemed non-existent. He let them see for themselves and for all their descendants the ruthlessness to which such a situation, even though it be but a temporary one, can bring a man. Until now, they had been unused to worrying about their sustenance. It was in their masters' interest to keep them alive and strong when they were slaves just as one cares for his working animals and beasts of burden.

But now they were to learn the proper way of providing sustenance for themselves and for their dependents. They would gather the bread which rained from Heaven only: "...their daily requirement each day so that I may test them whether they will walk in My Teaching or not" (*Shemos* 16:4). Whether "My Teaching" will be observed depends upon there being men who are content having their families' needs provided for one day at a time, cheerfully and happily enjoying today while carrying out all of its duties, leaving the worry for tomorrow to Him Who has provided for today and Who can be trusted to provide for tomorrow, too. Only such unreserved confidence in God will safeguard the observance of His Law against infringement caused by anxiety, real or imagined, about material hardship. He who has not learned to trust God for the next day will ultimately be led away from God and His Law by his persistent concern for future years. Hence, the saying of Rabbi Elazar Hamodai: "He Who created the day created its sustenance too." On this Rabbi Eliezer the Great commented: "Anyone who has enough to eat for today and says: 'What shall I have to eat for tomorrow?' — indeed he is among those who have little trust in God" (see *Mechilta, Beshalach* 2:4 and *Sotah* 48b).

AND GAVE US SHABBOS. Had the Shabbos, with its manifold benefits, been nothing more than a Divinely ordained day of rest, how great a blessing would it still have been.

For had Shabbos *not* been given to the Children of Yisrael for rest, had God *not* ordained it, then when would they have found rest? When can a man find time for himself, for his wife, and for his children? When can he find time for his spirit and soul? When can he find his Heaven on earth? One might answer: "When he has time." But when will that be? When is such a man allowed to find the time?

The material world goes about its work without respite. It never pauses and so, perpetually in motion, it wages its war for survival. Whatever does not ascend, descends; whoever marks time is trampled down. "Day and night shall never cease" (*Bereishis* 8:22). Can one then stop, say "Halt!" to his cares and anxieties about his physical existence? Can one simply rest his hand, his head, his soul and wipe away the sweat, smooth away the frown, and shake off the dust from the treadmill of life? When will he cease peering ahead at his next goal? When will he have the time to look behind and around — to gaze into the inner recesses of his soul and see what it was that he wanted and what he strove for, to see what he has become and what has become of him? One must ask himself: "When will I once and for all desist from the vexation of pursuing the future and rejoice in the happiness of the present — the joy of the present in my paradise on earth?"

126

Paradise? Who still dreams about a paradise on earth? The gates of the Garden of Eden closed behind us long ago. The Tree of Life no longer blooms for man; thorns and thistles grow by the wayside. By the sweat of his brow does man seek his bread. And the bread he finds he eats in worry and sadness. Without Shabbos, man toils restlessly. Without Shabbos, without a respite, he tortures himself with his anxiety. Even if each day a thousand minds were to ponder how to add to human knowledge — even if each day a thousand new inventions increased man's power, he would not become happier through his augmented knowledge. He would neither become more free nor his burden become lighter, by his increased power. "He that increases knowledge, increases sorrow" (*Koheles* 1:18). The more inventions, the more desires; the more power, the more toil.

The father strives with his neighbor, the scope of his pursuits extending as far as the boundaries of his hamlet, while the son competes against the whole world, reaching for the heavens where the sky is the limit. The smart son chases after a thousand objects of pleasure that were unknown to the simple father. He acquires them by the sweat of his brow, and in so doing, *worries* much about himself, his wife, and his children. But he has no time to *think* about himself, his wife and his children. In his anxiety over his household's survival, he becomes estranged from his family.

The concept of "making a living," consumes man to the point where the whole of life has become subjugated to the struggle for a living. Meanwhile, no one asks about the purpose and goal of living, about the value and significance of life. Making a living has become so great and gigantic a task that the sum of all human wisdom — the study of heaven and earth, lands and seas, virtue and ethics, even kindness and compassion — has no other than a purely economic value. And man, who was created in the image of God by resembling his Creator in wisdom, in kindness and in justice, man, who was to rejoice as did God in the work of his hands, is harnessed to the soil, dripping with sweat as he seeks his food. He does not hear the voice of God moving about, calling out, searching: "...Where are you?" (*Bereishis* 3:9).

Then, sent from Eden like the angel of God, Shabbos comes and approaches man and says: "In the Name of God, Stop! Your sole worry must not be for material provisions for yourself and your family. You are sinning against yourself, your wife, and children if your hand is unceasingly occupied in providing food. Have you no spirit, no heart, no soul assigned to your earthly existence wherewith to merit eternal life? Will you surrender your souls to suffering and

127

degeneration at the same time that you feed and pamper your bodies? An end to work! Your God has decreed it. You are forbidden to work. And this is the guarantee that you do not need to work: you will have accomplished enough if you have worked properly for six days. Do not deny your Heavenly soul — do not deny your God. Leave your work and come home with me."

Now indeed man stands where he belongs — his bursting chest relaxes, his violent pulse subsides. Now he takes off time for himself and casts off his burdens. He wipes his sweat-covered brow, and dusts off his body. The frown disappears, he raises his eyes and looks about — indeed, he smiles — and now he can hear the voice calling from the Garden of Eden. It beckons him to his wife's side, within the circle of his children. It brings Shabbos into his soul, into his home: and his dwelling is transformed. No home is too small to contain the Divine Presence entering upon the footsteps of Shabbos. The light radiating from within him doubles the illumination of the candles; the peace reposing within him adds spice to the Shabbos meal. Worry, tears, sorrow and sighing — all are banished from even the poorest of Jewish dwellings. "It is Shabbos — and to cry out is forbidden" (*Shabbos* 12a). "It is Shabbos — and funeral orations are proscribed" (*Bach*, in *Tur Shulchan Aruch, Orach Chayim, Siman* 287). Shabbos offers balm and comfort to all. Shabbos enriches and equalizes great and small. Shabbos proclaims to each and all: "Cast the burden of your path upon Hashem, and trust in Him, and He will bring it to pass" (*Tehillim* 37:5). If one has done his share, Hashem will do the rest. Consequently, Shabbos is a delight to him. Indeed, Shabbos is an order given in the Name of God for man to rest from his worry and anger. It shows him that God fights his battles, knows his suffering, and does his worrying for him. And He rejoices in lifting man's burdens from upon him if only he will entrust them to His hands.

Shabbos enriches and equalizes great and small! The possessions for which men struggle on weekdays distinguish the haves from the have-nots, for not everyone succeeds in the struggle. But the treasures of paradise that Shabbos supplies from its stores — the peace and relaxation, the fullness of joy in the presence of God — are provided for all in abundance and equality.

"Rabbi Levi said, 'If Yisrael were to observe even a single Shabbos properly, the son of David would come immediately, and they would be redeemed'" (*Yalkut, Tehillim* 95:7). Only the Shabbos of Hashem will succeed in effecting such magic. Only if God commands that one cease from his work, will he achieve the proper rest. Choosing a weekly rest day oneself would be in vain, even though one's hand might rest, his feet stand still, his body enjoy itself, for peace of mind and tranquility of heart come from God alone. Only if rest is God-ordained, will His command assure that one will rest well and securely and that he will find his life's fulfillment in Him.

Indeed, God gave us Shabbos — and only Shabbos gives rest to Yisrael.

AND FED US WITH MANNAH AND GAVE US SHABBOS. For thousands of years, man was oblivious to Shabbos. It had disappeared from the earth. Man bent his knee before his sensual desires. He trembled before the host of material forces that everywhere constrained his existence and endeavors. He regarded himself as being at war with nature. Every stone he wrested from the earth became a weapon with which to transform even history into a story of war and strife in which man oppressed man. War ruled the earth. Man's creative power expressed itself in developing ever more sophisticated weapons; his creative spirit expressed itself in cunning and trickery. Egotism, pleasure seeking, being and enjoying were life's goals, and in striving for these objectives man saw himself as alone.

The war of man against nature or man against man — this was what life meant. Desire and ambition, fear and hatred were life's motives. Man sought to save himself from nature and to exploit its powers for his own ends. Man sought to protect himself from the competition of his brother and to utilize his brother's struggle solely for his own benefit — this was the sum of man's ambitions once Shabbos had been lost to the world.

Shabbos was lost — and with it the belief in the One God, the Master Whose will and wisdom are manifest in the totality of the world and in the slightest movement of the smallest of any of its parts. Shabbos had disappeared — and with it, belief in the dignity and nobility of man. Gone was faith in man whom God had imbued with part of His own spirit, granted part of His freedom, with whom He had established a special covenant and whom He had destined to become, not a slave to nature or a tyrant over other men, but His voluntary servant. Gone was faith in he who was to be first in the choir of created beings into whose hands freedom, truth, justice, compassion and blessing were given.

With the disappearance of Shabbos, belief in the value of human activity was lost. Gone was the understanding that one thought freely conceived and acceptable to God, one word freely spoken and acceptable to God, one deed freely done and acceptable to God is

129

worth more than all the power of the mighty, physical forces of nature. Gone was the notion that man has merely to be good and he will find the earth at his feet. With the loss of belief in God, belief in the Divine nature of man was lost too. Gone was the belief in man's freedom of choice and in the Divine power of his thinking, speech and action. Gone was the belief that the Master of the universe had assured salvation and blessing to man's free, moral will, that neither man's knowledge of nature, nor the art of war, nor the cleverness of his cunning, nor the might of his power, but only the knowledge of God and the art of serving Him, the wisdom and compassion learned from God alone, would bring salvation to man on earth.

Shabbos was missing from the world — and for thousands of years, she stood before the Throne of Glory saying: *You gave each of the days a partner. Only I remained forgotten, neglected, alone* (see *Bereishis Rabbah* 11:8).

Now there was a certain family which had still preserved some spark of the knowledge of God. God had cast that family into the Egyptian crucible of forgetfulness of God. That family was enabled to feel in their own flesh the curse corrupting those who deified nature, who enslaved man, who lacked a Shabbos. And, finally, both the gods of Egypt and the Egyptian tyrants also saw the finger of God. They trembled before the pure spark contained within the heart of the slaves for whose sake the Divine finger had been lifted. Indeed, God showed them that the propertyless slave, the God-trusting servant was mightier than all the forces of atheism, whose power was based upon natural phenomena and the might of man. He broke the chains, tamed the turbulent waves and led Yisrael through the desert, there to foster the redemption of man — there to discover Shabbos.

"And the Children of Yisrael said unto them: 'Would that we had died by the hand of Hashem in the land of Egypt, when we sat by the fleshpots, when we ate bread to the full; for you have brought us forth into this wilderness, to make this whole assembly die of hunger.' And Hashem said to Moshe, 'Behold I am about to make bread rain from heaven for you; and the people shall go out and gather the daily requirement every day, so that I may test them, whether they will walk in My teaching or not. And it shall come to pass on the sixth day that they shall prepare that which they bring home, and it shall be twice as much as they gather daily.' ... 'See the Lord has given you Shabbos; therefore He gives you on the sixth day bread for two days; abide you every man in his place, let no man go out of his place on the seventh day'" (*Shemos* 16:3-5,29).

Shabbos awaited the arrival of the people of Yisrael as they entered the desert. Indeed, the entire forty years of wandering in the desert were but an education for Shabbos. Each argument and quarrel and complaint was in essence no more than a sin against the spirit of Shabbos. And if one reviews the entire history of Yisrael, he will find that this is the source of all the evil that ever befell Yisrael. The Shabbos spirit in its entirety had not penetrated the hearts of the people.

For forty years Shabbos was signed and sealed in Yisrael. Even a child could have no doubt which was the day of Hashem. "He blessed it with mannah and hallowed it with mannah" (*Bereishis Rabbah* 11:2). Shabbos announced its coming on Friday by the blessing that doubled Yisrael's portion of mannah. And every Shabbos proclaimed its Divine sanctity: *Let no man leave his place to gain his livelihood, for it [the Shabbos] is holy unto God. "*...Today you will not find it [any mannah] in the field" (see *Shemos* 16:29,25).

For forty years the people learned, "that man does not live by bread alone but by everything that proceeds out of the mouth of Hashem can man live" (*Devarim* 8:3).

For forty years the people learned that God requires man to be active, not to make his weekday a Shabbos. He is not, however, to become enslaved to his pursuit after food; he must not sacrifice his present on the altar of the future. God's blessing for tomorrow is as certain as His blessing for today. Let man trust in Hashem, let him rejoice in His blessing every day and rest securely on the seventh day — since it is only trust in God that will bring man blessing and protection, while whatever is hoarded as a result of disbelief will rot and become putrid.

And this seemingly simple law which our people were taught for forty years became the eternal heritage of the people of Yisrael. Indeed, simple as it may seem, it alone will bring sanctity and happiness, grace and blessing to mankind.

The power of Shabbos revives man. The Shabbos man is a new man. He looks with different eyes upon nature and history, at other men and at his God.

He neither kneels nor trembles before nature. He will not bend his knee to "moles and bats" (*Yeshayahu* 2:20). He has acquired in the Name of God his freedom from all the terrors of nature. His soul soars aloft to God, over and above all the majesty of nature. He has God alone in heaven and has "...no other desire on earth" (*Tehillim* 73:25).

He will not tyranize nature. He has acquired humility in the Name of God. Despite the power of his dominion over nature, he submits in humility to Hashem, the supreme God. He utilizes his dominion over nature only in the service of Divine salvation, in the service of God Who placed him in the garden of nature "to work it and to guard it" (*Bereishis* 2:15).

Neither will this man bow down or tremble before human power. He has acquired in the Name of God his freedom from the fear and deification of man. God is close to his humble dwelling — just as He is near to palaces. God takes account of those of His sons in their poor cradles just as He counts those clad in silk. God sees one's modest, quiet efforts just as clearly as He hears the trumpeting of glorious deeds. And if God is his help in his quiet pure creativity — what harm can other men do to him (see *Tehillim* 118:6-7)?

He is no enemy to human society. He has attained his freedom in the Name of God, freedom from envy and arrogance, from hatred and hostility, from vengeance and brute coercion. He does not evaluate himself by outward appearances beause he has a covenant with God. And, so, he sees God hovering over every man and will make every man his brother, in the Name of God. He sees every home as a holy habitation of providence. He will not lord it over the poor nor will he envy the rich. Generously will he rejoice over his friend's blessing, over the measure of wealth and glory that God has accorded to someone else. In his eyes "he who had gathered much had nothing left over, and he who had gathered little had no lack" for "each had gathered in accordance with his needs" (*Shemos* 16:19), in accordance with the portion allotted to him by God.

"Competition" — the word is both blessing and curse. Remove Shabbos from man and he will rush perspiring and dusty along the path of the pursuit of happiness. The generous eye that smiled at every participant in the road of life is corrupted into an evil and envious organ. The helping hand that was stretched out generously to all making the journey is now clenched in a mighty fist, poised to hit out from behind. The human heart in which mercy and compassion were to repose is now barred with seven locks of envy, jealousy and hatred. The human spirit which was a beacon of truth, justice and saving wisdom now degenerates into the robber's lamp of falsehood, iniquity and brute force. Indeed, such is competition and this is its curse. It divides human society and incites ceaseless strife among brothers blessed by God.

But the curse of competition is absent from the Shabbos man. He will not build his home on the ruins of his neighbor's. His foot will not step on his brother's neck. His brother's downfall will not raise him, and his brother's ascent will not bring him down. It is an easy matter for God to feed and sustain the millions of His creatures. And when the terror of envy departs from the Shabbos-heart of man, then the flowers of paradise, of grace and kindness, will of their own accord bloom within him. Man has been made a partner in promoting the happiness of his neighbor. And the choicest of all his blessings is the blessing that he has compassionately prepared for his brother.

Remove Shabbos from man, and he immediately believes that "his god is in his hands" (*Iyyov* 12:6). He will immediately "sacrifice unto his net and offer incense unto his drag, because by them their portion is fat and their food plenteous" (Chavakuk 1:16). Man becomes "as the fish of the sea, like the creeping things that have no ruler over them" (ibid. 14) If one takes Shabbos away from man, then he is deprived of his sole support, for he has been deprived of his God.

But give man Shabbos, and one has not only given him the God of the world, but the God of every home and the Lord of every soul, Who is enthroned on high and looks down below. By His protection and providence, God will make every home secure and save every soul. By this knowledge and holiness, every home will find its deliverance, every soul find its peace.

Give mankind Shabbos and one has broken his chains and healed his wounds.

AND GAVE US THE TORAH AND BROUGHT US INTO ERETZ YISRAEL. The Torah was given in the wilderness — but not because it originated in the obscurity of a hermit's gloomy meditations. God did not appear to the Children of Yisrael on the outer fringes of life, removed from reality. Neither did He appear to them in nebulous illusions of death and darkness or in moments of surrealistic ecstasy. God never said: *"Escape from the world in order to find Me."* On the contrary, He said: "I have not spoken in secret, in a place of a land of darkness: I did not say to Yaakov's seed, 'Seek Me in vain'..." (*Yeshayahu* 45:19).

God did not reveal supernatural secrets to be conjectured about or lift the veil from otherworldly realms. He did not make mankind "believe in" something; rather, "...I, Hashem, speak righteousness, I declare things that are right" (*ibid.*). What God revealed in the wilderness was His law!

True, God led His people into the desert. The desert was the ideal venue for the revelation of His Torah because it was virgin soil, unpolluted as yet by egotism and ambition, undefiled by the pursuit of vanity. He chose the desert, far from cities, far from society and inhabited lands, far from an already corrupt society, for whose

רַבָּן גַּמְלִיאֵל הָיָה אוֹמֵר. כָּל שֶׁלֹּא־אָמַר שְׁלֹשָׁה דְבָרִים אֵלּוּ בַּפֶּסַח לֹא־יָצָא יְדֵי חוֹבָתוֹ. וְאֵלּוּ הֵן.

פֶּסַח. מַצָּה. וּמָרוֹר:

regeneration the Divinely-inspired foundation needed first to be laid. All that was to come about was new and unprejudiced. The desert held no preconditions, it contained no national-political boundaries, it was open and accessible to all. It was there that God led Yisrael, the firstborn of the family of man. And there it was that He revealed His glory in all its majesty and dignity and in all its power and might. There He caused His Divine spirit to rest on man, destined to be redeemed by the light of His Torah, and there he caused heaven to touch the earth. *The way to Sinai leads through the wilderness, but afterward it leads, by means of the Torah, to a land flowing with milk and honey.* There the potential of the Torah was to achieve its fullest realization.

This is the road which God has shown to Yisrael and that is why every year on the anniversary of the Giving of the Torah in the desert, all Yisrael proceed from every part of Eretz Yisrael to the Temple of His Torah bringing their first fruits with them. At the altar of God, they will express their thanksgiving, for He has made His word come true and all the promises made in His Torah have been fulfilled in the flourishing land.

Promises of eternal life after death can easily be made by any imposter wishing to found a religion of his own. No one will return from there to confirm his promise or call it a lie. But only God can say: "...if you will hearken diligently unto My commandments...then I will give the rain of your land in its due season, the early rain and the late rain that you may gather in your grain, your wine and your oil. And I will give grass on your field for your cattle, that you may eat and be satiated" (*Devarim* 11:13-15).

But, if the hearts of the Children of Yisrael will be led astray, and they will turn aside to serve other gods, then... "The wrath of Hashem will be kindled against you, and He will hold back the heaven and there

134

RABBAN Gamliel used to say: Whoever does not explain the following three things at the Pesach festival has not fulfilled his obligation, namely:

PESACH, MATZAH, and MAROR.

will be no rain and the soil will not yield its produce and you will quickly be lost from off the good land which Hashem is giving to you" (ibid., 17).

Only God can promise that compliance with His word will result in such a blessing. Only God, Whose word rules over heaven and earth at one and the same time, Who controls both the germ within the seed and the nucleus of history, Who alone triggers both the process of nature and the development of events in time. He alone can lift up His Hand and declare: I, the one "Who shapes heaven and earth, the sea and all that is in them"; I am the One, "Who keeps faith forever" (Tehillim 146:6).

Because He gave us His Law — not a "belief" to tide us over, sad and trembling, until we reach another world, but the Torah and mitzvos to regulate life upon earth and convert its darkness into light — He can promise that if we keep His Law, He will come to join us in our world and dwell among us and give us blessing — and not that we may join Him in a world to come. The flourishing of our life on earth will make His Presence among us manifest, and the earth will once again become the joyous paradise He created it to be.

God's Torah will deliver man from the existence of evil in this world, and, precisely on this account, God's Torah is — first and foremost — Law. Faith may effect a change of the spirit and mind, but only deeds can effect the transformation of the world. Only a law-abiding life can surmount the thorns and thistles strewn by sin. Belief paired with falsehood in deed will never dispel the darkness on earth. Neither will the darkness recede before arbitrary actions. It will give way only before men's deeds in the Name of God, carried out in keeping with His order in the world, in compliance with His will, and in His service. The key to mankind's redemption is: Mitzvah — Law.

פֶּסַח שֶׁהָיוּ אֲבוֹתֵינוּ אוֹכְלִים בִּזְמַן שֶׁבֵּית הַמִּקְדָּשׁ הָיָה קַיָּם עַל־שׁוּם מָה. עַל־שׁוּם שֶׁפֶּסַח הַקָּדוֹשׁ בָּרוּךְ הוּא עַל בָּתֵּי אֲבוֹתֵינוּ בְּמִצְרַיִם. שֶׁנֶּאֱמַר וַאֲמַרְתֶּם זֶבַח־פֶּסַח הוּא לַיהוה אֲשֶׁר פָּסַח עַל־בָּתֵּי בְנֵי־יִשְׂרָאֵל בְּמִצְרַיִם בְּנָגְפּוֹ אֶת־מִצְרַיִם וְאֶת־בָּתֵּינוּ הִצִּיל וַיִּקֹּד הָעָם וַיִּשְׁתַּחֲווּ:

THE PASCHAL LAMB...FOR WHAT REASON. The Pesach Sacrifice represents the call of Providence to men in the dark hours of the night: *Sleep peacefully in the very midst of storm and stress; smile cheerfully in your sleep. Do not tremble when death and destruction rage in the streets. Do not despair if the dark and deadly mantle of violence covers you like a shroud. For God protects those forsaken in that dreadful hour of midnight. The darker the hour, the darker the night, the deeper your sun has set at your feet and the fainter your earthly stars grow above your head, the nearer is God to you. Thus does His eternal Providence watch over you in the very stillness of the night.* ליל שמורים הוא ליי. "This night had been a night of manifold solicitous care for Hashem" (*Shemos* 12:42).

And the Holy One, blessed be He, is not only the "One who watches, highest above all" (*Koheles* 5:7). His protection is not only collective, a protection for the world as a whole (which would have been indicated had the singular noun *shimur* been used in the pasuk), but an individual protection of the life and limb of every single one of His innumerable children (*shimurim* — plural). God's eye watches over every house and door — in the very hour of midnight. The lintel and door posts of every house where man draws his breath are holy unto Him. The pulse of the inhabitants is revealed to Him at the threshold, and He examines whether the very heart's blood of the members of the household has been offered and dedicated to Him. He sees the blood of the family offering daubed on every door post and lintel in His Name: "And He will see the blood on the lintel and on the two door posts" (*Shemos* 12:23).

Nor does He see the house and family alone. He counts every head and numbers every soul, all those who were counted for the family

136

✦ PESACH the Paschal lamb that our fathers used to eat at the time when the Holy Temple was still standing — for what reason? Because the Holy One, Blessed be He, passed over the houses of our fathers in Egypt, as it says: "And you shall say: 'It is a meal of a salvation performed through a hesitating pass-over, dedicated to Hashem Who hesitated as He passed over the houses of the Children of Yisrael in Egypt when He mortally smote the Egyptians and our houses He saved.' And the people bowed and prostrated themselves" (*Shemos* 12:27).

offering, "...according to the counting up of souls..." (*ibid.*, 4). His Providence is individual, extended to every single Jew — "...a night of manifold solicitous care for all the Children of Yisrael throughout their generations" (*ibid.* 12:42).

But the Pesach offering is even more than this. The Paschal lamb represents the call of the Shepherd to His flock and the response of the flock to its Shepherd: "...Go out and take unto yourselves lambs for your families and slaughter the Paschal lamb" (*ibid.*, 21). The Paschal lamb says to Yisrael that every individual is a part of God's flock as it is written: "And you My sheep, the sheep of My pasture, are men..." (*Yechezkel* 34:31). Pesach says to us: *See, the Holy One, blessed be He, not only cares for us, is not only near to us in the darkness of the night, not only takes us in when all have abandoned us, but He is also our Shepherd, our Guide and Leader, and we are to follow Him because* "...He shall feed His flock like a shepherd..." (*Yeshayahu* 40:11). *He alone knows the destination, and He alone knows how to lead us.*

Over land and seas, through fire and water He leads us, if we would only be willing to follow Him — to the most sacred of all goals: "He shall feed His flock like a shepherd, who gathers the lambs in his arm and carries them in his bosom, and gently leads those that nurse" (*ibid.*). "Go and cry in the ears of Yerushalayim, saying: 'Thus said the Lord: "I remember in your favor the affection of your youth, the love of your espousals, how you went after Me in the wilderness, in a land that was not sown"'" (*Yirmeyahu* 2:2).

137

The Paschal lamb also shows mankind and Yisrael another aspect of God, not only the Shepherd and the Protector, but also the Judge. Pesach reveals the Judge Who does not dispense salvation or wreak destruction by blind chance, but "...Who hesitated as He passed over the houses of the Children of Yisrael in Egypt when He mortally smote the Egyptians and our houses He saved..." (*Shemos* 12:27). He paused and weighed, He deliberated before bringing plague and destruction or help and survival.

The Pesach Sacrifice reveals the King of Justice, Who sent a warning message to the ruler on his throne on behalf of the subservient and oppressed slave, deprived of his rights and dignity: *This slave — this mass of slaves whom from your lofty throne you regard as lower than the lowliest of your subjects, to whom you deny every title to justice, property, family and home, to the free exercise of their abilities, to human dignity and life, whose marriages you have broken up, whose children you have drowned, whose backs you have whipped, whose spirit you have degraded, and whose bodies you have harnessed to your labor — this slave who languishes under the whip of your taskmasters, under the heavy load of your bricks is indeed* "My child," "the firstborn" *of My human family; he is* "Yisrael," *harbinger of the mighty reign of God* (see *Shemos* 4:22). "Let My people go that they may serve Me" (*ibid.*, 7:26). *Send out My people that they may dedicate their powers to My service. And if you refuse to send them out,* "...behold I shall slay *your* son, your firstborn" (*ibid.*, 4:23).

The ruler's ear remained deaf. "...Who is Hashem that I should hearken unto His voice..." (*ibid.*, 5:2). And then the midnight hour approached and with it the Divine verdict: "But also that nation whom they shall serve do I judge..." (*Bereishis* 15:14). The warning became reality "...when He mortally smote the Egyptians and our houses he saved" (*Shemos* 12:27). And the slave, the enslaved nation, was free.

The slave, the enslaved people, were free, But the slave had to become a man; the mass of slaves, a nation. They had to become man and nation by the will of God, through the might of the Omnipotent Creator. Let us see: What condition did the Holy One, Blessed be He, stipulate for man and nation to exist on earth? How did He transform the mass of slaves into man and nation? Let us read the "Magna Carta," in which God proclaimed the fundamental rights of the people of Yisrael.

It was on the tenth of Nissan, on "Shabbos Hagadol" (the Great Shabbos). The slave was still slave, having no property, no family, no home. This slave was neither husband nor father, wife nor mother, son nor daughter. The masses had no collective spirit that made them live as one; they had no common destiny to unify them socially. And then God called out to slave and horde. In the very presence of their oppressors, He restored to them property, home and family. He infused them with justice and compassion — justice which protected the individual and his title to freedom and compassion which linked individuals together in a bond of common dedication to the group. And thus He converted the horde into a nation, a community, a congregation. And to serve as the central point of this great nation, as its source of power and life, he set — the home.

He dispatched no messengers with tenuous words to the slaves' tents. He did not inscribe this "Magna Carta" on faded scrolls of parchment. But in the same way as He communicated His hallowed values to His people later on, through halachah, deed and commandment; as He had inscribed His covenant with Noach in the broken rays of the sun; as He had proclaimed His message of exile and redemption to Avraham in the Covenant between the Portions; as He had revealed the significance of Yisrael's struggles through Yaakov's wrestling in the night and perpetuated its significance through commandments in force throughout the generations — so did He proclaim and shape the eternal form of His people by means of halachah, deed and commandment. "...On the tenth of this month they shall take to them every man a lamb, according to their fathers' house, a lamb for a household" (*Shemos* 12:3). In this way He recognized them as possessors of property and independence. He gave recognition to the sanctity of their family ties in the past and into the future in their own individual houses. And just as He established justice to protect the home from robbery and housebreaking — "...you may not take any of the meat out of the house..." (*ibid.*, 46) — so did He join household to household in bonds of fellowship and voluntary cooperation through mutual help and support.

"And if the household be too small for a lamb, then shall he and his neighbor who is near to his house take one [together]..." (*ibid.*, 4). In this way He assigned the more prosperous household the duty of helping its less fortunate neighbor, making good the deficiency of the one through the supplement and support of the other. And precisely because the feeling of obligation unites them here — justice standing side by side with compassion, and compassion by the side of justice — precisely on account of this unity, neither rich nor poor lose their personal worth as free persons: "...according to the counting up of souls..." (*ibid.*). Conversely, only through the power of voluntary dedication and unity does each individual attain the highest self-fulfillment: "...according to every man's eating you [plural] shall make your count for the lamb" (*ibid.*).

This was the gift of Shabbos Hagadol. For four days each one learned to think of himself as a free man, as a link in a family chain stretching back into the past and as the starting point of an independent family life continuing into the future. During those four days, each learned to count himself and be counted — to count the number of souls to whom he was tied as trunk, branch, twig, and blossom in the life of a free family. Each learned to know the Law which protected his own group and, at the same time, his neighbor's circle as well. Each learned to recognize the obligation and love which unite all households together, not as unconnected adjacent rings, but as intertwined links, strong links in a single chain of love.

The fourteenth of Nissan arrived. "Your lamb shall be complete, without blemish, a male of the first year; you may take it from the sheep or the goats. And it shall be to you for a safekeeping until the fourteenth day of this month..." (*ibid.*, 5-6). And now, in addition to God's will which had conferred freedom, in addition to the blood that had created the families, to the rights that had created the circles, to the compassion that had linked the circles together — came the common history, the common destiny and mission. All these together transformed the individual and family, the home and groups of homes into a nation: "...and the whole assembly of the congregation of Yisrael shall slaughter it between the two evenings."

The mighty arm of God which redeemed them all from the same suffering and which carried them aloft on the eagles' wings of its power and grace, the single God-illumined past, present and future on which they were all henceforth to base their existence as a people — this is what transformed them into Yisrael, the people which revealed to the world the rule of God. Participation in a single task devolving upon all alike and in conjunction, united all the separate members of this people, all the representatives of the various sections, to form a community, and summoned the oldest and most competent among them to a council, which would be the new community's permanent and ever-ready focus and center.

And now, "...the whole assembly of the congregation of Yisrael shall slaughter it..." All these souls — their households, families, groups, this entire nation — all are moved by a *single* spirit and dedicate themselves to a *single* mission. All are called upon to be "שה," a sheep in the flock of a single Shepherd. They are to be "תמים," unblemished, to serve the Shepherd in every aspect of their nature, both physical and spiritual, to be "זכר," male, to serve as free, independent and powerful men, and to be "בן שנה," of the first year, to follow their Shepherd with the freshness and humility of a perpetual youth.

140

This idea of consecration is expressed and fulfilled in the life of the individual, household, family, community and nation, just as the tree reproduces itself again and again in trunk, branch, twig, leaf, bud and germ.

These constitute only a few excerpts from this "Magna Carta" in which God, after awakening His people from death, established it in eternal life. But the center of this noble structure, the blessed soil fertilizing this life, the foundation upon which all these values — freedom, justice, compassion, family ties, communal, congregational and national spirit, dedication, trust and obedience — are based was neither Temple nor State but *the home.* "And they shall take of the blood and they shall put it on the two door posts and on the lintel..." (*ibid.,* 7). The Rabbis deduce from here that our forefathers had three altars in Egypt: the lintel and the two door posts (*Mechilta, Bo*). The lintel symbolizes the roof, which protects man from nature; the door posts allude to the walls that separate the individual from society. Together they constitute the idea of "home."

The lessons which Yisrael learned at that midnight hour, the sacred rites which Pesach hallowed for them as their own possession, stood by our fathers and by us and have remained with us ever since. They assured our existence through the vicissitudes and storms of time. All other altars crumbled, all our other Temples were destroyed. But *the home* hallowed by the Pesach Sacrifice and by the angels it welcomed inside, the mutual affection of husband and wife, parents and children, the spirit of freedom, justice and brotherhood, of community, congregation and nation, the trusting obedience to God, with love and devotion — this home and the spirit of this Jewish home, have remained with us forever. They are what made this people, that had come to life, immortal.

From now on, this reborn people no longer needed to fear death. Even were it to forfeit its state, to be banished from its land, to have its Temple burnt, its altar crushed, its members scattered to the four corners of the earth, it would nevertheless everywhere erect its homes, everywhere gather its sons into household circles. Wherever any of its sons has pitched his tent, there has he saved his Jewish home, built his house to God. He has saved the life of his family — and if he is blessed abundantly, the life of the community is blessed as well. He has not only preserved himself but also all the angels of peace who protect and purify, save and redeem, who escorted the nation from the day of its birth onwards and who still constitute its pride and glory.

מַצָּה זוֹ שֶׁאָנוּ אוֹכְלִים עַל שׁוּם מָה. עַל שׁוּם שֶׁלֹּא הִסְפִּיק בְּצֵקָם שֶׁל אֲבוֹתֵינוּ לְהַחֲמִיץ עַד שֶׁנִּגְלָה עֲלֵיהֶם מֶלֶךְ מַלְכֵי הַמְּלָכִים הַקָּדוֹשׁ בָּרוּךְ הוּא וּגְאָלָם. שֶׁנֶּאֱמַר וַיֹּאפוּ אֶת־הַבָּצֵק אֲשֶׁר הוֹצִיאוּ מִמִּצְרַיִם עֻגֹת מַצּוֹת כִּי לֹא חָמֵץ כִּי גֹרְשׁוּ מִמִּצְרַיִם וְלֹא יָכְלוּ לְהִתְמַהְמֵהַּ וְגַם־צֵדָה לֹא־עָשׂוּ לָהֶם:

THIS MATZAH WHICH WE EAT — FOR WHAT REASON. Indeed, such was the nature of this newly-resurrected people. They had acquired freedom and independence. Divine Providence protected, guided and tested them according to the standards of Divine justice. They became obliged to live their lives as family, community and nation, bravely, justly and compassionately, dedicated to holiness, with the eternal freshness of youth. Thus, they became hallowed, clinging to the only God, sheltering beneath His protection and taking refuge in His stronghold. So they succeeded in celebrating their holidays as if in paradise, as a people dwelling alone — until the day comes when the rest of the nations "...will beat their swords into plowshares and their spears into pruning hooks" (*Michah* 4:3). At that time, they, too, will go up to the House of the God of Yaakov to learn of His ways and to walk in His paths (see *Yeshayahu* 2:3). Into their homes, too, will they welcome — instead of sword and spear, arrow and armor — the angels of justice and lovingkindness, of freedom and holiness. They, too, will return to dwell in the Garden of Eden which had been lost to man.

But what if even this nation, in the course of its long exile, should come to forget its origins? What if it forgets how it was wallowing in blood and only Divine *fiat* awakened it to renewed life?

❧MATZAH unleavened bread — this matzah

which we eat — for what reason? Because the dough of our fathers did not have time to become leavened before the King of kings, the Holy One, Blessed be He, revealed Himself to them and redeemed them. As it says: "And they baked the dough which they had brought forth from Egypt into unleavened cakes, for it was not leavened, because they had been driven out of Egypt and could not tarry, and even provisions they had not prepared for themselves" (*ibid.* 12:39).

What if this People forgets the One to Whom it owes its renewed life, and to Whom it belongs with every fiber of its being? What if subsequent generations examine their history, their family, their communal and national life — and find there only the ordinary elements present in the life of every society and nation? What if when they recall past events, they do not sing praises to their God, but place their laurels on the heads of their ancestors, regarding their forefathers as "men of valor" and Moshe as their hero? What if they proclaim: "Our hand is exalted, and not Hashem has wrought all this" (*Devarim* 32:27)?

And what if the very idea of the living God, which was to have hallowed their entire existence, becomes effaced because of this? What if — finally — all the angels of peace, freedom, justice, lovingkindness and holiness depart, and instead of the home being a perpetual paradise, the soil produces thorn and thistle, as happened with that Garden of Eden of the past?

Was not the world a paradise once? Did not the Heaven of peace extend over the head of man and the Divine Presence walk about in man's garden? Alas, the sun soon set on the Garden of Eden, for man's sensuality drove him from it. Jealously he rose up to kill his brother. In their quest for glory, men built themselves their tower. "Jealousy, lust and the quest for glory drive man from the world" (*Pirkei Avos* 4:21). This is the maxim inscribed on every page of human history. Do not these same evil angels threaten the restored Garden of Eden? Will not the family be destroyed by lust, the community disintegrate through jealousy, the nation in its quest for fame and prestige divest itself of the ornaments received at Sinai — it too becoming harnessed to the merciless and relentless chariot of godless ambition, trampling upon human bodies?

Therefore the Holy One, Blessed be He, provided them with a reminder to take with them from the darkness of exile to the light of redemption, namely, the combination of the sacrifice of freedom with the bread of dependence. "...With unleavened bread and bitter herbs shall they eat it" (*Bemidbar* 9:11). He banned the eating of leavened bread, the bread of independence, during the Festival of Freedom. He removed this bread of independence from Yisrael's diet, domain and use. "Seven days shall you eat unleavened bread; however on the first day you shall put away leaven out of your houses..." (*Shemos* 12:15). "...Nothing leavened shall be eaten" (*ibid.* 13:3). "...And there shall be no leavened bread seen with you, neither shall any leaven be seen with you in all your borders" (*ibid.*, 7). Holding the freedom sacrifice in one hand and the bread of slavery in the other, one shall tell his children and grandchildren repeatedly from Whom it was that they received their freedom and to Whom it is that they belong in this freedom. "...You have acquired this people" (*ibid.* 15:16). They shall remove, along with their leaven, all lust, jealousy and glory. They must remove from their bodily pleasures all the sensuality that degrades the family. They must remove from their homes the jealousy that erodes the life of the community. They must exclude from their pursuits and activities the quest for glory which undermines the life of the nation. They must sedulously foster justice, lovingkindness and holiness, lest they fall prey to glory, jealousy and lust. So will they preserve purity and holiness in their communal, national and family life.

"This matzah which we eat — for what reason? Because the dough of our fathers did not have time to become leavened before the King of kings, the Holy One, Blessed be He, revealed Himself to them and redeemed them."

Alas, the King of kings, the Holy One, Blessed be He, appears — but man fails to notice Him. Man lives as if he himself were king and master of his fate. But our forefathers did see Him; our forefathers learned to look upon Him; to them He was revealed! They were still slaves, eating the bread of servitude. They remained as they were —

144

letting their sons be drowned, toiling under heavy burdens, baring their backs to the harsh sting of the whip, having no heart to listen to Moshe and his tidings. Even later on, six hundred thousand armed men trembled at the sight of their overlords in pursuit, and they longed to return to the yoke of slavery with every new difficulty! They were the same slaves, and their masters were the same oppressors who had imposed so burdensome a yoke upon them as to leave them no time to bake their bread thoroughly and, so, it was eaten unleavened. But now to both of them — to both slave and oppressor — the light of the Divine Presence suddenly became visible. The oppressor was gripped with fear. The whip which had until now driven the slave to work, the arm that did not wish to give up the diligent, patient slave, now urged the slave to go forth to freedom, as it says, "...they were driven out of Egypt and could not tarry, neither had they prepared any provisions for themselves" (*ibid.* 12:39). Our Sages refer to this as "the Egyptian haste and the Israelite haste" (*Berachos* 9a). Both were in haste to depart from one another. Yisrael went out to freedom with the unleavened bread of slavery because they had not seized their freedom, but had received it from God. And because He had made them free, God acquired them forever for His service.

The human yoke had been cast off their necks forever. They were to be the freest men on earth, no longer subservient to the might of any human power — and at the same time they were to accept the yoke of the service of God. In this *service* they would discover their freedom; in it they had acquired their freedom and only by virtue of this service would they preserve it forever. Yisrael passed from the service of Pharaoh to the service of God: "...when you bring forth the people out of Egypt, you shall become servants of God..." (*Shemos* 3:12). As long as they serve the One God, no human power on earth will be master over them. Were they to disengage themselves from the service of the One God, they would once more become slaves to man. The service of God alone brought and brings them forth to freedom.

To serve God with all that one has received from His hands! Whatever one has received shall remain in his possession as the sacred property of God. To regard *everything* as given by God; to let no vestige remain of the overweening pride of the person who believes that he fashions his fate with his own hands; to let no memory remain of arrogant willfulness and sensual cravings — this constitutes the central clause of the "Magna Carta" of the People of Freedom. This is the paragraph dealing with chametz and matzah inscribed in the Declaration of Freedom of the Redemption from Egypt.

Matzah is the bread of the slave, the symbol of dependence. Chametz, by contrast, is the symbol of independence. Hence there is no Pesach without matzah, no freedom without total subjection to God. "You shall not offer the blood of My Meal Offering with leavened [products]..." (*ibid.* 23:18).

Hence, the Freedom Offering brought at the time when we commemorate the freedom that God and God alone granted us must be consumed only with matzah, the bread of the slaves, in order that we be reminded of our subjection and our complete helplessness at the moment we attained our freedom. It says to us that had Hashem not brought our forefathers from Egypt, we would have remained slaves there to this very day. Indeed, it tells us even more, for "Seven days shall you eat unleavened bread..." (*ibid.* 12:15), and, "seven days shall there be no leaven found in your houses..." (*ibid.*, 19). The number seven denotes the physical world. By being commanded not to receive benefit from leaven, not to eat it and not to see or find it for seven days, we are being instructed to remove from the physical world all thought of freedom that is independent of God, whether this be the satisfaction of our bodily needs, the employment of our material resources or the control of our property. This is the freedom clause in our charter of independence (see page 67).

Other peoples have credited the acquisition of their homes to their own efforts. Others have allowed themselves to be ruled by their own desires and to rule arbitrarily over their property. The community of Yisrael received everything from God. From His Hands they received their home and property, their physical freedom and the capability to utilize both these possessions and powers. And, so, they dedicate home and property, existence and life, power and possessions to God. And when the anniversary of their freedom comes round, they banish the signs of freedom from their midst and proclaim that all their possessions are dedicated to God even to this very day. If not for Hashem, their God, they would again find themselves in a house of bondage. Their masters would force them to bow their heads, they would confiscate their homes and property, and drown their sons "lest they multiply" (*ibid.* 1:10). They would once again be wallowing in their blood — and no one would pass over them, proclaiming: "In your blood, live!" (*Yechezkel* 16:6).

Just as all leaven is banned from Jewish homes on Pesach, the festival of the founding of these homes, so must chametz be banned from Yisrael's Temple, its altar and sacrifices at all times. True, Yisrael were destined to receive a land flowing with milk and honey. They would eat the bread of independence in that land, not in scarcity or poverty, as it says: "A land in which you shall not eat bread parsimoniously..." (*Devarim* 8:9). Yet they would acquire this honey of plenty and bread of independence from God's hand only as a reward for living according to His commandments.

On the anniversary of the Giving of the Torah, and during the ensuing weeks, the People of Yisrael appear in the Sanctuary before God and His altar. In their hands they bear the bread of independence and the honey of plenty — the two loaves and the first fruits. By word of mouth, they give thanks to God Who makes His promise come true, Who vouchsafes an abundance of blessing and independence to those that fear Him. "As an offering of first fruits shall you bring them [chametz and honey] near to God, but they may not go up on the altar in expression of willingness to please Hashem" (*Vayikra* 2:12).

There is no place for the bread of independence and the honey of plenty in the offerings through which the People of Yisrael give expression to their own existence, dedicate themselves to God, become pleasing to Him and sustain the Divine fire upon earth. "Every allegiance gift which you bring near to Hashem, may not be made leavened, for not the least leaven and fruit honey may you burn as an offering made of fire unto Hashem" (*ibid.*, 11). Yisrael does not embody within them those conditions which accord all other nations independence and abundance. Yisrael grew up and became a People as aliens, oppressed. Only from the Hand of God and by His Torah, did they, and will they, receive their land of independence and plenty.

On Pesach, the Festival commemorating the founding of the homes of Yisrael, each home is transformed into a Temple, every table into an altar, all bread a sacrificial meal. On this day obedience and dedication to God returns to dwell in our midst and before it, all signs of arrogance which pervert the essence of Yisrael depart — from our possessions, from our resources, and from our sustenance. Anyone who sings Halleluyah in the synagogue but eats the bread of self-esteem in his own home on this day has already denied the basic feature of Yisrael, and has already uprooted himself from the soil of his people, "...for whosoever eats that which is leavened, that soul shall be cut off from the congregation of Yisrael..." (*Shemos* 12:19).

The moment we remove all haughtiness from our acquisitions, our activities and our eating, we open the gates to the Divine Presence. Then we belong once more to God, we behold His glory, we become hallowed through His holiness. Before the effulgence of the Divine Presence all the evil agents of jealousy, pride and lust depart from us, and the angels of lovingkindness, justice and holiness take their place. They are the cherubim with beating wings and flaming swords that stand guard over the Garden of Eden that is our home.

מָרוֹר זֶה שֶׁאָנוּ אוֹכְלִים עַל־שׁוּם
מָה. עַל־שׁוּם שֶׁמֵּרְרוּ
הַמִּצְרִים אֶת־חַיֵּי אֲבוֹתֵינוּ בְּמִצְרָיִם. שֶׁנֶּאֱמַר
וַיְמָרְרוּ אֶת חַיֵּיהֶם בַּעֲבֹדָה קָשָׁה בְּחֹמֶר
וּבִלְבֵנִים וּבְכָל עֲבֹדָה בַּשָּׂדֶה אֵת כָּל־עֲבֹדָתָם
אֲשֶׁר עָבְדוּ בָהֶם בְּפָרֶךְ:

**THIS MAROR WHICH WE EAT — FOR WHAT REASON? BECAUSE
THE EGYPTIANS EMBITTERED THE LIVES OF OUR FATHERS IN
EGYPT.** Not just at that time, but again and again, as the Jews'
destiny unfolds, they will taste the bitterness of life which served to
bring about the regeneration of their forefathers. One must set his
heart on the lofty goal of redemption and then, he will learn to endure
all the suffering which must accompany him — indeed, was ordained
to accompany him — during this waiting period before the
redemption. One must remember, however, that no matter how bitter
one may find the present, the bitterness that his *forefathers*
experienced will make his troubles seem insignificant. All the
outstanding personalities of the Jewish people, beginning from the
time of Avraham, were purified in the crucible of suffering and were
tested in the melting pot of adversity. One must recognize that if not
for the bitter herbs, the Children of Yisrael would not have merited
the Pesach Sacrifice. Every deliverance that has been vouchsafed to
them was preceded by bitter birth pangs.

"Rabbi Shimon bar Yochai said: 'The Holy One, Blessed be He,
gave Yisrael three precious gifts, and all were given only through
suffering'" (*Berachos* 5a). He gave them the Torah, but only such
hearts and souls as had been purified in the crucible of suffering were
fit to receive it. "Forward strides the man whom You, God, do train by
discipline, and whom You teach out of Your Torah the while"
(*Tehillim* 94:12). He gave them Eretz Yisrael, but the road leading to
it crossed through the desert. "...As a man trains his son, so does
Hashem, your God, train you" (*Devarim* 8:5). "For Hashem, your
God, is bringing you to a good land..." (*ibid.*, 7). Finally, He gave

148

❧ MAROR the bitter herbs — this maror which

we eat — for what reason? Because the Egyptians embittered the lives of our fathers in Egypt, as it says: "And they [the Egyptians] embittered their lives with hard labor, with mortar and bricks and with all manner of work in the field; they embittered all their work which they made them do, with harshness" (*ibid.* 1:14).

them the World to Come, but only through suffering does one merit it. "For the commandment is a lamp and the Torah is light and the reproofs of instruction are the way of life" (*Mishlei* 6:23). Indeed Torah and mitzvos point out the goal and illuminate the path. However, in order that one follow the path which leads to his goal, in order that one choose to walk in the "way of life," one must be taught by reproofs of instruction. And so the maror is combined with the Pesach Sacrifice and the matzah.

The Paschal lamb tells one that there is an ever-watchful Guardian, Shepherd and Judge Who is involved in the world. It presents the concept of the importance of family, communal and national life, all based on justice, lovingkindness and holiness. Matzah teaches one to divest himself of all haughtiness in his pleasures, activities and acquisitions. But only the maror, or the bitter hours of trial in one's own life, can demonstrate to the individual that God is his personal Guardian, Shepherd and Judge. Only in periods of bitterness does one actually learn to appreciate the precious value to him of a pure family, communal and national life. Only through the crucible of the maror does one acknowledge his helplessness and lack of independence, and only there does he learn to cast his burden on Hashem. And so, only through the power of the bitter herbs are the truths symbolized by Pesach and matzah realized for the individual. Only through tasting the bitterness of maror can he taste the sweetness of the Pesach and matzah. Therefore Hillel would *combine* the Paschal lamb, matzah and maror and eat them *together* in order to fulfill what is written "...with unleavened bread and bitter herbs shall they eat it" (*Bemidbar* 9:11).

בְּכָל דּוֹר וָדוֹר חַיָּב אָדָם לִרְאוֹת אֶת־עַצְמוֹ
כְּאִלּוּ הוּא יָצָא מִמִּצְרַיִם. שֶׁנֶּאֱמַר וְהִגַּדְתָּ לְבִנְךָ בַּיּוֹם
הַהוּא לֵאמֹר בַּעֲבוּר זֶה עָשָׂה יהוה לִי בְּצֵאתִי
מִמִּצְרָיִם. לֹא אֶת־אֲבוֹתֵינוּ בִּלְבָד גָּאַל הַקָּדוֹשׁ בָּרוּךְ
הוּא אֶלָּא אַף אוֹתָנוּ גָּאַל עִמָּהֶם. שֶׁנֶּאֱמַר וְאוֹתָנוּ
הוֹצִיא מִשָּׁם לְמַעַן הָבִיא אֹתָנוּ לָתֶת לָנוּ אֶת הָאָרֶץ
אֲשֶׁר נִשְׁבַּע לַאֲבוֹתֵינוּ:

The matzos are covered and the cup is lifted and held
until the closing sentence "Who has redeemed Yisrael"
(according to some customs it is put down after
"Halleluyah" and the matzos are uncovered, then lifted
again for the berachah "Who redeemed us..." and
the matzos covered once again).

לְפִיכָךְ אֲנַחְנוּ חַיָּבִים לְהוֹדוֹת
לְהַלֵּל לְשַׁבֵּחַ לְפָאֵר
לְרוֹמֵם לְהַדֵּר לְבָרֵךְ לְעַלֵּה וּלְקַלֵּס לְמִי שֶׁעָשָׂה
לַאֲבוֹתֵינוּ וְלָנוּ אֶת־כָּל הַנִּסִּים הָאֵלֶּה הוֹצִיאָנוּ
מֵעַבְדוּת לְחֵרוּת מִיָּגוֹן לְשִׂמְחָה מֵאֵבֶל לְיוֹם
טוֹב וּמֵאֲפֵלָה לְאוֹר גָּדוֹל וּמִשִּׁעְבּוּד לִגְאֻלָּה
וְנֹאמַר לְפָנָיו שִׁירָה חֲדָשָׁה הַלְלוּיָהּ:

LET US THEREFORE RECITE BEFORE HIM A NEW SONG:
HALLELUYAH! "Rabbi Yehoshua ben Levi said: 'The Book of
Tehillim was said in ten expressions of praise. The greatest of all is
Halleluyah since this contains His Name and His praise at one and
the same time'" (*Pesachim* 117a).

In every single generation one is obligated to look upon himself as if he personally had gone forth out of Egypt, as it says: "And you shall relate to your child on that day, saying: 'It is because of this that Hashem acted for me when I came forth out of Egypt'" (*ibid*. 13:8). Not only our fathers did the Holy One, Blessed be He, redeem, but us, too, He redeemed together with them, as it says: "And He brought *us* out from there that He might bring us home to give to us the land which He had sworn to our fathers" (*Devarim* 6:23).

The matzos are covered and the cup is lifted and held until the closing sentence "Who has redeemed Yisrael" (according to some customs it is put down after "Halleluyah" and the matzos are uncovered, then lifted again for the berachah "Who redeemed us ..." and the matzos covered once again).

❧ THEREFORE we are

obliged to avow thanks, to praise His mighty acts, to laud, glorify, exalt, proclaim His might, bless, extol and celebrate Him Who wrought all these miracles for our fathers and for us. He brought us forth from slavery into freedom, from sorrow into joy, from mourning into festivity, and from darkness into great light, and from subjugation into redemption. Let us therefore recite before Him a new song: Halleluyah!

The Name יה (related phonetically to כה and כח) is always used to designate a revelation of the might of God. It denotes His working and rule. The praise voiced by Halleluyah, then, expresses the revelation of God as manifested both in His Might, the salvation itself — and in the inspiration and soaring of the spirit — the song to which

151

הַלְלוּיָהּ הַלְלוּ עַבְדֵי יהוה הַלְלוּ אֶת־שֵׁם
יהוה: יְהִי שֵׁם יהוה מְבֹרָךְ מֵעַתָּה וְעַד־עוֹלָם:
מִמִּזְרַח שֶׁמֶשׁ עַד־מְבוֹאוֹ מְהֻלָּל שֵׁם יהוה: רָם עַל־
כָּל־גּוֹיִם יהוה. עַל הַשָּׁמַיִם כְּבוֹדוֹ: מִי כַּיהוה
אֱלֹהֵינוּ. הַמַּגְבִּיהִי לָשָׁבֶת. הַמַּשְׁפִּילִי לִרְאוֹת
בַּשָּׁמַיִם וּבָאָרֶץ: מְקִימִי מֵעָפָר דָּל. מֵאַשְׁפֹּת יָרִים
אֶבְיוֹן: לְהוֹשִׁיבִי עִם־נְדִיבִים. עִם נְדִיבֵי עַמּוֹ:
מוֹשִׁיבִי עֲקֶרֶת הַבַּיִת אֵם־הַבָּנִים שְׂמֵחָה הַלְלוּיָהּ:

this salvation gives rise. Indeed, song, the loftiest and most sublime
aspiration of the human spirit, is, in the Divinely inspired poet, a
work of God. As the Psalmist, King of Yisrael, testifies of himself, it is
God's spirit that speaks through him, and it is His words that hover
on his tongue (*Shemuel* II, 23:2).

   This, too, is what is expressed in the Song at the Sea (see *Shemos*
15:2). Both עזי — my victory, and זמרת, my song, are יה — a
manifestation of God's might. Not only my salvation, but the rapture
that this salvation has awakened in me is an act of God. Hence, in all
the verses referring to song the personal pronoun "my" is missing. It
does not read זמרתי but זמרת (see *Shemos* 15:2, *Tehillim* 118:14,
Yeshayahu 12:2). Both the singer's outward fate and his innermost
emotions reveal the presence of God.

**HALLELUYAH! PRAISE BY PROCLAIMING HIS MIGHTY ACTS, O'
SERVANTS OF HASHEM.** Halleluyah is the call that goes out to
Yisrael as the servants of God to render their service, their
contribution to the advancement and realization of God's purposes
on earth by proclaiming the ways in which He has revealed himself
through His mighty acts. In this manner the "Name" of God, that is,
the recognition and worship of Him, is "blessed" — spread abroad to
an ever-increasing extent.

Halleluyah! Praise by proclaiming His mighty acts, o' servants of Hashem, praise by proclaiming His mighty acts, the Name of Hashem. Blessed be the Name of Hashem from this time forth and unto eternity. True from the rising of the sun until its setting, the Name of Hashem is lauded in praises of His mighty acts. For Hashem is high above all nations, His glory is beyond the heavens. But Who is like Hashem our God, Who though enthroned on high, looks down so low, into the heavens and upon the earth? He raises out of the dust him who has sunk low and lifts the defenseless up from the dunghill. To set him next to princes, next to the princes of his people. He causes the barren woman of the house to sit as a joyous mother of children; Halleluyah! (*Tehillim* 113).

TRUE FROM THE RISING OF THE SUN UNTIL ITS SETTING. It is imperative that the true recognition of God be broadcast throughout the world. True, the earth has never been entirely without some awareness of God, some concept of His transcendent existence and grandeur. From east to west, wherever men dwell on earth, they know of One God Who stands in majesty high above all the powers in the world that man is wont to worship.

BUT WHO IS LIKE HASHEM. God was recognized by mankind as the "Most High" even before Yisrael was sent into its midst (see *Bereishis* 14:19). Not the awareness that God is "on high," but the conviction that He is "near," that He peers far into the heavens and into the earth and is close in His rule even to the lowliest of creatures, is what distinguishes the Jewish concept of God from the ones held by the other nations. This is the attitude which motivates Yisrael when they call Him "our" God, the Guide of our destinies, the Leader of our deeds, Who has revealed Himself to us by His word and by His mighty acts. This is what the rest of mankind should learn from Yisrael and through Yisrael concerning the One God.

בְּצֵאת יִשְׂרָאֵל מִמִּצְרָיִם בֵּית יַעֲקֹב מֵעַם לֹעֵז:
הָיְתָה יְהוּדָה לְקָדְשׁוֹ יִשְׂרָאֵל מַמְשְׁלוֹתָיו: הַיָּם רָאָה
וַיָּנֹס. הַיַּרְדֵּן יִסֹּב לְאָחוֹר: הֶהָרִים רָקְדוּ כְאֵילִים.
גְּבָעוֹת כִּבְנֵי צֹאן: מַה לְּךָ הַיָּם כִּי תָנוּס. הַיַּרְדֵּן תִּסֹּב
לְאָחוֹר: הֶהָרִים תִּרְקְדוּ כְאֵילִים. גְּבָעוֹת כִּבְנֵי־צֹאן:
מִלִּפְנֵי אָדוֹן חוּלִי אָרֶץ. מִלִּפְנֵי אֱלוֹהַּ יַעֲקֹב: הַהֹפְכִי
הַצּוּר אֲגַם־מָיִם. חַלָּמִישׁ לְמַעְיְנוֹ־מָיִם:

HE RAISES OUT OF THE DUST. The affairs of earth and those
concerning human society (verses 7,8), as well as the physical order of
things (verse 9) are all under His direct guidance and care. He who
suffers may look directly to Him to better his unhappy lot.

WHEN ISRAEL WENT FORTH FROM EGYPT. Yisrael is that nation
which proclaims the complete and unequivocal dominion of God.
Egypt represents that state, mighty and arrogant, which idolizes the
power of man and nature. The House of Yaakov is the *family* of
Yaakov who stand opposed by culture and spirit to the Egyptians, a
people of alien tongue.

This is the only instance in Tanach where we find the term לֹעֵז. In
Rabbinic terminology, any non-Hebraic tongue is called לֹעֵז, and לוֹעֵז
denotes a person who speaks an alien language. In Rabbinic
literature, לוֹעֵז may also mean "to ridicule." Hence עַם לוֹעֵז may mean
either "a people of alien tongue" or "a people who ridicule Jewish
ethics and the Jewish way of life."

Our fathers passed the supreme test. They were able to go forth
from Egypt as Yisrael; they left a people of alien tongue as the House
of Yaakov. Even though they had dwelt in a state that worshiped only
the power of nature and men, they had lost nothing of their own
concept of God which taught them to render homage to His
dominion alone. Moreover, even though they had lived among
people who were alien to them both spiritually and morally and even
though politically speaking, they had been entirely absorbed into the

When Yisrael went forth from Egypt, the House of Yaakov from a people of alien tongue. Yehudah became His sanctuary, Yisrael His sphere of dominion. The Sea saw it and fled, the Jordan sought to turn backward. The mountains skipped like rams, the hills like young sheep. What ails you, o' Sea, that you flee, o' Jordan, that you turn backward; o' mountains, that you skip like rams, o' hills, like young sheep? Tremble, o' earth, before the Master, before the God of Yaakov. Who turns the rock into a pool of water, pebbles into a fountain of water (*ibid.* 114).

state and its population, they had still retained their own morals and family purity. According to a statement in the Midrash, the House of Yaakov was "even as a child, encompassed by its mother's womb" so that what had to be done was "to take a nation unto Himself from out of the midst of another nation" (*Devarim* 4:34).

YEHUDAH BECAME HIS SANCTUARY. When Yisrael went forth from Egypt, Yehudah became the sanctuary of God. In contrast to the concept of power represented by Egypt and the other nations, Yehudah now represented the concept of Divine might. It became God's own, sacred to Him, dedicated to the acknowledgement of his dominion and to the worship of Him alone. (Therefore the feminine form היתה is employed here with reference to Yehudah, indicating that Yehudah had been divested of all arrogance and conceived of itself solely as a dependent of God). And the "family of Yaakov," which had now grown into the "people of Yisrael," constituted not ממשלתו, one great circle in the midst of which God would sit enthroned as a ruler, but was ממשלותיו, a multitude of spheres, tribes, families, houses, in the midst of each and every one of which·God reigned alone. In each entity within the people of Yisrael, God's will and His Law shaped and guided the life of the entire nation as well as that of every single individual.

When Yehudah thus became God's sanctuary and Yisrael a kingdom of God on earth, He caused all the physical world — the seas, the rivers, the mountains and hills, those physical supports of the stage of

בָּרוּךְ אַתָּה יהוה אֱלֹהֵינוּ מֶלֶךְ הָעוֹלָם אֲשֶׁר גְּאָלָנוּ וְגָאַל אֶת אֲבוֹתֵינוּ מִמִּצְרַיִם וְהִגִּיעָנוּ הַלַּיְלָה הַזֶּה לֶאֱכָל בּוֹ מַצָּה וּמָרוֹר. כֵּן יהוה אֱלֹהֵינוּ וֵאלֹהֵי אֲבוֹתֵינוּ יַגִּיעֵנוּ לְמוֹעֲדִים וְלִרְגָלִים אֲחֵרִים הַבָּאִים לִקְרָאתֵנוּ לְשָׁלוֹם שְׂמֵחִים בְּבִנְיַן עִירֶךְ וְשָׂשִׂים בַּעֲבוֹדָתֶךְ וְנֹאכַל שָׁם מִן הַזְּבָחִים וּמִן הַפְּסָחִים (יֵשׁ אוֹמְרִים בְּמוֹצָאֵי שַׁבָּת: מִן הַפְּסָחִים וּמִן הַזְּבָחִים) אֲשֶׁר יַגִּיעַ דָּמָם עַל קִיר מִזְבַּחֶךְ

human and world history — to sense the coming of that great moment, the significance of which extended far beyond the confines of the Jewish people. *And if you shall ask the fleeing sea, the river that flows backwards, the hills and mountains that rise and sink again: "What is the meaning of this moment? What does this upheaval of earth's nature proclaim?" Then they will answer: "It is the Master, Who at this moment begins His dominion over all the earth; it is the God of Yaakov, Who has just taken out for Himself that most powerless of peoples, that people which had sunk below all the nations of the world. He has done this in order to demonstrate through Yisrael the omnipotence and presence on earth of His rule and to show that men and nations do not live simply for the purpose that they might develop and exercise their power. It is before Him, Who is 'on high' but at the same time 'very near,' before the 'Master' and 'God', that the earth is to go into travail. It is to feel the birth pangs of a life that renews its vigor. He changes the most compact and solid rock, into a receptacle for the collection of fresh waters, and the hard pebbles, into a spring that pours forth from within them."*

✤BLESSED be You, Hashem our God, King of

the universe, Who redeemed us and redeemed our fathers from Egypt and enabled us to attain this night, on which to eat matzah and maror. So Hashem, our God and God of our fathers, enable us to attain other festivals of assembly and of pilgrimage which approach us in peace, rejoicing in the building of Your city and joyful in Your sacrificial service; and we shall eat there from the sacrifices and from the Pesach offerings (on *Motzai Shabbos* some say: from the Pesach offerings and from the sacrifices) whose blood will be sprinkled on the sides of Your altar for gracious acceptance, and we shall thank You with a new

---

Should not this transformation perhaps also proclaim to the earth that, in view of this work of God, begun with Yisrael's entry into the history of nations, the hearts of men which had hitherto been solid and closed like rocks will eventually open to receive the Divine truths and that the Divine spark dormant within the stony human heart will be caused to awaken and unfold?

AND WE SHALL THANK YOU WITH A NEW SONG. One must distinguish between שירה and שיר. שירה sings of the invisible aspect of Divine rule in the events of the present, while שיר refers to those signs of His sovereignty that will become apparent only some day in the future. שיר and particularly שיר חדש are always employed with reference to the eventual, ultimate redemption of the world to which all the developments of history will lead.

Our Sages explain the difference between the two words thus: "All of the songs of the past are referred to in the feminine form, for just as a woman gives birth to offspring, so the salvations of the past gave birth to other states of subjugation. However, the salvation of

157

לְרָצוֹן וְנוֹדֶה לְךָ שִׁיר חָדָשׁ עַל גְּאֻלָּתֵנוּ וְעַל
פְּדוּת נַפְשֵׁנוּ. בָּרוּךְ אַתָּה יהוה גָּאַל יִשְׂרָאֵל:

One should intend to fulfill the requirement of
drinking the second of the four cups of wine.

בָּרוּךְ אַתָּה יהוה אֱלֹהֵינוּ מֶלֶךְ הָעוֹלָם
בּוֹרֵא פְּרִי הַגָּפֶן:

The required amount of the second cup is drunk,
within the required period of time, while
reclining to the left.

the future is referred to in the masculine form, for just as a man does not bear offspring, so the salvation of the future will not give birth to any more troubles and tribulations" (*Mechilta, Beshalach*). The masculine form, שיר, refers to that salvation which will be the final, splendid goal of the entire march of time and not a mere stepping stone to some other eventual redemption.

FOR OUR REDEMPTION AND FOR THE DELIVERANCE OF OUR SOULS. The term geulah expresses the ultimate fulfillment of all our hopes. It means more than do the terms הצלה, תשועה, פדות. These refer to the external aspects of our deliverance, whereas geulah implies the personal concern and sense of responsibility of a goel, the Redeemer in Whom all redemption and deliverance are vested.

The term geulah in everyday usage denotes a legal claim for the restoration of a forfeited person or object, both by right and as an obligation. The right to make this claim, as well as the onus, derives from kinship, so much so that the term goel is synonymous with "relative." It implies the entire consequence of the family bond — that a man's personal rights and title to property are a part of the rights of the entire family. Independence or property lost by one

158

song for our redemption and for the deliverance of our souls. Blessed be You, Hashem, Who has redeemed Yisrael.

One should intend to fulfill the requirement of drinking the second of the four cups of wine.

Blessed be You, Hashem our God, King of the universe, Who creates the fruit of the vine.

The required amount of the second cup is drunk, within the required period of time, while reclining to the left.

constitute a loss for his relative as well, and so, the latter arises to take on the cause of his relation who has become powerless and destitute. This is the idea of geulah and goel in Jewish law and life.

As for the redemption of Yisrael and humanity — though mankind has expended its entire store of virility and morality and though Yisrael has forfeited its independence, energy, even the consciousness of its mission as well as the power and strength to carry it out, yet: "their Redeemer lives" (see *Iyyov* 19:25). The One Who lives forever, the God of Yisrael and the Redeemer of mankind, He is their Goel. Every human soul that has lapsed, every Jewish man or woman who has opted out of his or her mission, humanity forfeiting its destiny, Yisrael not attaining theirs — they are *His* loss! "When a man suffers," Rabbi Meir teaches us, "the Divine Presence expresses it thus: '*My* head is heavy, *My* arm is heavy'" (*Sanhedrin* 46a). And in the words of Yeshayahu: "In all their troubles, He is troubled" (63:9).

"Hashem will not cast off His People, nor forsake His inheritance" (*Tehillim* 94:14). He has life for every death, strength for all weakness, freedom and independence for any enslavement. Mankind and the Jewish People are His! He rises up on their behalf when they are prostrated. He is their Father, redeeming them from bondage and perdition to freedom and life.

From the time the hands are washed until after eating the korech, no unnecessary speaking is allowed. Therefore, the leader of the Seder should now explain to all the participants (especially children) all the instructions they will need to know concerning the eating of the matzah and the maror.

It is unlikely that there will be enough matzah on the Seder plate for all of the assembled. Furthermore, since the leader of the Seder is required to distribute from his matzah to those assembled, to have to measure and distribute the required amount after the blessing would constitute an unnecessary lapse of time between the berachah and the fulfilling of the mitzvah. Therefore, it is advisable that everyone have the measured, required amount of matzah from other, shemurah matzos before him (see Required Measurements and Amounts, page 37, before he goes to wash his hands. After the leader of the Seder will have recited the berachah and have measured the required amount for himself, he will easily and quickly be able to distribute bits of the leftover matzah to all assembled to eat together with their portions.

All present wash their hands (a washbasin is brought to the leader of the Seder) and recite the following berachah (one who washed his hands before the karpas and is sure that they have been kept clean, should first contaminate them by touching his shoe or the like):

בָּרוּךְ אַתָּה יהוה אֱלֹהֵינוּ מֶלֶךְ הָעוֹלָם אֲשֶׁר קִדְּשָׁנוּ בְּמִצְוֹתָיו וְצִוָּנוּ עַל נְטִילַת יָדָיִם:

ROCHTZAH. Man's actions should always be performed in a demonstrably human, as opposed to animalistic, manner. To do so, he must strive to subordinate his animal passions. This does not mean that one ought to despise, neglect or destroy his animal element. Rather, the ultimate aim of his actions should be to

Rochtzah

From the time the hands are washed until after eating the korech, no unnecessary speaking is allowed. Therefore, the leader of the Seder should now explain to all the participants (especially children) all the instructions they will need to know concerning the eating of the matzah and the maror.

It is unlikely that there will be enough matzah on the Seder plate for all of the assembled. Furthermore, since the leader of the Seder is required to distribute from his matzah to those assembled, to have to measure and distribute the required amount after the blessing would constitute an unnecessary lapse of time between the berachah and the fulfilling of the mitzvah. Therefore, it is advisable that everyone have the measured, required amount of matzah from other, shemurah matzos before him (see Required Measurements and Amounts, page 37, before he goes to wash his hands. After the leader of the Seder will have recited the berachah and have measured the required amount for himself, he will easily and quickly be able to distribute bits of the leftover matzah to all assembled to eat together with their portions.

All present wash their hands (a washbasin is brought to the leader of the Seder) and recite the following berachah (one who washed his hands before the karpas and is sure that they have been kept clean, should first contaminate them by touching his shoe or the like):

❧BLESSED be You, Hashem our God, King of the universe, Who has sanctified us by His commandments and commanded us concerning the washing of the hands.

accomplish a reconciliation between the animal and spiritual elements he contains. How? By according the animal element only as much importance as God has allotted it and by using it only for accomplishing those aims for which God has conjoined it to man. If one spiritualizes his animal element and hallows it as originally

161

מוֹצִיא

If the leader of the Seder is to make the berachos over the matzah and maror for all assembled (as is the custom in many homes), then he and they must have that in mind while the berachos are being made, and everyone should have in mind that it is his intention to fulfill his duty to eat matzah on Pesach night.

The leader of the Seder, or each participant, if he is to make his own berachos, takes all three matzos in his hand (the two whole ones for lechem mishneh and the broken one between them for lechem oni) and says the following berachah:

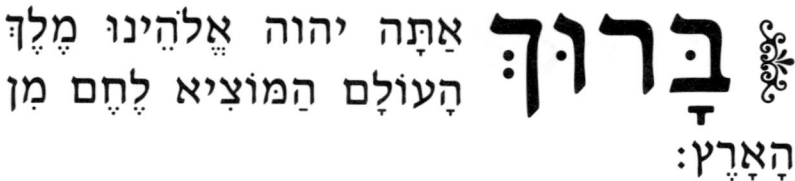

בָּרוּךְ אַתָּה יהוה אֱלֹהֵינוּ מֶלֶךְ הָעוֹלָם הַמּוֹצִיא לֶחֶם מִן הָאָרֶץ:

intended, then he will stand as a humanly Divine being with his whole life, including its physical aspect, in the service of God.

One of the ways to educate towards this aspiration, this aim of human perfection, is wisely connected by our Sages to the eating of meals. Although in itself a physical function, the eating of a meal can be ennobled and elevated above other animal functions by the fact that the organ which enables one to eat is, at the same time, servant to the activity that stamps one as human — speech.

By serving the functions of eating and of speech, the mouth, as it were, constitutes the bond of reconciliation between the spiritual and the animal elements within man. The meal, then, was designated by the Sages as the first step towards the ennoblement of the animal in man. One's table is to be transformed into an altar, and he is to approach his meal as if partaking of the sanctified foods in the Temple.

Eating only for pleasure is not a *human* activity — and the same is true for every other bodily function — if it is prompted only by the desire for the sensation of pleasure which God has associated with the satisfaction of every physical demand. If, however, one eats only as much as he needs and with the intention to gain from it the strength

Motzi

BLESSED be You, Hashem our God, King of the universe, Who causes bread to grow forth from the earth.

necessary for leading a life vigorous with righteousness and love, pleasing to God, then one's eating becomes elevated to a human level and it becomes a Divine service. In the same way, any bodily function can become a Divine service, provided it is done with the intention, for the purpose, in the measure and manner that God demands and teaches by His Word.

Consequently, one should approach his meal as he would an act of holiness, as a priest would dedicate himself to the sacrificial service, dedicating his hands by washing them even for the eating of ordinary bread. This will teach that one can consecrate even animal-physical actions such as eating through human-spiritual intent and elevate them to the level of Divine service. As one strives to elevate the animal within the sphere of the spiritual, one achieves that reconciliation between body and soul, that ennoblement, which is the highest task in life. Then, his table will become an altar and bring atonement, purity, and sanctification. This is what the Sages wish to express with their beautiful dictum: "As long as the Temple stood, the altar was the source of purity and atonement. Now that the Temple is no longer, the table of the Jewish house has taken its place" (*Chagigah* 27a).

מַצָּה

He now releases the bottom matzah from his grip and
says the following berachah, with the intention that it
refer also to the matzah of the korech and
afikoman which will be eaten later on:

בָּרוּךְ אַתָּה יהוה אֱלֹהֵינוּ מֶלֶךְ
הָעוֹלָם אֲשֶׁר קִדְּשָׁנוּ
בְּמִצְוֹתָיו וְצִוָּנוּ עַל אֲכִילַת מַצָּה:

In some communities the matzah is dipped in salt, but
in most it is not.

The required amounts of matzah (see Required
Measurements and Amounts, page 37) are then eaten
by all of the participants, while reclining on the
left side, within the required period of time.

WHO HAS SANCTIFIED US BY HIS COMMANDMENTS. One recites
this berachah in order to summon his attention to the proper attitude
required from him before performing mitzvos. He must be aware that
he is about to fulfill them because they are Divine commandments
given by God for the purpose of rendering man holy. Therefore, a
berachah is pronounced only before the performance of those mitzvos
which are designed to rectify and enrich one's thoughts and volition,
thereby exerting a sanctifying influence upon him, such as matzah,
shofar, megillah, tzitzis, and the like. However, mitzvos whose only
intent and purpose is to yield immediate, practical results such as the
giving of charity, returning of stolen property, returning of a pledge
given as security for a loan, and the like, whose effective performance
is not directly dependent upon one's mood or frame of mind, are not
preceded by a berachah.

We believe that we have thus found a key to the system of the
blessings to be recited before performing mitzvos. The only exception
to this rule would be the berachah recited prior to the construction of

164

Matzah

*He now releases the bottom matzah from his grip and
says the following berachah, with the intention that it
refer also to the matzah of the korech and
afikoman which will be eaten later on:*

🌿 **BLESSED** be You, Hashem our God, King of the universe, Who has sanctified us by His commandments and commanded us concerning the eating of matzah.

*In some communities the matzah is dipped in salt, but
in most it is not.*

*The required amounts of matzah (see Required
Measurements and Amounts, page 37) are then eaten
by all of the participants, while reclining on the
left side, within the required period of time.*

a guardrail to prevent people from falling off a roof (see *Devarim* 22:8, *Avudraham* Chapter 3 and *Chorev* paragraph 678).

MATZAH. Through one's observance of the prohibition of chametz, one affirms the deliverance of Yisrael from Egypt and, indeed, the very existence of Yisrael as a nation is entirely God's doing and that one does not harbor any egotistical or prideful thoughts to the contrary. If one acknowledges and accepts this aspect of Yisrael's existence, and if he does so gladly, sacrificing his whole self for the name of Yisrael, then one can achieve complete surrender to God. One demonstrates all this — he affirms and accepts and acknowledges — by partaking of matzah on the first night of Pesach (or, for those outside the borders of Eretz Yisrael, the first two nights). When one eats the matzah, one should do so gladly, as one who shares in Yisrael's lot in all its changes, as one who shares in Yisrael's duties and her onward march, however varied and difficult, all as God has destined it.

165

מָרוֹר

The leader of the Seder then takes a kezayis of maror (see Required Amounts and Measurements, page 38), dips it briefly in charoses, and shakes off the excess charoses. After putting aside one such kezayis for himself, he proceeds to distribute similar portions to all present. Everyone should have in mind that it is his intention to fulfill the requirement of eating maror on Pesach night. He, or each participant, if he is making his own berachos, then says the following berachah with the intention that it refer also to the maror of the korech which will be eaten later on:

בָּרוּךְ אַתָּה יהוה אֱלֹהֵינוּ מֶלֶךְ הָעוֹלָם אֲשֶׁר קִדְּשָׁנוּ בְּמִצְוֹתָיו וְצִוָּנוּ עַל אֲכִילַת מָרוֹר:

All the assembled eat their portions of maror, not reclining, within the required period of time.

כּוֹרֵךְ

The leader of the Seder takes a kezayis of the third, unbroken matzah, places upon it a kezayis of maror, dips it in the charoses (some shake off the charoses and some do not), and distributes similar portions to the other participants. Before eating the korech the following is said:

זֵכֶר לְמִקְדָּשׁ כְּהִלֵּל. כֵּן עָשָׂה הִלֵּל בִּזְמַן שֶׁבֵּית הַמִּקְדָּשׁ הָיָה קַיָּם. הָיָה כּוֹרֵךְ (פֶּסַח) מַצָּה וּמָרוֹר וְאוֹכֵל בְּיַחַד. לְקַיֵּם מַה שֶּׁנֶּאֱמַר עַל־מַצּוֹת וּמְרֹרִים יֹאכְלֻהוּ:

Everyone eats his portion, while reclining to the left, within the required period of time.

166

Maror

The leader of the Seder then takes a kezayis of maror (see Required Amounts and Measurements, page 38), dips it briefly in charoses, and shakes off the excess charoses. After putting aside one such kezayis for himself, he proceeds to distribute similar portions to all present. Everyone should have in mind that it is his intention to fulfill the requirement of eating maror on Pesach night. He, or each participant, if he is making his own berachos, then says the following berachah with the intention that it refer also to the maror of the korech which will be eaten later on:

BLESSED be You, Hashem our God, King of the universe, Who has sanctified us by His commandments and commanded us concerning the eating of maror.

All the assembled eat their portions of maror, not reclining, within the required period of time.

Korech

The leader of the Seder takes a kezayis of the third, unbroken matzah, places upon it a kezayis of maror, dips it in the charoses (some shake off the charoses and some do not), and distributes similar portions to the other participants. Before eating the korech the following is said:

This is in remembrance of the Temple, according to the custom of Hillel. Thus did Hillel at the time when the Temple was standing: He would combine (the Paschal lamb,) the matzah and the maror and eat them together in order to fulfill what is written: "...with unleavened bread and bitter herbs shall they eat it" (*Bemidbar* 9:11).

Everyone eats his portion, while reclining to the left, within the required period of time.

167

שֻׁלְחָן עוֹרֵךְ

It is customary to eat eggs at the beginning of the meal and not to eat roasted meat of any kind. Some do not dip any food. Although one may not drink wine between the first and second cups or between the third and fourth, at the meal, between the second and the third cups, one is permitted to do so provided that he is cautious not to become drowsy as a result. One should recline throughout the meal unless it is uncomfortable.

One may not eat so much that he has no appetite for the afikoman.

One should be careful to finish the meal early enough for the afikoman to be eaten before midnight. The meal is not to be considered as a "break" in the Seder, and, consequently, as a time for levity, lightheadedness and idle talk. On the contrary, it is a part of the service and should be treated with the proper dignity and in the festive yom tov spirit. It is appropriate to discuss the Exodus and to sing zemiros of thankfulness to Hashem during this time.

Shulchan Orech

SHULCHAN ORECH. The Torah intends one to understand that the aim of the observance of Shabbos and festivals is not to raise one to a superhuman level. How difficult this would be — since we are men, not angels. Man's task is to serve God as a human being, through the very fact of his being a human. Clearly this is the reasoning behind the requirement that one put aside his everyday tasks and concerns during these times and enjoy himself before God. The Torah requires that man make his sensual aspect, that which he shares with the animal world, a part of the celebration. In this way one realizes that his whole life — from his most spiritual thoughts down to his bodily pleasures — can and should be a Divine service, permeated with the spirit of Shabbos and yom tov. In the Jewish view, even gratification of the senses is a Divine service if it is controlled by law and dedicated to that holy aim which God's wisdom set for it. It should be this way with everything, be it bodily pleasure or intellectual or artistic attainment.

No part of one's life may be completely devoted to the animal-like, to gratification of the senses only — one must purify, sublimate and refine everything into Divine service by observing the Divine law. That is why Seudos Shabbos and yom tov are mitzvos, and one should add whatever he can, however small, to his usual meal, for the celebration of Shabbos and yom tov. And whenever one partakes of food on Shabbos or on yom tov, he should remember to do so with the intention to consecrate even his bodily needs to the holy service of God, for it is there, in the sublimation of one's physical desires, that the consecration of one's whole being begins, indeed, is founded.

Some families are accustomed to studying at the Seder table a portion of the laws governing the eating of the Paschal lamb. Here is the order of these laws, as arranged by Rabbi Yaakov Emden, of blessed memory, to be recited as a memorial so as to fulfill verbally the commandment to eat of the Paschal lamb on this night.

אכילת בשר הפסח בליל חמשה עשר של חודש האביב מצות עשה מן התורה, שנאמר ואכלו את הבשר בלילה הזה צלי אש ומצות על מררים יאכלוהו.

מצוה מן המובחר לאכול בשר הפסח אכילת שובע, לפיכך אם הקריב שלמי חגיגה בארבעה עשר אוכל מהם תחילה, אחר כך אוכל בשר הפסח כדי לשבוע ממנו. ואם לא אכל אלא כזית יצא ידי חובתו, ושניהם אינם נאכלים אלא צלי אש.

וצריכים ברכה לכל אחד בפני עצמו. על הפסח אומר אשר קדשנו במצותיו וצונו לאכול הפסח, ועל החגיגה, לאכול הזבח.

TO EAT THE FLESH OF THE PASCHAL LAMB ON THE NIGHT OF THE FIFTEENTH DAY OF THE MONTH OF SPRING [NISSAN] IS A POSITIVE TORAH COMMANDMENT. The Paschal lamb was slaughtered on the fourteenth, בין הערבים (*Shemos* 12:6), *between the two mixtures of day and night.* The first mixture occurs when darkness has already started to intrude upon the light — when the day begins to dwindle. The second occurs when there is still some daylight mingled with the darkness — when the last ray of daylight retreats from before the night. The time for slaughtering the Pesach Sacrifice, then, was from the moment that the sun had passed its zenith until the beginning of the actual night, that is, the whole afternoon of the fourteenth of Nissan. This was the dividing time between slavery, to which the fourteenth still belonged, and deliverance, which, from nightfall, the fifteenth was to bring about but which had already "dawned" during the afternoon. It was the moment when the two aspects of the redemption were to begin: the external one of "...and I shall redeem you with an outstretched arm..." (*Shemos* 6:6) and the inner one of "And I will take you to Me for a people..." (*ibid.*, 7), the selection by God of Yisrael as His People. It was the space of time which prepared Yisrael for its elect

*Some families are accustomed to studying at the Seder
table a portion of the laws governing the eating of the
Paschal lamb. Here is the order of these laws, as
arranged by Rabbi Yaakov Emden, of blessed memory,
to be recited as a memorial so as to fulfill verbally the
commandment to eat of the Paschal lamb
on this night.*

To eat the flesh of the Paschal lamb on the night of the fifteenth day of
the month of spring [Nissan] is a positive Torah commandment, as it
says: "And they shall eat the flesh in that night, roasted with fire; with
unleavened bread and with bitter herbs shall they eat it" (*Shemos*
12:8).

The mitzvah is best performed by eating the flesh of the Paschal
lamb until satiated; hence, if a Jew offered up Festival Peace Offerings
on the fourteenth, he eats of them first and then finishes with the flesh
of the Paschal lamb, thereby becoming satiated. If he ate no more of
the Paschal lamb than an amount the size of an olive, he has
nevertheless fulfilled his obligation, and both the festival offering
and the Paschal lamb are eaten only roasted by fire.

A separate blessing is mandatory for each. On the Paschal lamb
one recites "...and commanded us to eat the Pesach," while on the
Festival Offering one says "...to eat the sacrifice."

status of being placed under God's guidance, of becoming "the sheep
of His flock" (see *Yechezkel* 34:31).

The act of shechitah, the slaughter of the Paschal lamb, symbolically expressed Yisrael's total relinquishment of any previous or
alternative way of life in favor of this new status. However, it would
be a mistake to understand this as an act of self-destruction or
annihilation. Rather, the sacrifice of the Paschal lamb was an
essential prerequisite for achieving through Divine grace a higher
level of existence. Immediately upon its slaughter we are commanded
to fulfill the mitzvah of Receiving the Blood. The blood of the
sacrificial offering is taken up and received for this new, loftier level
of existence.

The idea of the sacrifice being a preparation for life on a higher
level is particularly true for the Pesach Sacrifice since, in the first
place, it was only slaughtered in order to be consumed by the very
persons who, by means of it, dedicated themselves entirely to God.
There is no other sacrificial offering in which the eating of it is so
essential (see *Pesachim* 78b *et seq.*). Only of the Pesach offering is it

171

הפסח טעון הלל באיכלתו, ואמר רב משום רבי חייא כזיתא פסחא והלילא פקע איגרא.

אין צולין את הפסח על גבי כלי אבן או כלי מתכת ולא בשפוד של מתכת. כיצד צולין אותו? מביאין שפוד של רמון — תוחבו מתוך פיו עד בין נקובתו, ותוחב כרעיו ובני מעיו בשפוד למעלה מפיו של טלה, ותולהו לתוך התנור והאש למטה.

אין הפסח נאכל נא ומבושל, ואינו נאכל בשתי חבורות ואין מוציאין מחבורה לחבורה, ולא האוכל רשאי לאכול משני פסחים, שאין נמנים על שני פסחים כאחת.

said: "Its only purpose is to be eaten" (*Pesachim* 76b).

The Pesach Sacrifice symbolizes one's freedom and independence. And what else can it mean to be "free and independent" than to have the free use and enjoyment of oneself? To be able to realize one's physical and spiritual potential, to determine one's own purpose and to develop oneself toward that purpose — this is the very essence of independence. Accordingly, in the case of *this* offering, it is essential that it be eaten by the same persons to whom it belongs, those whose self-sacrifice its slaughter is to represent. The Pesach offering symbolizes the independence and gaining of one's self, to be obtained by giving oneself up to God. This self-identity had, until then, been absorbed and lost in the personality of the Egyptian taskmaster. It follows that: "If they slaughtered it not intending it for consumption, or not intending it for the persons belonging to it...it is invalid" (*Pesachim* 61a). For a Pesach slaughtering not intended for the persons belonging to it implies enslavement; and if it is not intended for consumption, it implies an act of self-destruction without the benefit of independence.

THE PASCHAL LAMB IS EATEN NEITHER HALF-COOKED NOR COOKED WITH WATER. Indeed, the Torah commands: "You may not eat of it half-cooked nor cooked in water as usual..." (*Shemos* 12:9).

נא means half-cooked, incomplete, while בשל מבשל במים is its opposite, thoroughly cooked by means of an addition such as water or

172

A requirement for the eating of the Paschal lamb is the recitation of the Hallel. Rav said in the name of Rabbi Chiyah: "an amount the size of an olive of the Paschal lamb and the Hallel 'shattered the roof'" [so large were the groups of people who ate of the Pesach together].

The Paschal lamb is not roasted upon stone or metal or with a metal spit. How was it roasted? A spit of pomegranate wood was brought and thrust through the mouth to the buttocks, its legs and innards were skewered on the spit above the mouth of the sheep and the sheep was suspended in an oven with the fire burning underneath.

The Paschal lamb is eaten neither half-cooked nor cooked with water, nor in two groups. It is not taken from one group to another, and one is not permitted to eat from two lambs, since one is not permitted to be listed for two lambs at the same time.

any other liquid. The freedom received from the Hand of God and symbolized by the Paschal lamb came to Yisrael complete, and no addition was required from human hands.

Moreover, the significance of roasting the entire lamb, "...its head with its legs and with its innards" (*ibid.*), is that this independence, this redemption came all at once (see Rashi's commentary on the *Mishnah, Pesachim* 74a). All at once, Yisrael's bonds were released. The fetters fell away from head, hand and foot, and from all attempts to gain nourishment — indeed from life itself. This enumeration of "its head" etc., is proof of the symbolic character of the Pesach Sacrifice.

IT IS NOT TAKEN FROM ONE GROUP TO ANOTHER. The fundamental significance of every individual Jewish home as the structural basis on which the Divine nation rests is indicated through the laws of the Pesach Sacrifice.* The commandment of "In one house shall it be eaten..." (*Shemos* 12:46) and the prohibition against removing the flesh outside the house (see above verse), served to elevate each Jewish household, however varied its individual character, to the highest level of sanctity, like that of the Mikdash, Yisrael's national sanctuary. The Mikdash is considered a focal, self-contained, living entity, holding fast everything which is dedicated to

---

* See "The Pesach Sacrifice," page 8.

ואינו נאכל אלא למנוייו (בשעת שחיטה) ישראל מהול טהור
בן ברית. וכשם שמילת בניו ועבדיו מעכבתו מלשחוט הפסח
כך מעכבתו מלאכול בו.

השובר עצם בפסח הטהור לוקה, ואפילו שלא בליל פסח.
לפיכך שורפין עצמות הפסח בכלל הנותר מבשרו כדי שלא
יבואו בהן לידי תקלה.

it. As long as the object remains within the Temple's domain, it
achieves its purpose, but once removed from its precincts, it can no
longer be of any use. The comparison is to the flesh of a mortally
wounded animal which also loses its purpose to be eaten, by virtue of
its being terefah: "'...flesh torn by beasts in the field, you shall not
eat...' (*Shemos* 22:30) — once meat passes beyond its bounds it is
forbidden" (*Zevachim* 82b).

Similarly, every home, represented by the household of the group
making the Pesach Sacrifice, becomes a self-contained, holy entity
from which no member and no portion might become estranged by
virtue of the requirement that the flesh may not be transferred. True,
the Pesach Sacrifice may be eaten by two groups, but, in that case,
each group must form a separate, closed circle of its own (according to
the Rambam the groups must even be separated by actual walls
[*Mishneh Torah* "Laws of the Pesach Sacrifice" 9:3]) and every
person is allowed to eat of his sacrifice only within that one space.

No portion of the meat of the offering was to be brought outside its
own assigned area. Whatever was taken outside the circle became
passul, unfit, just as was the case with every offering taken outside its
own assigned circumference within the boundaries of the Sanctuary
(which could be the precinct of the Temple, or the walls of
Yerushalayim, as the case may be).

And just as the foundation of the Jewish People was established
symbolically upon the principle of the separation of homes, as one
sees from the assignment of every person to a specific place
representing his own family circle for the Pesach, so one finds at the
time of the actual building of the nation, that the first and most basic
rule is the counting and recounting of the People of Yisrael according
to their families and their fathers' houses. Because of Yisrael's quality

174

The Paschal lamb is eaten only by those who have applied to eat from it (at the time of slaughter), by Jews who are circumcised, ritually pure, and members of the covenant. Just as a person's uncircumcised sons and uncircumcised slaves disqualify him from slaughtering a Paschal lamb, so, too, they disqualify him from eating it.

Whoever breaks a bone of a ritually pure Paschal lamb is liable for lashes, even if it is not on the night of Pesach. Hence, the bones of the lamb are burned together with the remains of its flesh, so as to avoid committing any offense.

of purity and chastity, it naturally seeks to create groupings, that is, families. And it is these families which are the pride of Yisrael and the source of its immortality (see also the *Midrash Esfah* quoted in the *Yalkut Shimoni* on the verse: "and it came to pass after the plague" [*Bemidbar* 25:19]). יוחסין שלהם — "their genealogy" — this is the precious gem which only the Jewish People possess. And the first and foremost requirement for its preservation is the sign of the covenant with Avraham — the circumcision of all males. This requirement is also one of the necessary qualifications for being allowed to participate in the Pesach offering (see *Shemos* 12:48).

WHOEVER BREAKS A BONE OF A RITUALLY PURE PASCHAL LAMB IS LIABLE FOR LASHES. The Torah commands: "...and no bone shall you break thereof" (*Shemos* 12:46). A sacrificial offering consists primarily of the blood and muscular flesh, that is, that part of the animal which is active, as it is written: "And you shall offer your elevating-offerings, the flesh and the blood..." (*Devarim* 12:27; see also *Zevachim* 86a). The bones of the animal, which are considered to be its passive part, its supporting framework, are excluded from the offering. As explained before (see page 169), in symbolic terms, the Pesach offering represents the dedication of one's being and his conscious actions to God. By making this dedication, the Jew accomplishes the recovery of his own, true personality. This is expressed by the act of eating the sacrifice, for then one symbolically demonstrates the regaining of one's personality and the restoration of his freedom of will.

This restitution of freedom primarily affects the flesh, the active aspect of one's personality. However, the bones are closely bound up

175

אין רשאין לאכול מגדי הרך אלא מה שנאכל בשור הגדול.

הפסח אינו נאכל אלא עד חצות הלילה הזה. בשר חגיגה
שעלה עם הפסח על השולחן וכן כל התבשילין העולין עמו
מתבערין עמו, ואינן נאכלין אלא עד חצות כפסח.

with the flesh since it is only by virtue of their attachment to the skeletal structure that the muscles can function. Accordingly, the bones represent the *means* through which man can exercise his free will. Whenever they are mentioned as being connected to flesh — עצם שיש בו בשר — they represent the means by which a said activity is made possible.

When such means are used in the service of one's free will which is itself dedicated to God (in symbolic terms, as long as the flesh is ritually pure), they acquire an importance in themselves and they must be respected and shielded from destruction. However, means which do not enable one to accomplish deeds which are pure and holy are worthless, and, therefore, the prohibition against fracturing a bone applies only to a bone which has at least an amount of meat the size of an olive on it and that meat is ritually pure.

If one takes this precept together with the two mitzvos preceding it in the Torah — "In one house shall it be eaten; you may not take any of the meat outside, out of the house..." (*Shemos* 12:46) — one learns: Let no person withdraw from his family, no flesh be taken from the person, and no bone from the flesh. The sanctity of the home should encompass all and everything.

THE PASCHAL LAMB MAY BE EATEN ONLY UNTIL MIDNIGHT [OF THE FIFTEENTH]. The Sages reduced the period during which the Paschal lamb may be eaten as a preventive measure. According to Torah law this period should last until morning, as it says: "And you shall let nothing of it remain until the morning; and that which does remain of it until morning, you shall burn with fire" (*Shemos* 12:10).

In the Temple, in regard to offerings, it was understood that the night followed the day, and the term "day" signified "from one morning till the next." It has already been stated (see page 170) that the main purpose for slaughtering the Paschal lamb was in order to eat it. Slaughter not followed by eating represents self-destruction —

176

Only what is edible in a full-grown ox may be eaten of a tender lamb.

The Paschal lamb may be eaten only until midnight [of the fifteenth]. The remaining flesh of the Festival Offering that was set on the table together with the Paschal lamb, and the remainder of all cooked foods placed on the table as well, are all burned together with the remainder of the Paschal lamb. All are eaten only until midnight, like the Paschal lamb itself.

since no independent existence follows from it. Similarly, eating that which was not ritually slaughtered beforehand symbolizes independence not preceded by dedication to God. Consequently, it is necessary that the Paschal lamb be eaten on the same day that it was slaughtered, so that the slaughtering and the eating be connected in time. With the advent of the next morning, the day of the sacrifice has passed. Whoever leaves over any flesh which could be eaten thereby in effect asserts that it is possible to acquire independence without sacrifice. Such a possibility must be negated by the act of burning.

In general, burning any offering which became unfit for the Temple service represents the rejection of ideas counter to the concept of the Temple and the reinstatement of the correct view, since whatever renders them unfit places them in opposition to the ideals of the Temple. Accordingly, such burning is considered one of the Temple rites. This is clearly indicated by the fact that burning leftover and rejected sacrificial flesh may only be performed by day, just as is the rule with the rites of Slaughtering and the Sprinkling of the Blood of the offerings.

THE PASCHAL LAMB IN EGYPT...ITS BLOOD HAD TO BE SPLASHED BY MEANS OF A BUNCH OF HYSSOP ON THE LINTEL AND BOTH DOOR POSTS. The foundation upon which the structure of Yisrael is built is not its free and independent *individuals*, but free and independent *homes* united by the bonds of blood or by free choice. Only within the context of the family will the individual be able to realize himself. Hence, the blood which had been offered was taken up and dashed on the lintel and door posts of the houses where those who had sacrificed the lamb would eat it, this eating symbolizing the regaining of freedom and independence, (see page 170, as it says:...on the two door posts and on the lintel, upon the houses wherein they will eat it" (*Shemos* 12:7).

177

חלוק פסח מצרים מפסח דורות בג' דברים, שהוא היה מקחו מבעשור וטעון הגעת דם באגודת אזוב על המשקוף ושתי המזוזות ושנאכל בחפזון.

זו היא מצות אכילת הפסח, הרחמן יזכנו לאכול בעיר מקדשנו במהרה בימינו, ויקוים בנו מקרא שכתוב כי לא בחפזון תצאו ובמנוסה לא תלכון כי הלך לפניכם ה' ומאספכם אלהי ישראל. כימי צאתנו מארץ מצרים יראנו נפלאות, ודבר אלהינו יקום לעולם ימינו רוממה עושה נוראות.

צָפוּן

At the end of the meal, preferably before midnight (see tables, pages 286-9), everyone must eat a kezayis of the afikoman in remembrance of the Korban Pesach. It is

The lintel and door posts represent the idea of home. Indeed, the concept "home" is comprised of two components: social protection against human beings and physical protection against the elements. Social protection is afforded by the walls, represented by the door posts, physical protection by the roof, represented by the lintel. The slave who had now become a free man — a father and a member of his family, rather than the property of the taskmaster — became the owner of door posts and a lintel, protected by God against man and nature. Yet, before he could expect such Divine protection, he needed first to dedicate himself to God by abandoning entirely his previous existence, symbolized by the slaughter of the Paschal lamb. Only afterwards was he to acquire "the use and enjoyment of himself," represented by the eating of the Pesach Sacrifice, and this in a house protected by God. Such was indicated by the blood of the sheep dashed on the door posts and lintel, "upon the houses wherein they will eat it." It was not the walls that would protect them against human forces or the roof against the elements. Only God within the walls and under the roof would protect those who had dedicated themselves to Him by their sacrifice.

The Paschal lamb in Egypt differed from that of all subsequent generations in three respects: the Pesach of Egypt had to be taken on the tenth day; its blood had to be splashed by means of a bunch of hyssop on the lintel and both door posts; and it had to be eaten in haste.

This is the mitzvah of eating the Paschal lamb. May the All Merciful grant us the merit to eat it in the city of our Temple speedily and in our days, and may the Biblical prediction be fulfilled through us: "For you shall not go out in haste, neither shall you go by flight, for Hashem goes before you, and the God of Yisrael will be your rear guard" (*Yeshayahu* 52:12). May He show us wonders as in the days when we went forth from Egypt, and may the word of our God endure forever. His right hand is exalted, doing awesome deeds.

Tzafun

preferable to eat a second kezayis in remembrance
of the matzah which was eaten with it.

The pieces of afikoman are broken from the larger part
of the broken middle matzah which was hidden away at
the beginning of the Seder for this purpose. If it is lost
or there is not enough for all of the participants,
any shemurah matzah may be used.

It is customary to allow the children to "steal" the
afikoman at the beginning of the Seder and to "buy" it
back from them now to show how precious this mitzvah
is to us. However, the bargaining should not take too
long, so as not to delay the eating of the afikoman
before midnight.

All the participants should eat the required amount of
the afikoman while reclining to the left and within the
required period of time, having in mind that it is their
intention to fulfill their duty to eat the afikoman.

After the afikoman, it is forbidden to eat or drink
anything except for the last two cups of wine,
and water, tea, or the like.

שִׁיר הַמַּעֲלוֹת בְּשׁוּב יהוה אֶת שִׁיבַת צִיּוֹן הָיִינוּ כְּחֹלְמִים: אָז יִמָּלֵא
שְׂחוֹק פִּינוּ וּלְשׁוֹנֵנוּ רִנָּה אָז יֹאמְרוּ בַגּוֹיִם הִגְדִּיל יהוה לַעֲשׂוֹת עִם
אֵלֶּה: הִגְדִּיל יהוה לַעֲשׂוֹת עִמָּנוּ הָיִינוּ שְׂמֵחִים: שׁוּבָה יהוה אֶת
שְׁבִיתֵנוּ כַּאֲפִיקִים בַּנֶּגֶב: הַזֹּרְעִים בְּדִמְעָה בְּרִנָּה יִקְצֹרוּ: הָלוֹךְ יֵלֵךְ
וּבָכֹה נֹשֵׂא מֶשֶׁךְ הַזָּרַע בֹּא־יָבֹא בְרִנָּה נֹשֵׂא אֲלֻמֹּתָיו:

A SONG OF ASCENTS. When Hashem will turn to us again and bring about
our return to Tzion, then we shall awaken as if from a dream. It will seem to
us that we had lived through the long, long years of our exile as in a dream, a
long nightmare during which, absorbed in ourselves, we had taken little
notice of the changes which had gone on around us and of the impact which,
unknown to us, our wanderings had had upon the nations with which we had
come in contact during our dispersion. Whatever the conception we might
have had of these things during our exile, our understanding of them will
become much clearer once our Galus has ended. Then we shall exult, and our
rebirth to a new life will be so unexpected and so obviously a miracle that the
nations will then say: "Hashem has done great things with these."

But the nations have not noticed, nor have they had any understanding of
the great things which Hashem did for us even long before, throughout our
exile. They did not know it then, nor do they know it now; Hashem has done
great things with us at all times, as proven by the fact that, throughout our
grievous suffering, we have remained glad and serene. This Divine miracle,
which only we ourselves sensed and experienced, and which lasted
throughout the centuries of Galus, is quite equal in significance to our
eventual wondrous redemption which will be such that all eyes will be able to
see its miraculous nature. We were happy even when we had no cause at all for
laughter or exultation; we have retained vigor of both heart and spirit, and,
despite all our tribulations, we enjoyed quiet happiness, an inner
contentment, which was brought about solely by God's invisible nearness, of
which our foes, of course, had no conception.

The Psalmist foresees that the "return of God to our captivity," the time

180

Barech

A Song of Ascents. When Hashem will turn once more to the return of Tzion, we will have been like those who dream. Then our mouth will fill with laughter and our tongue with exultation; then they will say among the nations: "Hashem has done great things with these." Hashem has done great things with us at all times; we have remained glad. Turn, Hashem, to our captivity once more, as the springs in the South. Those who sow in tears will reap in exultation. Though he who bears the measure of seed goes on his way weeping, he shall surely come home with exultation, bearing his sheaves (*Tehillim* 126).

when He will again truly guide and shape our destinies as of old, changing our banishment into redemption and a return to Tzion, may not come about gradually and imperceptibly. Instead this miracle may come to pass suddenly, like the gushing forth of springs of living waters in the arid wilderness of the south, and the rigors of Yisrael's exile may remain unabated until the coming of that day of deliverance.

We will have sown in tears but reaped in exultation. When Hashem sent His people into exile among the nations, He changed ישראל into יזרעאל, the *"victors of God"* into "the *sowers* of God" (see *Bereishis* 32:29 and *Hoshea* 2:2). Yisrael was to disseminate the seeds of truth concerning God and the destiny of mankind into the fields of mankind's future. And Yisrael has fulfilled this vocation as "God's sower" through the Divine Book which nations everywhere have accepted from their hands, as well as through the living commentary which it has given to the doctrine taught in this Book by virtue of its conduct, in private and public life alike. For every aspect of Yisrael's life was directed to all that was spiritual, humane and pure and ran its course with self-sacrificing devotion, in morality and loyalty, to duty. True, this process of dissemination was completed under the impact of a fate sodden with tears. But the time of harvest will come in the end, and the seed sown with tears will open in the form of ever-growing homage paid on earth to truth and right, morality and mercy, as the duty and destiny of mankind. Then the "sower of God," who originally had sown the seeds for all this and had to water them with his tears, will be allowed to rejoice and exult in this harvest. Therefore, however long he may walk on his way in tears, carrying the measure of seed for the acre of mankind, he will surely return home one day with exultation, bearing his sheaves.

181

The third cup is filled for birkas hamazon. If the cup is not clean, it must first be washed and rinsed. It is customary to wash the hands with mayim acharonim. Although a guest is usually honored with leading birkas hazimun, on Pesach night it is customary for the leader of the Seder to do so, although he may appoint another participant. One should have in mind that he is fulfilling the requirement of reciting birkas hamazon. The cup is held throughout birkas hamazon and one should not recline.

If there are at least three adult males eating together at the Seder, the assembled say the following (if there are at least ten adult males, the words in parentheses are added):

Leader: רַבּוֹתַי נְבָרֵךְ:

The others respond: יְהִי שֵׁם יהוה מְבֹרָךְ מֵעַתָּה וְעַד עוֹלָם:

The leader repeats the above verse and says: בִּרְשׁוּת מָרָנָן וְרַבָּנָן וְרַבּוֹתַי נְבָרֵךְ (אֱלֹהֵינוּ) שֶׁאָכַלְנוּ מִשֶּׁלּוֹ:

The others respond: בָּרוּךְ (אֱלֹהֵינוּ) שֶׁאָכַלְנוּ מִשֶּׁלּוֹ וּבְטוּבוֹ חָיִּינוּ:

The leader repeats the above verse and says:

בָּרוּךְ הוּא וּבָרוּךְ שְׁמוֹ:

בָּרוּךְ אַתָּה יהוה אֱלֹהֵינוּ מֶלֶךְ הָעוֹלָם הַזָּן אֶת הָעוֹלָם כֻּלּוֹ בְּטוּבוֹ בְּחֵן בְּחֶסֶד וּבְרַחֲמִים הוּא נוֹתֵן

BIRKAS HAZIMUN. No other craving is so apt to turn man into a self-centered creature viewing every other human being only as a rival on the path to happiness than the urge to satisfy the hunger for food. It is most probably for this reason that the Sages, seeking as they did to educate and discipline by their ordinances, put such stress upon the communal element in the act of eating. When three or more persons have eaten bread together, they are commanded to have one member of the group call upon the rest of those assembled to recite *birkas hamazon* together. In this manner they are to proclaim and recall the truth that it is the One God (and when ten adult males are gathered around the table, that it is אלהינו, the One God Who is the common God of all the Jewish people) of Whose bounty they have all partaken

182

The third cup is filled for birkas hamazon. If the cup is not clean, it must first be washed and rinsed. It is customary to wash the hands with mayim acharonim. Although a guest is usually honored with leading birkas hazimun, on Pesach night it is customary for the leader of the Seder to do so, although he may appoint another participant. One should have in mind that he is fulfilling the requirement of reciting birkas hamazon. The cup is held throughout birkas hamazon and one should not recline.

If there are at least three adult males eating together at the Seder, the assembled say the following (if there are at least ten adult males, the words in parentheses are added):

Leader: Gentlemen, we wish to say Grace.
The others respond: Blessed be the Name of Hashem from this time forth and unto eternity.
The leader repeats the above verse and says: With your permission, let us bless Him (our God) from Whose bounty we have eaten.
The others respond: Blessed be Him (our God) from Whose bounty we have eaten, and through Whose goodness we live.
The leader repeats the above verse and says:

Blessed be He, and Blessed be His Name.

BLESSED be You, Hashem our God, King of

the universe, Who nourishes the whole world with His goodness, with favor, lovingkindness

and Whose goodness has enabled them all to live and to remain alive.

This communal act of homage to God as the sole Father, Preserver and Sustainer Who is equally near to all should remove any and all feelings of jealous rivalry from men's hearts and implant in their place sentiments of kinship for all of their brethren under the common Fatherhood of God. One is not to regard his brother's prosperity as prejudicial to his own welfare; instead, one must know that He Who is the Father of all men is sufficiently rich and kind to give to every human soul at all times that which is good and beneficial for it.

BIRKAS HAMAZON. For a Jew, there must be no dichotomy between that part of life which is devoted to prayer and that part which is

לֶחֶם לְכָל־בָּשָׂר כִּי לְעוֹלָם חַסְדּוֹ. וּבְטוּבוֹ
הַגָּדוֹל תָּמִיד לֹא חָסַר לָנוּ וְאַל־יֶחְסַר לָנוּ מָזוֹן
לְעוֹלָם וָעֶד. בַּעֲבוּר שְׁמוֹ הַגָּדוֹל כִּי הוּא אֵל זָן
וּמְפַרְנֵס לַכֹּל וּמֵטִיב לַכֹּל וּמֵכִין מָזוֹן לְכָל־
בְּרִיּוֹתָיו אֲשֶׁר בָּרָא. בָּרוּךְ אַתָּה יהוה הַזָּן אֶת־
הַכֹּל:

occupied by his daily concerns. Life must not be divided for him into
hours of prayer, when he stands before God and hours of activity,
when he does not walk before Him. What value would prayer have if
it did not return one to active life in a holier, stronger, more God-
filled state, indeed if it did not transform one's whole life into Divine
service? But man so lives his life that, although he witnesses all
around him and even within himself gifts of God, he does not think of
them as gifts or that they are from God. Nature and the human world,
the great stage upon which man lives, is nothing but the revelation of
God; yet he has no eye for Him. All one enjoys is but a gift from God.
Even so, men equip themselves with God's gifts for a life estranged
from Him because they do not think that they are God's gifts! Even
the duties which are to educate one towards God do not do so, when
one practices them by rote, not thinking of them as Divine
institutions. Even the unusual moments of life do not turn men's
minds to God, for they do not choose to understand them as being sent
and guided by God. They do not understand that it is only by serving
God completely, in the fullness of one's soul, that one can
successfully achieve his mission.

For this reason, the Sages instituted berachos to accompany one's
awakening and his going to sleep, his appreciation of nature and of
the human world, his pleasures and his every fulfillment of the
educative mitzvos,* and every extraordinary moment of his life: thus
do they show one God everywhere *in* life, so that every person devote
his all to Him, so that he understand his task is to view himself, his
position in life, his pleasures and his duties — in sum, his whole
existence — with the same holiness he views God Himself.

---

*See commentary, page 164.

184

and compassion. He gives food to all flesh because His lovingkindness endures forever. And through His great goodness we have never lacked nor shall we ever lack food, for His great Name's sake. For He is God Who feeds and sustains all beings, does good to all and prepares food for all His creatures which He has created. Blessed be You, Hashem, Who gives food to all.

The duty to pronounce a berachah is a Biblical, as opposed to a Rabbinic, commandment in two cases: after the eating of bread and before the study of Torah. *After* eating bread, one becomes aware of the vigor and strength it gives him and recognizes that this strength is a gift of God and, therefore, must be used only in the service of He Who granted it. *Before* learning the Torah, *before* occupying oneself with the teaching coming from God, one should be conscious of the fact that it comes from God and was given for life, so as to learn from it the nature of life and its duties, this being the only spirit in which the study of the Torah succeeds and leads to its true purpose.

The Sages extended by analogy the Biblical command of saying a berachah *before* the study of the Torah to the saying of a berachah *before* eating bread, so that not only should the strength gained from eating be used solely for the service of God but that right from the start, one's intention is to eat solely in order to gain the strength necessary for serving God. The eating, when sanctified by such an intention, becomes purely human,* as holy as every other commandment that one performs. They likewise extended the Biblical command of saying a berachah after eating bread to the saying of a berachah after studying Torah — when this was publicly done — so that each person should have its purpose before his eyes and regard it as the God-given law of his existence not only during the study of Torah, but also in every aspect of daily living (*Berachos*, 21a). As *berachos* hallowing man's spiritual and physical life were already commanded, they extended the idea and added berachos to infuse and sanctify his entire existence. They composed berachos for awakening and going to sleep, for the enjoyment of nature and the human world,

---

*See commentary, page 160.

185

נוֹדֶה לְּךָ יהוה אֱלֹהֵינוּ עַל שֶׁהִנְחַלְתָּ
לַאֲבוֹתֵינוּ אֶרֶץ חֶמְדָּה טוֹבָה וּרְחָבָה. וְעַל
שֶׁהוֹצֵאתָנוּ יהוה אֱלֹהֵינוּ מֵאֶרֶץ מִצְרַיִם וּפְדִיתָנוּ
מִבֵּית עֲבָדִים וְעַל בְּרִיתְךָ שֶׁחָתַמְתָּ בִּבְשָׂרֵנוּ וְעַל
תּוֹרָתְךָ שֶׁלִּמַּדְתָּנוּ וְעַל חֻקֶּיךָ שֶׁהוֹדַעְתָּנוּ וְעַל חַיִּים
חֵן וָחֶסֶד שֶׁחוֹנַנְתָּנוּ וְעַל אֲכִילַת מָזוֹן שָׁאַתָּה זָן
וּמְפַרְנֵס אוֹתָנוּ תָּמִיד בְּכָל־יוֹם וּבְכָל עֵת וּבְכָל
שָׁעָה:

וְעַל הַכֹּל יהוה אֱלֹהֵינוּ אֲנַחְנוּ מוֹדִים לָךְ
וּמְבָרְכִים אוֹתָךְ יִתְבָּרַךְ שִׁמְךָ בְּפִי כָּל־חַי תָּמִיד
לְעוֹלָם וָעֶד. כַּכָּתוּב וְאָכַלְתָּ וְשָׂבָעְתָּ וּבֵרַכְתָּ אֶת־
יהוה אֱלֹהֶיךָ עַל־הָאָרֶץ הַטֹּבָה אֲשֶׁר נָתַן־לָךְ. בָּרוּךְ
אַתָּה יהוה עַל הָאָרֶץ וְעַל הַמָּזוֹן:

רַחֵם יהוה אֱלֹהֵינוּ עַל יִשְׂרָאֵל עַמֶּךָ וְעַל
יְרוּשָׁלַיִם עִירֶךָ וְעַל צִיּוֹן מִשְׁכַּן כְּבוֹדֶךָ וְעַל מַלְכוּת
בֵּית דָּוִד מְשִׁיחֶךָ וְעַל הַבַּיִת הַגָּדוֹל וְהַקָּדוֹשׁ שֶׁנִּקְרָא
שִׁמְךָ עָלָיו. אֱלֹהֵינוּ אָבִינוּ רְעֵנוּ זוּנֵנוּ פַּרְנְסֵנוּ

for pleasure, for the observance of duties, and for the most important
moments of one's life.

HE GIVES FOOD TO ALL FLESH. In Devarim 8:1, Yisrael is told that
the one condition for the fulfillment of God's promise of life and
prosperity for His people and the preservation of the land upon
which Yisrael is to live and grow is that the people of Yisrael
faithfully fulfill His Divine Law: "All the commandments...shall
you observe to do that you may live...". In verses 2-4, Yisrael is asked

We thank You, Hashem our God, because You have given as a heritage to our fathers a desirable, good and spacious land; and because You brought us forth, Hashem our God, from the land of Egypt and delivered us from the house of bondage; as well as for Your covenant which You have sealed in our flesh; and for Your Torah which You have taught us; for Your statutes which You have made known to us; and for the life, favor, and lovingkindness which You have bestowed upon us; and for the food, for You feed and sustain us constantly every day, in every season, and at every hour.

For all this, Hashem our God, we thank You and bless You, Blessed be Your Name by the mouth of all living things constantly and forever, even as it is written: "When you have eaten and are satisfied, you shall bless Hashem your God for the good land which He has given you." Blessed be You, Hashem, for the land and for the food.

Have compassion, Hashem our God, on Yisrael Your People, and on Yerushalayim Your city, and on Tzion, the Abode of Your glory, and on the kingdom of the house of David, Your Anointed, and on the great and the holy House over which Your Name was proclaimed. Our God, our Father, tend us, feed us,

---

to remember its journey through the wilderness so replete with trials and lessons for the future; it is bidden to recall at all times God's direct care and concern, as visibly demonstrated by the wondrous mannah and by its miraculous survival throughout its wanderings until it entered the fertile and fruitful Promised Land.

Immediately thereafter, Yisrael is told: "And when you have eaten and are satisfied, then you shall bless Hashem, your God, for the good land which He has given you" (*ibid.*, 10). This Scriptural commandment is the basis for birkas hamazon, the grace recited after

וְכַלְכְּלֵנוּ וְהַרְוִיחֵנוּ וְהַרְוַח־לָנוּ יהוה אֱלֹהֵינוּ מְהֵרָה מִכָּל צָרוֹתֵינוּ. וְנָא אַל־תַּצְרִיכֵנוּ יהוה אֱלֹהֵינוּ לֹא לִידֵי מַתְּנַת בָּשָׂר וָדָם וְלֹא לִידֵי הַלְוָאָתָם כִּי אִם לְיָדְךָ הַמְּלֵאָה הַפְּתוּחָה הַקְּדוֹשָׁה וְהָרְחָבָה שֶׁלֹּא נֵבוֹשׁ וְלֹא נִכָּלֵם לְעוֹלָם וָעֶד:

(On Shabbos add:)

רְצֵה וְהַחֲלִיצֵנוּ יהוה אֱלֹהֵינוּ בְּמִצְוֹתֶיךָ וּבְמִצְוַת יוֹם הַשְּׁבִיעִי הַשַּׁבָּת הַגָּדוֹל וְהַקָּדוֹשׁ הַזֶּה כִּי יוֹם זֶה גָּדוֹל וְקָדוֹשׁ הוּא לְפָנֶיךָ לִשְׁבָּת־בּוֹ וְלָנוּחַ בּוֹ בְּאַהֲבָה כְּמִצְוַת רְצוֹנֶךָ וּבִרְצוֹנְךָ הָנִיחַ לָנוּ יהוה אֱלֹהֵינוּ שֶׁלֹּא תְהֵא צָרָה וְיָגוֹן וַאֲנָחָה בְּיוֹם מְנוּחָתֵנוּ וְהַרְאֵנוּ יהוה אֱלֹהֵינוּ בְּנֶחָמַת צִיּוֹן עִירֶךָ וּבְבִנְיַן יְרוּשָׁלַיִם עִיר קָדְשֶׁךָ כִּי אַתָּה הוּא בַּעַל הַיְשׁוּעוֹת וּבַעַל הַנֶּחָמוֹת:

אֱלֹהֵינוּ וֵאלֹהֵי אֲבוֹתֵינוּ יַעֲלֶה וְיָבֹא וְיַגִּיעַ וְיֵרָאֶה וְיֵרָצֶה וְיִשָּׁמַע וְיִפָּקֵד וְיִזָּכֵר זִכְרוֹנֵנוּ וּפִקְדוֹנֵנוּ וְזִכְרוֹן אֲבוֹתֵינוּ וְזִכְרוֹן מָשִׁיחַ בֶּן דָּוִד עַבְדֶּךָ וְזִכְרוֹן יְרוּשָׁלַיִם עִיר קָדְשֶׁךָ וְזִכְרוֹן כָּל עַמְּךָ בֵּית יִשְׂרָאֵל

partaking of bread. Even after completing an ordinary activity such as eating a meal, Yisrael is to preserve and nurture in its heart the conviction which the miracle of the gift of the Heavenly mannah has instilled into it in the wilderness — namely, that each and every home and soul on earth is favored by God's direct, immediate care and concern. Hence, Yisrael is to look upon every piece of plain bread as no less a direct gift of God than the mannah which was sent down from Heaven to their fathers long ago when they journeyed through the wilderness.

YAALEH VEYAVO. The Torah states that all the temidim and musafim sacrifices were accompanied by the sounding of the sustain us, and nourish us, and relieve us, and speedily grant us relief, Hashem our God, from all our troubles. And, Hashem our God, let us not be in need of the gifts of human hands, or of their loans, but only of Your hand, which is full, open, holy and generous, so that we may not be ashamed nor blush with shame forever and ever.

(On Shabbos add:)

Be pleased, Hashem our God, and fortify us by Your commandments and by the commandment pertaining to the seventh day, this great and holy Shabbos, for this day is great and holy before You, that we may refrain thereon from every manner of work and rest upon it in love in accordance with the commandment of Your will. In Your favor, Hashem our God, grant us rest so that there be no distress, no grief or sighing on the day of our rest, and let us, Hashem our God, behold the consolation of Tzion, Your city, and the rebuilding of Yerushalayim, the city of Your Sanctuary, for You are the Master of all salvation and the Master of all consolation.

Our God and God of our fathers, may our remembrance and the consideration of us and the remembrance of our fathers, and the remembrance of Mashiach the son of David Your servant, and the remembrance of Yerushalayim, Your holy city, and the remembrance of all Your people, the House of Yisrael, rise and come, reach You and be seen, be

chatzotzeros (trumpets) (*Bemidbar* 10:10). These soundings were meant to be a symbolic expression of Yisrael's cry to God for help (*ibid.*, 9). Accordingly, it says of them: "...and they will be to you for a memorial before your God..." The present prayer, beginning with Yaaleh veyavo, utters in words that same thought as was symbolized by the sound of the chatzotzeros in the Temple, with the one difference that the chatzozeros were sounded each day (see *Mishnah Sukkah* 53b) and Yaaleh veyavo is recited only on Rosh Chodesh and on festivals.

"The remembrance of our fathers" denotes the past, from which we receive the covenant made by God with our ancestors; "the

לְפָנֶיךָ לִפְלֵיטָה לְטוֹבָה לְחֵן וּלְחֶסֶד וּלְרַחֲמִים
לְחַיִּים וּלְשָׁלוֹם בְּיוֹם חַג הַמַּצּוֹת הַזֶּה. זָכְרֵנוּ יהוה
אֱלֹהֵינוּ בּוֹ לְטוֹבָה וּפָקְדֵנוּ בוֹ לִבְרָכָה וְהוֹשִׁיעֵנוּ בוֹ
לְחַיִּים וּבִדְבַר יְשׁוּעָה וְרַחֲמִים חוּס וְחָנֵּנוּ וְרַחֵם
עָלֵינוּ וְהוֹשִׁיעֵנוּ כִּי אֵלֶיךָ עֵינֵינוּ כִּי אֵל מֶלֶךְ חַנּוּן
וְרַחוּם אָתָּה:

וּבְנֵה יְרוּשָׁלַיִם עִיר הַקֹּדֶשׁ בִּמְהֵרָה בְיָמֵינוּ.
בָּרוּךְ אַתָּה יהוה בּוֹנֵה בְרַחֲמָיו יְרוּשָׁלַיִם אָמֵן:

בָּרוּךְ אַתָּה יהוה אֱלֹהֵינוּ מֶלֶךְ הָעוֹלָם הָאֵל
אָבִינוּ מַלְכֵּנוּ אַדִּירֵנוּ בּוֹרְאֵנוּ גּוֹאֲלֵנוּ יוֹצְרֵנוּ
קְדוֹשֵׁנוּ קְדוֹשׁ יַעֲקֹב רוֹעֵנוּ רוֹעֵה יִשְׂרָאֵל הַמֶּלֶךְ
הַטּוֹב וְהַמֵּטִיב לַכֹּל שֶׁבְּכָל יוֹם וָיוֹם הוּא הֵטִיב הוּא
מֵטִיב הוּא יֵיטִיב לָנוּ. הוּא גְמָלָנוּ הוּא גוֹמְלֵנוּ הוּא
יִגְמְלֵנוּ לָעַד לְחֵן וּלְחֶסֶד וּלְרַחֲמִים וּלְרֶוַח הַצָּלָה
וְהַצְלָחָה בְּרָכָה וִישׁוּעָה נֶחָמָה פַּרְנָסָה וְכַלְכָּלָה
וְרַחֲמִים וְחַיִּים וְשָׁלוֹם וְכָל טוֹב וּמִכָּל טוּב לְעוֹלָם
אַל יְחַסְּרֵנוּ:

remembrance of Mashiach" indicates the future linked with the
promise of the restoration of the dynasty of David; "the remembrance
of Yerushalayim," refers to our own present day in which
Yerushalayim and its ruins await with hope the time when they can
truly fulfill their destiny as the Holy City of God.

accepted and heard, considered and remembered for deliverance and for well-being, for favor and lovingkindness, for compassion, for life and for peace on this day of the Festival of Unleavened Bread. Remember us this day, Hashem our God, for good, be mindful of us for blessing, and save us for life; and in the promise of salvation and compassion, spare us and favor us, and be compassionate with us and save us, for our eyes look up to You; for You, o' God, are a gracious and compassionate King.

And rebuild Yerushalayim, the city of holiness,* speedily in our days. Blessed be You, Hashem, Who in His compassion rebuilds Yerushalayim, Amen.

Blessed be You, Hashem our God, King of the universe, o' God, our Father, our King, our Mighty One, our Creator, our Redeemer, our Maker, our Holy One, the Holy One of Yaakov, our Shepherd, the Shepherd of Yisrael, o' King, Who is kind and Who does good to all! He alone has done good to us day after day; it is He alone Who does good; and it is He alone Who will do good to us in the future. He alone has caused our destiny to bear ripe fruit; it is He alone Who causes it thus to ripen; and He alone, will continue to cause it thus to ripen, for favor, and for lovingkindness and compassion, and for relief, rescue and success, for blessing and salvation, for consolation, sustenance and nourishment, and for compassion, and for life, and for peace and all good. And with all the good may He never cause us to become wanting.

---

* עיר הקודש is traditionally translated "the holy city." The Hebrew word עיר, however, is feminine and should be modified by the corresponding feminine adjective הקדושה. HaGaon HaRav Yaakov Kaminetsky zt"l commented that הקודש in this case is not an adjective but a noun and the term should therefore be interpreted "the city of holiness."

הָרַחֲמָן הוּא יִמְלוֹךְ עָלֵינוּ לְעוֹלָם וָעֶד. הָרַחֲמָן
הוּא יִתְבָּרַךְ בַּשָּׁמַיִם וּבָאָרֶץ. הָרַחֲמָן הוּא יִשְׁתַּבַּח
לְדוֹר דּוֹרִים וְיִתְפָּאַר בָּנוּ לָעַד וּלְנֵצַח נְצָחִים
וְיִתְהַדַּר בָּנוּ לָעַד וּלְעוֹלְמֵי עוֹלָמִים. הָרַחֲמָן הוּא
יְפַרְנְסֵנוּ בְּכָבוֹד. הָרַחֲמָן הוּא יִשְׁבּוֹר עֻלֵּנוּ מֵעַל
צַוָּארֵנוּ וְהוּא יוֹלִיכֵנוּ קוֹמְמִיּוּת לְאַרְצֵנוּ. הָרַחֲמָן
הוּא יִשְׁלַח לָנוּ בְּרָכָה מְרֻבָּה בַּבַּיִת הַזֶּה וְעַל שֻׁלְחָן
זֶה שֶׁאָכַלְנוּ עָלָיו. הָרַחֲמָן הוּא יִשְׁלַח לָנוּ אֶת אֵלִיָּהוּ
הַנָּבִיא זָכוּר לַטּוֹב וִיבַשֶּׂר לָנוּ בְּשׂוֹרוֹת טוֹבוֹת
יְשׁוּעוֹת וְנֶחָמוֹת.

הָרַחֲמָן הוּא יְבָרֵךְ (אֶת [אָבִי מוֹרִי] בַּעַל הַבַּיִת
הַזֶּה וְאֶת [אִמִּי מוֹרָתִי] בַּעֲלַת הַבַּיִת הַזֶּה). אוֹתִי
(וְאֶת אִשְׁתִּי / בַּעְלִי וְאֶת זַרְעִי) וְאֶת כָּל אֲשֶׁר לִי
וְאֶת כָּל הַמְסוּבִּין כָּאן. אוֹתָם וְאֶת בֵּיתָם וְאֶת
זַרְעָם וְאֶת כָּל אֲשֶׁר לָהֶם אוֹתָנוּ וְאֶת כָּל אֲשֶׁר לָנוּ
כְּמוֹ שֶׁנִּתְבָּרְכוּ אֲבוֹתֵינוּ אַבְרָהָם יִצְחָק וְיַעֲקֹב בַּכֹּל
מִכֹּל כֹּל כֵּן יְבָרֵךְ אוֹתָנוּ כֻּלָּנוּ יַחַד בִּבְרָכָה שְׁלֵמָה
וְנֹאמַר אָמֵן:

בַּמָּרוֹם יְלַמְּדוּ עֲלֵיהֶם וְעָלֵינוּ זְכוּת שֶׁתְּהֵא
לְמִשְׁמֶרֶת שָׁלוֹם. וְנִשָּׂא בְרָכָה מֵאֵת יהוה וּצְדָקָה
מֵאֱלֹהֵי יִשְׁעֵנוּ וְנִמְצָא חֵן וְשֵׂכֶל טוֹב בְּעֵינֵי אֱלֹהִים
וְאָדָם:

192

May the Compassionate One reign over us to all eternity. May the Compassionate One be blessed in heaven and on earth. May the Compassionate One be praised from generation to generation, glorified through us for all eternity, and garbed in majesty through us for everlasting. May the Compassionate One grant us an honorable livelihood. May the Compassionate One break our yoke from off our neck and lead us upright to our land. May the Compassionate One send abundant blessing into this house, and upon this table at which we have eaten. May the Compassionate One send us Eliyahu the Prophet, may he be remembered for good, to bring us good news of salvation and consolation.

May the Compassionate One bless ([my father, my teacher] the master of this house, and [my mother, my teacher] the mistress of this house) me, (my wife/husband and children) and all that is mine, and all that sit here, both them, their household, their children and all that belongs to them, also us and all that is ours, even as our fathers, Avraham, Yitzchak, and Yaakov were blessed in everything, from everything and with everything, so may He bless all of us together with a perfect blessing and let us say, Amen.

May their and our merits be pleaded on High so that it may contribute to enduring peace, and that we may receive a blessing from Hashem and kindness from the God of our salvation, and obtain worthiness of favor and understanding of the good in the sight of God and man.

הָרַחֲמָן הוּא יַנְחִילֵנוּ יוֹם שֶׁכֻּלוֹ שַׁבָּת וּמְנוּחָה לְחַיֵּי
הָעוֹלָמִים:

הָרַחֲמָן הוּא יַנְחִילֵנוּ יוֹם שֶׁכֻּלוֹ טוֹב. יוֹם
שֶׁכֻּלוֹ אָרוּךְ. יוֹם שֶׁהַצַּדִּיקִים יוֹשְׁבִים וְעַטְרוֹתֵיהֶם
בְּרָאשֵׁיהֶם וְנֶהֱנִים מִזִּיו הַשְּׁכִינָה וְיִהְיֶה חֶלְקֵנוּ
עִמָּהֶם:

הָרַחֲמָן הוּא יְזַכֵּנוּ לִימוֹת הַמָּשִׁיחַ וּלְחַיֵּי
הָעוֹלָם הַבָּא. מִגְדּוֹל יְשׁוּעוֹת מַלְכּוֹ וְעוֹשֶׂה חֶסֶד
לִמְשִׁיחוֹ לְדָוִד וּלְזַרְעוֹ עַד עוֹלָם. עֹשֶׂה שָׁלוֹם
בִּמְרוֹמָיו הוּא יַעֲשֶׂה שָׁלוֹם עָלֵינוּ וְעַל כָּל יִשְׂרָאֵל
וְאִמְרוּ אָמֵן:

יְראוּ אֶת יהוה קְדֹשָׁיו כִּי אֵין מַחְסוֹר לִירֵאָיו.
כְּפִירִים רָשׁוּ וְרָעֵבוּ וְדֹרְשֵׁי יהוה לֹא יַחְסְרוּ כָל טוֹב.
הוֹדוּ לַיהוה כִּי טוֹב כִּי לְעוֹלָם חַסְדּוֹ. פּוֹתֵחַ אֶת יָדֶךָ
וּמַשְׂבִּיעַ לְכָל חַי רָצוֹן. בָּרוּךְ הַגֶּבֶר אֲשֶׁר יִבְטַח
בַּיהוה וְהָיָה יהוה מִבְטַחוֹ. נַעַר הָיִיתִי גַּם זָקַנְתִּי
וְלֹא רָאִיתִי צַדִּיק נֶעֱזָב וְזַרְעוֹ מְבַקֶּשׁ לָחֶם. יהוה עֹז
לְעַמּוֹ יִתֵּן יהוה יְבָרֵךְ אֶת עַמּוֹ בַשָּׁלוֹם:

On Shabbos add:

May the Compassionate One let us inherit that day which shall be all Shabbos and rest for life everlasting.

May the Compassionate One let us inherit that day which is altogether good. That everlasting day, the day when the righteous sit with crowns upon their heads, enjoying the radiance of the Divine Presence — and may our portion be among them.

May the Compassionate One make us worthy of reaching the days of the Mashiach and life everlasting; He Who is a tower of salvation to His King and shows lovingkindness to His Anointed, to David and his descendants forever. May He Who makes peace in His High places, make peace for us and for all of Yisrael, and let us say, Amen.

O' fear Hashem, you who are sanctified to Him, for there is no want for them that fear Him. Young lions have become poor and suffered hunger, but they who seek Hashem shall never want for any good thing. Avow it to Hashem that He is good, that His lovingkindness endures forever. You open Your hand and satisfy the desire of every living thing. Blessed is the man who trusts in Hashem, and to whom Hashem is also the source of His trust. I was young and I have grown old, but I have never seen a righteous man forsaken whose progeny was forced to beg for bread. May Hashem grant to His people the power to be victorious over all; may Hashem bless His people with peace.

*One should have in mind that it is his intention to
fulfill the requirement of drinking the third of the
four cups of wine.*

בָּרוּךְ אַתָּה יהוה אֱלֹהֵינוּ מֶלֶךְ
הָעוֹלָם בּוֹרֵא פְּרִי הַגָּפֶן:

*The required amount of the third cup is drunk, within
the required period of time, while reclining
to the left.*

הַלֵּל

*A special cup for Eliyahu Hanavi is now poured
and the door is opened to indicate that it is leil
shimurim, "a night which enjoys the protection of
Hashem." In some homes, the fourth cup for everyone
is poured now, too, but some wait until before the
recitation of the Hallel. Some follow the custom of
standing when they open the door.*

שְׁפוֹךְ חֲמָתְךָ אֶל הַגּוֹיִם אֲשֶׁר לֹא יְדָעוּךְ וְעַל
מַמְלָכוֹת אֲשֶׁר בְּשִׁמְךָ לֹא קָרָאוּ: כִּי אָכַל אֶת יַעֲקֹב
וְאֶת נָוֵהוּ הֵשַׁמּוּ: שְׁפָךְ עֲלֵיהֶם זַעְמֶךָ וַחֲרוֹן אַפְּךָ
יַשִּׂיגֵם: תִּרְדֹּף בְּאַף וְתַשְׁמִידֵם מִתַּחַת שְׁמֵי יהוה:

196

One should have in mind that it is his intention to fulfill the requirement of drinking the third of the four cups of wine.

❧ BLESSED be You, Hashem our God, King of the universe, Who creates the fruit of the vine.

The required amount of the third cup is drunk, within the required period of time, while reclining to the left.

Hallel

A special cup for Eliyahu Hanavi is now poured and the door is opened to indicate that it is leil shimurim, "a night which enjoys the protection of Hashem." In some homes, the fourth cup for everyone is poured now, too, but some wait until before the recitation of the Hallel. Some follow the custom of standing when they open the door.

Pour out Your wrath toward the nations that do not know You and on the kingdoms that have not proclaimed Your Name. For he has devoured Yaakov, and they have laid waste his habitation (*Tehillim* 79:6-7). Pour out Your perceptible wrath over them, and let the fire of Your anger overtake them (*ibid.* 69:25). Pursue them with anger and destroy them from under the Heavens of Hashem (*Eychah* 3:66).

197

The door is closed (and everyone is seated if they stood), and those who have not already done so pour the fourth cup. Although Hallel is usually said standing, on Pesach night we recite it while seated. However, one should not do so in a reclining position but, rather, sit respectfully, as if in the presence of a king. Some are accustomed to hold the cups in their hands throughout the recitation of the Hallel and some do not. One should have in mind that it is his intention to fulfill the requirement of reciting Hallel on Pesach night.

לֹא לָנוּ יהוה לֹא לָנוּ כִּי לְשִׁמְךָ תֵּן כָּבוֹד עַל חַסְדְּךָ עַל אֲמִתֶּךָ: לָמָה יֹאמְרוּ הַגּוֹיִם אַיֵּה נָא אֱלֹהֵיהֶם: וֵאלֹהֵינוּ

NOT TO US. "Not to us..." is perhaps an elliptical phrase offering the possibility of several interpretations. It could mean: "It is not for our own sake that we await or request anything at all from You, but rather...", etc. Or perhaps the "give honor" in the second half of the verse may serve to complete the first half: *Not to us, not to us give honor so that we may find recognition and favor among the nations but only so that the truth of Your existence and of Your will and rule should receive the recognition due it.*

"...For the sake of Your lovingkindness, for the sake of Your truth." The names of God — Hashem and Elohim — respectively, indicate the two basic traits of God's rule: מדת החסד — the attribute of mercy by which He blesses and advances all that is good and which is manifested in the concept of חסד — lovingkindness; and מדת הדין — the attribute of justice, which is manifested in the concept of אמת — the truth and faithfulness by which He trains all of His children to love and pursue all that is good and right. Following the second interpretation of this verse offered above, the Psalmist says: *May you, o' Hashem, cause Your rule, woven from the warp and woof of lovingkindness and truth to be demonstrated in our cause, so that Your Name may be recognized by all the nations.* However, one reads not על חסדך ועל אמיתך — for the sake of Your lovingkindness *and* for the sake of Your truth but על חסדך על אמיתך — for the sake of Your lovingkindness, for the sake of Your truth. The ways of God differ from each other only in the form they take. Actually, the motive at

NOT to us, Hashem, not to us, but to Your own Name give honor, for the sake of Your lovingkindness, for the sake of Your truth. Wherefore shall the nations say: "Where now is their God?" But our God is in the

their basis is one and the same in every instance. God's lovingkindness is truth and His truth is lovingkindness.

WHERE NOW IS THEIR GOD. This question, asked by the nations, could be understood in one of two ways. It could mean that Yisrael has proclaimed openly and repeatedly its reliance upon God's help; therefore, Yisrael now feels that if this help did not materialize, the other nations would all ask: *Where is their God, on Whom they have relied?* But, if so, the reply in the following verse, "...our God is in the Heavens...," would not be appropriate. Hence, one would have to understand the question asked by the nations as motivated by Yisrael's forsaken state, which gives the nations reason to doubt God's ability to render help. These doubts would then be refuted by the statement in verse 3 which, in effect, says that God has always been able to bring about that which it was His will to bring about. Or, and this seems more probable, the interpretation of verses 2 and 3 should be as follows: *The idols of paganism are visible to the physical, earth-bound eye, but no one can discern any achievement on their part. On the other hand, the God of Yisrael is physically invisible, but everyone can readily see what He has accomplished.*

More than anything else, the heathen world took exception to the concept of an invisible God, a concept which Yisrael brought with it when it entered into the midst of the nations. Specifically because of

199

בַּשָּׁמַיִם כֹּל אֲשֶׁר חָפֵץ עָשָׂה: עֲצַבֵּיהֶם כֶּסֶף
וְזָהָב מַעֲשֵׂה יְדֵי אָדָם: פֶּה לָהֶם וְלֹא יְדַבֵּרוּ
עֵינַיִם לָהֶם וְלֹא יִרְאוּ: אָזְנַיִם לָהֶם וְלֹא יִשְׁמָעוּ
אַף לָהֶם וְלֹא יְרִיחוּן: יְדֵיהֶם וְלֹא יְמִישׁוּן
רַגְלֵיהֶם וְלֹא יְהַלֵּכוּ לֹא יֶהְגּוּ בִּגְרוֹנָם: כְּמוֹהֶם

this, we ask Hashem to make His acts and ways, His lovingkindness and truth plainly visible to the nations through the course the destiny of His nation will take. For if the heathens will not perceive any such acts of God, they will continue to ask: "Where now is their God?" And, yet, even though "our God is in the Heavens," that is, invisible, "everything is as He has willed to bring it about," as stated in the next verse. These achievements proclaiming His will and His omnipotence bear witness to the fact that He does indeed exist and rule over all things.

It appears, then, that in verse 3 the cantillation points indicate that כל is the subject and אשר חפץ עשה is the predicate. The thought of this verse would then be: *Of course our God is invisible and in the Heavens, but every living being is only such as He had desired it to be and such as He brought about. True, our God cannot be seen by the human eye, but everything in the visible world attests to His will and to His power, and all the visible universe is the work of His free creation.*

חפץ and עשה, an absolutely unfettered will and an absolute power for which nothing is impossible — these are the prime attributes which distinguish the One and Only God from all the "gods" devised by human folly. In view of the above, it is entirely appropriate that the verses immediately following should be a description of these idols which men would foolishly adore.

THEIR IDOLS... DO NOT SPEAK... SEE... HEAR... SMELL... TOUCH... WALK... BREATHE... We explained in Devarim (4:28), where language similar to that of this psalm appears, that there existed in paganism a dual concept of idols. The common people worshiped the images made by human hands because they believed that a deity actually dwelt within these images. The statements here apply to them very much in the literal sense. But they are no less

200

Heavens; everything is as He has willed to bring it about. Their idols of silver and gold are the work of human hands; they have a mouth, but they do not speak; they have eyes, but they do not see; they have ears, but they do not hear; they have a nose, but they do not smell; [they have] their hands, but they cannot touch with them; [they have] their feet, but they do not walk; they can utter no sound

applicable to the more educated heathens who viewed the image as only a representation of natural forces personified. For like the graven images themselves, the forces of nature which the heathens worshiped are also entirely without mind or will of their own.

As we are told in Devarim, idols neither perceive things ("neither see nor hear") nor are they aware of stimuli that impinge upon the senses ("neither eat nor smell"). Hence, in this psalm, it is quite correct to add that they are not capable of commanding ("they do not speak"), of free and deliberate action ("they cannot touch"), or of movement toward any goal ("they do not walk"). Indeed, they are entirely devoid of even elementary intellect ("they can utter no sound"). All these false gods which men would worship are blind, lacking in freedom, and purely physical in nature. Thus, they are not only beneath the level of man himself, but also far, far below the level of any other living thing, because even the most primitive organism enjoys the Divine gift of some elementary ability to perceive and to wish or desire.

Heathen folly endows the statues that represent its idols with a mouth, eyes, and ears, thus indicating the belief that these idols can actually command and that they possess the ability to perceive things through the intellect. But this is deception, either deliberate or unwitting. Indeed, even the nose, which merely indicates an ability to perceive physically, does not really fulfill the function attributed to it in the idols.

"Their hands...their feet" (In this verse, one does not read "they have hands...they have feet" but "their hands...their feet." However, the expression used repeatedly in the previous verses, "they have," should be understood to apply here, too. Thus, the verse should be understood as saying *they have their hands...they have their feet*): Hands and feet are absolutely essential to a figure

201

יִהְיוּ עֹשֵׂיהֶם כֹּל אֲשֶׁר בֹּטֵחַ בָּהֶם: יִשְׂרָאֵל
בְּטַח בַּיהוה עֶזְרָם וּמָגִנָּם הוּא: בֵּית אַהֲרֹן
בִּטְחוּ בַיהוה עֶזְרָם וּמָגִנָּם הוּא: יִרְאֵי יהוה
בִּטְחוּ בַיהוה עֶזְרָם וּמָגִנָּם הוּא:

representing a god, for they are the organs of creativity and of locomotion toward a goal. They are the attributes of power and of free will, of מעשה and of חפץ (cf. verse 3). Hence, to a heathen mind, a god without hands and feet is simply not a god at all. Therefore, the Gemara teaches that even the sculptured representation of a hand or a foot would in itself constitute an image of idolatrous worship (*Avodah Zarah* 41a).

ימישין, the causative of מיש, synonymous with למשש, "to touch," indicates *they do not cause their hands to touch.* Touch is the primitive beginning of the deliberate handling of things, the understanding of them; a person touches an object when he wants to know, at a basic level, what is before him. Hence, the use of this expression here is very significant. The forces of nature, which heathen folly endows with Divine qualities, do exert a powerful influence upon the environment. This cannot be denied, for it is because of their influence that they have become the object of idolatrous worship and have caused men to fall trembling before them. Yet, despite their impact on other living things, they still lack the qualities of deliberation and free will. They lack even the most primitive indication of deliberate independent motion or attempts at such motion.

"Their feet": Human beings have provided their images with the organs of locomotion toward a goal, because it is presumed that these idols have such ability. But the fact of the matter is that they do not possess the power which would render them capable of any deliberate motion toward a goal or destination out of their own free will.

"They can utter no sound with their throat": Since it is not "heart," or "tongue", but "throat" that is mentioned here as the organ of הגה, and the throat is an organ through which only inarticulate sounds can be made, הגה in this case most likely designates an animal sound. Even though the idols are pictured as having a throat, they do not with their throat. They who make them shall become like them; indeed, everyone who trusts in them. O' Yisrael, trust in Hashem; He is their help and their shield. O' house of Aharon, trust in Hashem; He is their help and their shield. O' you who fear Hashem, trust in Hashem; He is their help and their shield (*Tehillim* 115:1-11).

possess even the animal's elementary faculty for emitting sounds in response to a stimulus or perception.

THEY WHO MAKE THEM SHALL BECOME LIKE THEM. Those whose concept of a god — and, hence, their ideals as well — belongs to the realm of nature, fettered and entirely devoid of freedom, and those who put their trust in the blind power of a force that acts without any consciousness of its own, thus entrusting their fate and success to such a force, divest themselves of all the splendor of intelligent moral freedom. They themselves sink to a level where they become subject to the blind impulse of their physical urges and instincts. They become even as their idols are. And since they put their trust in these figments of folly, they forfeit all their moral grandeur and significance as human beings and, lost and helpless, they perish.

O' YISRAEL, TRUST IN HASHEM. In contrast to the rest of the world, which labors under delusions, puts its trust in folly, and is about to perish through deception, Yisrael is called upon at all times to put its trust in Hashem. He is not only the Source of the past and the future, but He also determines every moment that is to be and is ready at all times to open the gate to a new future. Trust in Hashem is not an idle delusion. To all those who trust in Him in truth, He proves to be an עזר and a מגן, a help in the discharging of their task and a shield against all threats of destruction by enemy hands. However, the help Yisrael may expect from God is demonstrated not only in protection against enemies from without but also in assistance in the fulfillment of its mission. Therefore, Yisrael is described by three different classifications. First, there is "Yisrael," denoting the people which has been sent among the nations with the task of bringing them the message of God. Within Yisrael there is the "House of Aharon," whose task is such that its position in Yisrael is very similar to that

יהוה זְכָרָנוּ יְבָרֵךְ יְבָרֵךְ אֶת בֵּית יִשְׂרָאֵל יְבָרֵךְ
אֶת בֵּית אַהֲרֹן: יְבָרֵךְ יִרְאֵי יהוה הַקְּטַנִּים עִם
הַגְּדֹלִים: יֹסֵף יהוה עֲלֵיכֶם עֲלֵיכֶם וְעַל בְּנֵיכֶם:

which Yisrael itself holds among the nations. Finally, there are those
who "fear Hashem," a label describing every single individual whose
task is, foremost, to see that he personally conduct himself in
accordance with the fear of God, that he lead a life of duty such as
constitutes true homage to God, and that he be "God's messenger and
priest" first of all to himself. If all Yisrael will be truly "Yisrael," in
the sense of the word as explained above, if the priests will be true sons
of Aharon also in their conduct and spirit, if every single individual
within Yisrael will strive after the fear of God, then everyone, the
priestly family as well as each and every single individual, may
confidently trust in Hashem. He is the Help and the Shield of
"Yisrael," of the sons of Aharon, and of all those that truly fear Him.
He will help "Yisrael" discharge its mission among the nations; He
will assist the sons of Aharon in the fulfillment of their task in the
midst of "Yisrael," and He will aid every individual who fears Him in
his efforts towards his own spiritual refinement. And, finally,
Hashem will protect them all against any who would oppose them.

HASHEM, WHO HAS BEEN MINDFUL OF US, HE WILL BLESS.
Hashem, through the help, protection and preservation that has been
ours, has proven that He has been mindful of us at all times, that He
has never forgotten us or left us to our own devices. Neither has He left
our fate to chance and accident. In like manner, He will also bless us
by granting progressively growing prosperity to the House of Yisrael
among the nations, to the House of Aharon in the midst of Yisrael,
and to all those everywhere who fear Hashem.

Here, where one reads of the increase to be brought about by God's
blessing, Yisrael is called "the House of Yisrael," the closed national
entity among the nations in which, beginning with its first Patriarch,
each new member has enlarged the circle of those that bear the destiny
of this house. In like manner the descendants of Aharon form "the
House of Aharon," a closed entity of its own within Yisrael, a group
which also inherited its task from its patriarch and passes it on to each
of its descendants.

204

Hashem, Who has been mindful of us, He will bless. He will bless the House of Yisrael; He will bless the House of Aharon; He will bless those who fear Hashem, the small together with the great; Hashem will give you increase, to you and to your children.

"Those who fear Hashem," on the other hand, do not constitute such a closed unit, for one cannot speak of a "House of those who fear Hashem." However, the prosperity of the *home* of every individual who fears Hashem is all the more in need of special Divine Providence so that his children, of their own free will, may become part of their parents' home. In this voluntary union they will acquire all the spiritual and moral traits which their parents seek to perpetuate through them so that they, in turn, may take these spiritual treasures and nurture them and pass them on to their own descendants, for all time to come. Thus, together with their own children and descendants, they will remain a part of their ancestral home. Since there is no group of "those who fear Hashem" but rather each individual seeks to inculcate in his children these values, this particular blessing for a "house" that fears Hashem is phrased differently. Instead of saying "He will bless the House of those who fear Hashem," the blessing in verse 13 reads: "He will bless those who fear Hashem, the small together with the great," so that the young may retain an eternal link with the old and the children with their parents, so that the blessing of the parents may be transferred to the children. And the blessing continues, in verse 14, that *Thus you shall grow, and, in the same degree, your children, too, will grow progressively*. The reason, as explained in verse 15, is that, "Blessed are you for Hashem, the Maker of heaven and earth." It is לי and not מיי. You are blessed, not *from* Hashem, but *for* Hashem; you are blessed by Hashem because the blessing that has come to you actually benefits the work which Hashem seeks to have advanced by mankind on earth! For He is "the *Maker* of heaven and earth," Who not only called heaven and earth into being at the time of Creation, but even today constantly shapes the process of development resulting from the concerted collaboration of heaven and earth so that it may work toward the goal He has set.

Verses 9-15 thus constitute a timeless appeal made by Yisrael to its brethren; it is the fruit of that experience which should be passed on in Yisrael from generation to generation.

בְּרוּכִים אַתֶּם לַיהוה עֹשֵׂה שָׁמַיִם וָאָרֶץ: הַשָּׁמַיִם
שָׁמַיִם לַיהוה וְהָאָרֶץ נָתַן לִבְנֵי אָדָם: לֹא הַמֵּתִים
יְהַלְלוּ־יָהּ וְלֹא כָּל יֹרְדֵי דוּמָה: וַאֲנַחְנוּ נְבָרֵךְ יָהּ
מֵעַתָּה וְעַד עוֹלָם הַלְלוּיָהּ:

אָהַבְתִּי כִּי יִשְׁמַע יהוה אֶת קוֹלִי תַּחֲנוּנָי: כִּי
הִטָּה אָזְנוֹ לִי וּבְיָמַי אֶקְרָא: אֲפָפוּנִי חֶבְלֵי מָוֶת
וּמְצָרֵי שְׁאוֹל מְצָאוּנִי צָרָה וְיָגוֹן אֶמְצָא: וּבְשֵׁם יהוה

THE HEAVENS ARE THE HEAVENS OF HASHEM. Verse 16 continues
the thought presented by "the Maker of heaven and earth" earlier
(verse 15), and thus gives us another reason why we should trust in
Hashem. At the same time, it demonstrates another feature that
distinguishes the true God from the idols raised by heathen folly. We
are told not simply that "the heavens are Hashem's," but "the
heavens are the heavens of Hashem," meaning that the fact that they
fulfill their purpose as heavens is solely God's concern; He alone can
effect this. But He has given the earth to man. He has appointed man
as His representative and co-worker who is to see to it that the earth
fulfills the purpose for which God has created it. From this we can
deduce that the purpose of God's rule does not consist in death and
destruction, but in the advancement of life and in having man
develop and unfold to the greatest possible extent. The gods of
paganism are depicted as envying man and being inimical to human
happiness. The word of God calls them "idols that withhold and
deny," עצבים and אלילים (see Hirsch, commentary to *Bereishis* 3:16),
for paganism viewed death and destruction as the demonstration of
the greatness and power of its gods. Hashem, the true God, the God of
Yisrael, is not so. It is not the dead and those who go down in silence
that proclaim His power. It is life, growth, and development that
declare His greatness and might. Therefore, Yisrael knows that it —
the nation which He has sent forth to attest to His greatness and
might among men — will never die. It shall walk through the ages,
"from this time forth and forever," as the immortal people, and, in

Blessed are you for Hashem, the Maker of heaven and earth. The heavens are the heavens of Hashem, but He has given the earth to the children of men. It is not the dead that proclaim God's might, and not all those who go down into silence. But as for us, we will bless the mighty God from this time forth and forever. Halleluyah! (*ibid.*, 12-18).

I love my voice, indeed, my supplications, for Hashem will hear. For He has inclined His ear to me in the past, and I will call [upon Him] in my fateful days. [When] the pains of death oppressed me, when the straits of the grave gained hold of me, when I faced trouble and sorrow, [when] I call upon the Name of

the course of this vigorous, persevering life, "we will bless the mighty God." Yisrael shall do its part in the furtherance and fulfillment of the works and goals of God.

I LOVE MY VOICE. The last psalm concluded on a note of confidence that Yisrael's destiny, in fulfillment of which God aims to show His might, is not death and the grave, but the overcoming of death and destruction. This psalm now adds the thought that God has already delivered Yisrael many times in the past and, thus, Yisrael is confident that its pleas will always be heard. For this reason, even a situation which will cause Yisrael to appeal to God for help and to beg repeatedly for His favor will fill Yisrael with a certain sense of exaltation, because, as it were, Yisrael senses the bliss of redemption even in advance of actual deliverance. The object of אהבתי, "I love," is קולי תחנוני, "my voice, indeed, my supplications," and the phrase כי ישמע יי, "for Hashem will hear," is an interjection in the Hebrew text meaning: *For I know Hashem will hear me.* The thought of verse l is: "I love," literally, *I have come to love my voice that calls. I love even my repeated pleas for Divine favor, for I know that Hashem will hear me,* for, as the psalm continues, *He has already inclined His ear to me in the past.* יום, "day," with endings such as יומו or יומך frequently denotes the day of decision for a person, usually in an unhappy, fateful sense. So here, too, ימי means "my fateful days."

אֶקְרָא אָנָּא יהוה מַלְּטָה נַפְשִׁי: חַנּוּן יהוה וְצַדִּיק
וֵאלֹהֵינוּ מְרַחֵם: שֹׁמֵר פְּתָאִים יהוה דַּלּוֹתִי וְלִי
יְהוֹשִׁיעַ: שׁוּבִי נַפְשִׁי לִמְנוּחָיְכִי כִּי יהוה גָּמַל עָלָיְכִי:
כִּי חִלַּצְתָּ נַפְשִׁי מִמָּוֶת אֶת עֵינִי מִן דִּמְעָה אֶת רַגְלִי
מִדֶּחִי: אֶתְהַלֵּךְ לִפְנֵי יהוה בְּאַרְצוֹת הַחַיִּים:
הֶאֱמַנְתִּי כִּי אֲדַבֵּר אֲנִי עָנִיתִי מְאֹד: אֲנִי אָמַרְתִּי
בְחָפְזִי כָּל הָאָדָם כֹּזֵב:

HASHEM PROTECTS THE UNAWARE. The word פתאים here, rather than denoting the concept of inattention or carelessness, refers to the unaware, the innocent or guileless, who are the victims of events or acts brought about by others and which they could not have foreseen, had no reason to expect and which therefore strike them פתאום, suddenly. The thought behind this is: *When our own insight and foresight fails, Hashem protects us.*

RETURN... MY SOUL, TO YOUR RESTING PLACES. מנוחיכי is not derived from מנוחה, rest, but is the plural form of מנוח, meaning the site where one finds rest, as in אבקש לך מנוח (*Ruth* 3:1). גמל עליכי means: *He is the one Who has caused that which has come upon you to ripen.* Whatever life may bring, one should find peace of mind in the knowlege that whatever has happened has been brought about by God Himself.

BUT WHEN YOU HAVE DELIVERED MY SOUL FROM DEATH. The fact that we have here a direct appeal to God, a change from verses 1-7 where God is mentioned only in the third person, shows that verse 8 introduces a new idea, and together with the verses that follow, it forms one thought. That thought is: *The realization that it was You Who have delivered my soul from death, that but for Your intervention I would have perished long ago, guards "my eye from tears and my foot from stumbling." This awareness of Your deliverance takes all the bitterness from my fate and sustains me, so that, even when I walk through the most grievous trials, my foot will not take a false step. It gives me the confidence that "I shall walk on before Hashem in the lands of the living."* That is, *I know that I shall fulfill to the end the task given me by God in the midst of the nations*

Hashem: "I beseech You, o' Hashem, deliver my
soul." Then Hashem deals graciously [with me] and is
just, and our God takes pity. Hashem protects the
unaware; I had been brought low, but He grants me
new life. Return again and again, o' my soul, to your
resting places, for it is Hashem Who has caused to
ripen that which has come over you. But when You
have delivered my soul from death, my eye from tears
and my foot from stumbling. Then I shall walk on
before Hashem in the lands of the living. So firmly
convinced was I that I said it, I, who was so greatly
afflicted. I said it during my hasty flight: "All
mankind is deluded" (*ibid.* 116:1-11).

*of any era, because I am the one nation which by reason of God's will
is immortal.*

SO FIRMLY CONVINCED WAS I. The statement כל האדם כזב,
"All mankind is deluded," in verse 11 is the object of both אדבר (verse
10) and אמרתי (verse 11). חפז is the hasty walk of the fugitive as in
בחפזה לנוס (*Shemuel* II 4:4) and אשר השליכו ארם בחפזם (*Melachim* II
7:15). כזב does not occur in the kal form in any other instance. The
term for "to deceive another" or "to utter a falsehood" is כזב in the
piel form. Therefore, כזב in the kal form would most probably mean
"to labor under a delusion." The Psalmist says: *I was so firmly
convinced of the authenticity of my mission* (האמנתי) *though it was so
contrary in spirit to the rest of mankind, that I, who was so terribly
afflicted and dependent, dared say aloud during my flight and
wandering through the world,* "All mankind is deluded." Yisrael was
עני, the most powerless, dependent people among the nations. It was
always in a state of חפז; no place on earth offered permanent sojourn
to its wandering feet; it had to be prepared at all times for expulsion.
Nevertheless, it had the courage to speak out (אדבר) in the presence of
its overlords the truth of its conviction, its protest against the error of
the rest of the world. Yisrael had the strength, too, not to act contrary
to its avowed principles in its intercourse with those in whose
countries it happened to dwell but, rather, to proclaim (אמרתי) those
very principles.

מָה אָשִׁיב לַיהוה כָּל תַּגְמוּלֹהִי עָלָי: כּוֹס
יְשׁוּעוֹת אֶשָּׂא וּבְשֵׁם יהוה אֶקְרָא: נְדָרַי לַיהוה
אֲשַׁלֵּם נֶגְדָה נָּא לְכָל־עַמּוֹ: יָקָר בְּעֵינֵי יהוה הַמָּוְתָה
לַחֲסִידָיו: אָנָּא יהוה כִּי אֲנִי עַבְדֶּךָ אֲנִי עַבְדְּךָ בֶּן

WHAT SHALL I DO FOR HASHEM. The terms עני and חפז in verses 10 and 11 denote the final stage of Yisrael's sorely tried wanderings upon earth. Yisrael now says: *What is it that I must do for Hashem in return once all the things which He seeks to ripen to full maturity will have come to me?*

I SHALL RAISE THE CUP OF SALVATION'S MANY FORMS. כוס is the term denoting a fate appointed or meted out by Hashem (see *Yirmeyahu* 25:15,17; *Yeshayahu* 51:17, 22; *et al.* See also *Tehillim* 11:6). Thus, the thought of verse 13 is: *I shall interpret* (or accept and take up) *the many forms of salvation that have come my way as granted and meted out to me by Hashem,* "and בשם יי אקרא." *I shall continue and complete the mission begun by my first ancestor to call upon men in the name of Hashem* (see *Bereishis* 12:8). Yisrael will be fully qualified thus to "call men unto God" only once it will hold in its hands כוס ישועות, the abundance of demonstrations of Divine salvation for which the Name of Hashem will shine forth for every human eye to see.

I WILL FULFILL MY VOWS TO HASHEM. Yisrael says: *I shall then fulfill all that I have vowed to Hashem during the long centuries of my exile as resolutions to be fulfilled once I will be delivered.* The additional "heh" in נגדה changes נגד into a wish: "O' would that it were in the presence of all of His people:" *would that all of His scattered sons be gathered round Him once more in one united group, and would that all the rest of mankind who find their way back to Hashem be united with us to form* עמו — *one society of men belonging to Hashem.* Thus we read: "And many nations shall join themselves to Hashem on that day and shall be my people..." (*Zechariah* 2:15).

PRECIOUS IN THE EYES OF HASHEM. The generation that will be redeemed one day and then start upon the full discharge of its mission

But what shall I do for Hashem in return, once all His ripened bounties will have come upon me? I shall raise the cup of salvation's many forms and call in the Name of Hashem. I will fulfill my vows to Hashem; o' would that it were in the presence of all His people. Precious in the eyes of Hashem is even the ebb of life that has come to his devoted ones. If, Hashem, I am Your servant, I am Your servant only as the son of Your handmaid, o' You Who has now

is entirely free of any presumptuousness with regard to the generations which have preceded it and died in exile. Instead, it pays high tribute to all that these generations have achieved, even though, for the most part, they remained passive and patiently bore the sufferings of exile. מותה mitigated by the additional "heh" does not mean "death," but "the ebbing away of life," that is, a state akin to death. Or it is to be understood abstractly as the prefix ל: It is "a state leading to death," "going down toward the grave." This summarizes the entire sad history of Yisrael's past. The thought of verse 15 is that Hashem sets great value even on a sad fate such as this, even on suffering such as this, if only it is borne by "His devoted ones," borne with love and devotion by men who, even within the narrow straits to which misfortune has confined their lives, still live for the practical fulfillment of their duties.

IF, HASHEM, I AM YOUR SERVANT. The Psalmist is saying: *Hashem, if I am Your servant, then I am such only because I am the son of Your handmaid, I, whose bonds you have now loosed.* This means: The generation which has been found sufficiently mature to be redeemed acknowledges that for whatever abilities and qualifications it might possess to meet the demands of its new future it owes thanks to the generations of the past. Through centuries of trials and tribulations, these past generations have remained faithful in the service of Hashem as His "handmaid." Thus, by passing on to their descendants all that was true and noble in their lives, they have become the "mother" of the new generation of the future. All of past Jewish history is "Your handmaid," and I am "the son of Your handmaid."

211

אֲמָתֶךָ פִּתַּחְתָּ לְמוֹסֵרָי: לְךָ אֶזְבַּח זֶבַח תּוֹדָה וּבְשֵׁם
יהוה אֶקְרָא: נְדָרַי לַיהוה אֲשַׁלֵּם נֶגְדָה נָא לְכָל עַמּוֹ:
בְּחַצְרוֹת בֵּית יהוה בְּתוֹכֵכִי יְרוּשָׁלָיִם הַלְלוּיָהּ:

הַלְלוּ אֶת יהוה כָּל גּוֹיִם שַׁבְּחוּהוּ כָּל הָאֻמִּים:
כִּי גָבַר עָלֵינוּ חַסְדּוֹ וֶאֱמֶת יהוה לְעוֹלָם הַלְלוּיָהּ:

*If there are at least three participants at the Seder, the
leader chants each of the following four verses aloud,
and the others respond by repeating the first verse each
time, followed by the suceeding verse, just as it is
recited in shul.*

כִּי לְעוֹלָם חַסְדּוֹ:	הוֹדוּ לַיהוה כִּי טוֹב
כִּי לְעוֹלָם חַסְדּוֹ:	יֹאמַר נָא יִשְׂרָאֵל
כִּי לְעוֹלָם חַסְדּוֹ:	יֹאמְרוּ נָא בֵית אַהֲרֹן
כִּי לְעוֹלָם חַסְדּוֹ:	יֹאמְרוּ נָא יִרְאֵי יהוה

I WILL BRING YOU OFFERINGS. The Psalmist continues: *By thus
proclaiming by my thanksgiving offering the acknowledgment of my
debt to You, I also call upon all mankind to render homage to Your
Name.* "I will fulfill my vows..." is a repetition of what has already
been said in verse 14, but here the thought is supplemented by the
addition of "In the courts of the House of Hashem, in your midst, o'
Yerushalayim..." in verse 19. Yisrael's salvation and that of the rest of
mankind belongs to the future, but, with the coming of that future,
Tzion and Yerushalayim will by no means have outlived their
purpose. Instead, the realization of this future is inextricably linked
to Tzion, because it is the Sanctuary of God, and to Yerushalayim,
because it is the City of Hashem. Both Tzion and Yerushalayim can
attain the full glory of their mission only in that future. Thus one
finds in Yeshayahu: "...I will comfort you, and you shall be
comforted in Yerushalayim" (66:13). It will be from Tzion and
Yerushalayim that all the nations will be brought together around
Hashem (see *Yeshayahu* 2:2,3).

212

loosened my bonds. I will bring You offerings to acknowledge my debt of gratitude, and call in the Name of Hashem. I will fulfill my vows to Hashem; o' would that it were in the presence of all His people. In the courts of the House of Hashem, in your midst, o' Yerushalayim, Halleluyah! (*ibid.*, 12-19).

O' proclaim the praise of Hashem's mighty acts, all you nations; laud Him, all you tribes of mankind. For His lovingkindness was mighty over us, and the faithfulness of Hashem endures forever, Halleluyah! (*ibid.*, 117).

If there are at least three participants at the Seder, the leader chants each of the following four verses aloud, and the others respond by repeating the first verse each time, followed by the succeeding verse, just as it is recited in shul.

Avow it to Hashem, that He is good,
　　that His lovingkindness endures forever.
Say it now, o' Yisrael,
　　that His lovingkindness endures forever.
Say it now, o' House of Aharon,
　　that His lovingkindness endures forever.
Say it now, o' those that fear Hashem,
　　that His lovingkindness endures forever (*ibid.* 118:1-4).

O' PROCLAIM THE PRAISE OF HASHEM'S MIGHTY ACTS. "O' proclaim..." is a call which the redeemed nation of Yisrael will one day address to the rest of mankind, summoning them all to render homage to Hashem. The "us" mentioned in the passage "for His lovingkindness was mighty over us..." refers to Yisrael and all the nations which Yisrael addresses here. With this same lovingkindness He has guided them all back from their estrangement and has won them for His service once again; and His faithfulness will reign over them forever.

AVOW...THAT HIS LOVINGKINDNESS ENDURES FOREVER. That the lovingkindness of Hashem endures forever, in times of sorrow no less than in days of joy and happiness, is a fact that has been

מִן הַמֵּצַר קָרָאתִי יָּהּ עָנָנִי בַמֶּרְחַב יָהּ: יהוה לִי
לֹא אִירָא מַה יַּעֲשֶׂה לִי אָדָם: יהוה לִי בְּעֹזְרָי וַאֲנִי
אֶרְאֶה בְשֹׂנְאָי: טוֹב לַחֲסוֹת בַּיהוה מִבְּטֹחַ בָּאָדָם:
טוֹב לַחֲסוֹת בַּיהוה מִבְּטֹחַ בִּנְדִיבִים: כָּל גּוֹיִם
סְבָבוּנִי בְּשֵׁם יהוה כִּי אֲמִילַם: סַבּוּנִי גַם סְבָבוּנִי

experienced by Yisrael in its mission among men, by the House of Aharon in its calling in the midst of Yisrael, and by every God-fearing man in general in his own endeavors towards his spiritual refinement. It is this everlasting Divine lovingkindness that all three groups are called upon to proclaim now in a spirit of homage and thanksgiving to Hashem.

Verses 5-20 constitute such an acknowledgment of grateful thanks voiced by Yisrael, in which Yisrael looks back upon its difficult past through which Hashem has led it to the lofty pinnacle of deliverance.

FROM OUT OF THE STRAITS, I CALLED. מרחביה is one word, like הללויה, according to Pesachim 117a. It denotes one single concept, namely, the Divine "breadth," liberation from every sensation of constricting anxiety, an enlargement, a blessed ease and relief, which only God can provide and which causes anyone confined in the "straits" of oppression to sense that God is near. Verses 6-9 mention this awareness of God's nearness which makes man free.

HASHEM WAS FOR ME. The Psalmist exclaims: *I sensed that Hashem was with me, and when I was utterly forsaken by men on earth, I still knew no fear even though all of mankind was against me. And even when men were at my side to help me, I viewed them simply as messengers of Hashem, as part of His plan. I regarded the aid they rendered me as help coming to me from God Himself, and therefore I could look calmly upon those who hated me. When men came to my*

214

From out of the straits I called upon God; He answered me through the breadth of Divine relief. Hashem was for me; therefore I did not fear; what can man do to me? If Hashem is for me through my helpers, I shall calmly look upon those who hate me. It is better to look to Hashem than to trust in man. It is better to look to Hashem than to trust in noblemen. All the nations surrounded me; it was with the Name of Hashem that I faced them. They surrounded me; indeed, they closed in about me; it was with the Name

aid, I did not put my trust in such assistance as they gave me, but I trusted in God alone, Whose work I beheld in this help I received from human hands. Hence, I did not despair even when I lacked such aid and saw only men's hatred round about me.

IT IS BETTER TO LOOK TO HASHEM. חסה ב־ is an intensified form of חזה and means "to look with confidence toward help that is still far away." In contrast, בטח ב־ denotes trust in the efficacy of help that is already apparent. Thus the thought of verses 8-9 is: *It is better to look with confidence toward the help of God, though it be far off, than to trust in the aid of men, though it is present even now and even if these are "noble men" according to social status and character, men who are capable of doing as they please and are willing to do so.*

ALL THE NATIONS SURROUNDED ME. Yisrael continues: *I have manifested such confidence in Hashem's deliverance throughout my history, and it has proven to be good.* This three-time repetition of סבבוני, סבוני, סבוני, is a motif which frequently recurs throughout Yisrael's history and seems to refer to three specific periods of that history: the period from Yehoshua until the destruction of the First Temple, followed by the period of the Second Temple until its destruction, and finally the era of exile and dispersion. The שלמים form of סבב, when viewed in relation to the form סוב that is ordinarily used, seems to denote a closer "surrounding" than would just סוב. The word אמילם is derived from מול, meaning "opposite" or "face to

215

בְּשֵׁם יהוה כִּי אֲמִילַם: סַבּוּנִי כִדְבוֹרִים דֹעֲכוּ כְּאֵשׁ
קוֹצִים בְּשֵׁם יהוה כִּי אֲמִילַם: דָחֹה דְחִיתַנִי לִנְפּוֹל
וַיהוה עֲזָרָנִי: עָזִּי וְזִמְרָת יָהּ וַיְהִי לִי לִישׁוּעָה: קוֹל

face," (or, as in the verb form להמיל: "to meet face to face"). אמילם is
spelled with a פתח instead of צירה because of the סוף פסוק. During the
first period of its history, Yisrael suffered primarily at the hands of its
neighboring nations. They all surrounded it, and in the end it was
still only "with the Name of Hashem" that Yisrael faced them. So
long as Yisrael lacked confidence, it succumbed to its foes. And
Yisrael's survival, despite the cessation of its independent statehood,
was due solely to the power of God's Name. During the era of the
Second Commonwealth, Yisrael suffered oppression at the hands of
nations from both near and far, and it was only when the Jewish
People were inspired with confidence by the Name of Hashem that
they came away victorious when they went out to meet these foes.
Whenever Yisrael has attempted to involve itself in politics in the
manner of the other nations and has placed its trust in the help offered
by other states, it has thereby brought about its own ruin and incurred
the loss of its independence. It was with the Name of Hashem, and
with nothing but the Name of Hashem, that Yisrael went into exile
and dispersion. It was surrounded by a host of enemy nations the
extent of whose territory was almost as great as that of the entire earth.
It was as if Yisrael had come into a swarm of bees from which there
was no escape; and every foe could and did employ his sting upon it.
Yet Yisrael's enemies could never quite attain their goal. Thousands
of years later, Yisrael can look back and tell itself: דעכו (this is the pual
form) — *a higher, invisible Power has put them out like a fire of
thorns.* The simile "like a fire of thorns" may come from the idea of
the smarting, burning sting of the bees. What is it that has given
Yisrael the strength to face unflinchingly these long, long centuries of

216

of Hashem that I faced them. They surrounded me like bees; they were put out as the fire of thorns; it was with the Name of Hashem that I faced them. True, you have struck me again and again that I might fall, but Hashem helped me. God was my strength and song, and this has become my salvation. Therefore let

torture? It was only "with the Name of Hashem" that Yisrael could face all its foes and every peril and win the victory of continued survival.

YOU HAVE STRUCK ME AGAIN AND AGAIN. The use of the second person in this verse shows that all the foregoing words of the psalm were directed to the nations which had already been summoned in the previous psalm to praise Hashem. Now they are addressed as one single unit, perhaps for the reason that they were actually united as one in their hostility and opposition to Yisrael. Yisrael tells the enemy: *You have struck me again and again so that I might fall. It was your intention that I fall, and I would have, had it not been for God's help. He was at my side, and therefore I was able to resist you; I grew calm and serene; I roused myself to song. Indeed, this strength of mine and my inspired song was* יה. *It was the power of God which was demonstrated in my strength and my inspiration to song, which was not* זמרתי, *"my own song,"* at all. This has become my salvation; it was this that permitted me to acquire renewed vigor in the midst of all my affliction. The statement "God was my strength and song, and this has become my salvation" makes one view the whole, long period of Yisrael's exile as a direct demonstration of Hashem's power, an act of God even as the splendid moment of the splitting of the Sea of Reeds was. In fact, the importance of Yisrael's exile could be said to surpass that of the miracle at the shores of the Sea of Reeds, because the latter took only moments, while the former can be measured in terms of thousands of years.

217

רְנָּה וִישׁוּעָה בְּאָהֳלֵי צַדִּיקִים יְמִין יהוה עֹשָׂה חָיִל:
יְמִין יהוה רוֹמֵמָה יְמִין יהוה עֹשָׂה חָיִל: לֹא אָמוּת
כִּי אֶחְיֶה וַאֲסַפֵּר מַעֲשֵׂי יָהּ: יַסֹּר יִסְּרַנִּי יָהּ וְלַמָּוֶת
לֹא נְתָנָנִי: פִּתְחוּ לִי שַׁעֲרֵי צֶדֶק אָבֹא בָם אוֹדֶה יָהּ:
זֶה הַשַּׁעַר לַיהוה צַדִּיקִים יָבֹאוּ בוֹ:

(Each of the following verses is repeated:)

אוֹדְךָ כִּי עֲנִיתָנִי וַתְּהִי לִי לִישׁוּעָה: אודך אֶבֶן

LET THE VOICE OF REJOICING AND SALVATION BE IN THE TENTS OF THE RIGHTEOUS. This Divine aid that has come to Yisrael will bring the joyous tidings of salvation far beyond the Jewish People to the tents of all the righteous men of the world: *The saving right hand of Hashem, which has proven in the past to be exalted over all things, still is omnipotent even now and will be so for all time to come.*

I SHALL NOT DIE. Yisrael says: *This is my destiny — that I shall never die. Through the greatest dangers to life I am to wander upon earth as the immortal nation; I am to pass through the entire course of mankind's development as well as my own history in order to recount the acts of Divine omnipotence which I experience on this journey. Hashem in His almighty power has not spared me from sufferings in order to chastise and discipline me, but He has not intended that I die.*

OPEN FOR ME THE GATES OF RIGHTEOUSNESS. Yisrael says: *Now that through my sufferings I have become a better nation and I am sufficiently mature to fulfill my destiny, open for me once again the gates of the Sanctuary of God's Law, which teaches and demands the practice of righteousness in everyday life. When I strayed from the paths of righteousness, these gates were closed to me. But now that I have returned to the ideals of righteousness taught by the House of Hashem, now that I have become worthy of the Sanctuary again, I may once more enter through its portals and there declare my debt of* the voice of rejoicing and salvation be in the tents of the righteous: "The right hand of Hashem does valiantly. The right hand of Hashem has ever proven exalted. The right hand of Hashem does valiantly still." I shall not die, but I shall live and recount the works of God. God has chastised me heavily, but He has not turned me over to death. Open for me the gates of righteousness; I will enter into them and avow [my debt to] God. This gate is Hashem's, the righteous shall enter into it. *(Each of the following verses is repeated:)* I will avow [my debt to] You, for You have

---

gratitude to God and render Him my homage. צדק is the ideal of righteousness as taught by God, the realization of which constitutes the sum total of one's life's duty. He whose life is dedicated to the practice of such צדק is a צדיק.

THIS GATE IS HASHEM'S. The gate of the Sanctuary of the Law is the gate of Hashem as well. There is *no other way* to God than by the path which leads from the practical righteousness of daily life as taught by His Law. And not only the sons of Yisrael, but all those who render homage to such God-taught righteousness are invited to enter into the gate of the Sanctuary of His Law. Thus the Sages also comment in Toras Kohanim (on *Vayikra* 18:5): "And so, it does not say (*Yeshayahu* 26:2) 'Open the gates that Priests, Levites and Israelites may enter in,' but rather 'that the righteous nation that keeps faithfulness may enter in.' Similarly, it does not say (*Tehillim* 118:20) 'This gate is Hashem's; Priests, Levites, and Israelites shall enter into it,' but rather 'the righteous shall enter into it.'" Yisrael precedes the rest of mankind only to act as a guide that shows the way, and it is only in this spirit that Yisrael is the first among the nations to proclaim its homage and grateful thanks to Hashem.

I WILL AVOW [MY DEBT TO] YOU. *I avow to You that You have answered me and have become my salvation,* or: *I will acknowledge You* because *You have answered me and have become my salvation.*

219

מָאֲסוּ הַבּוֹנִים הָיְתָה לְרֹאשׁ פִּנָּה: אֶבֶן מֵאֵת יהוה
הָיְתָה זֹּאת הִיא נִפְלָאת בְּעֵינֵינוּ: מֵאֵת זֶה הַיּוֹם עָשָׂה
יהוה נָגִילָה וְנִשְׂמְחָה בוֹ: זה

If there are at least three participants at the Seder, the
leader chants each of the following four verses aloud,
and the others repeat after him:

אָנָּא יהוה הוֹשִׁיעָה נָּא:
אָנָּא יהוה הוֹשִׁיעָה נָּא:
אָנָּא יהוה הַצְלִיחָה נָּא:
אָנָּא יהוה הַצְלִיחָה נָּא:

THE STONE WHICH THE BUILDERS DISDAINED. The architects
who labored on behalf of the supposed welfare of the nations did not
even think that they could include Yisrael as one building block
among all the other stones. Thus, scornfully, they left Yisrael to lie by
the wayside, and, behold, now it is none other than Yisrael that has
become the chief cornerstone of the edifice of man's salvation.

THIS IS HASHEM'S DOING. The final and universal recognition of
Yisrael, who had hitherto been scorned and misunderstood by the
nations of the world, the recognition of Yisrael's unique significance
in the building of mankind's salvation, has been brought about in
such a manner that the finger of God is unmistakably demonstrated
therein.

HASHEM HAS MADE THIS DAY. It is Hashem Who has brought
about this day when Yisrael, redeemed, returns to its Divine

220

answered me and have become my salvation. ɪ... The
stone which the builders disdained has become the
chief cornerstone. The... This is Hashem's doing; it is
marvelous in our own eyes. This... Hashem has made
this day; we will rejoice in Him and delight. Hashem...
(*ibid.*, 5-24).

If there are at least three participants at the Seder, the
leader chants each of the following four verses aloud,
and the others repeat after him:

We beseech You, o' Hashem, grant new life.
We beseech You, o' Hashem, grant new life.
We beseech You, o' Hashem, cause us to prosper.
We beseech You, o' Hashem, cause us to prosper.

(ibid., 25)

Sanctuary, crowned by universal recognition. Hence, there is reason
to rejoice and be glad in *Him*, in Hashem (see *Yalkut Shimoni* to
Yishayahu remez 505). גיל, related to קול, is vocal rejoicing,
exultation. שמח, related to צמח, is quiet, inner joy, delight.

WE BESEECH YOU. "We beseech you..." is the call voiced by the
nations that follow Yisrael's lead. At last they have realized that they
can expect true salvation only from Hashem, and therefore they direct
their plea to Him.

The salvation for which man may hope and strive for is two-fold in
character: ישועה and הצלחה. ישועה is the undimmed vigor of one's
own life and existence; ישע is the true שי. הצלחה is the unhampered
prospering of all work and endeavors. It is for both of these that they
beseech Hashem.

בָּרוּךְ הַבָּא בְּשֵׁם יהוה בֵּרַכְנוּכֶם מִבֵּית יהוה:
ברוך אֵל יהוה וַיָּאֶר לָנוּ אִסְרוּ חַג בַּעֲבֹתִים עַד
קַרְנוֹת הַמִּזְבֵּחַ: אֵל אֵלִי אַתָּה וְאוֹדֶךָ אֱלֹהַי אֲרוֹמְמֶךָ:
אֵלִי הוֹדוּ לַיהוה כִּי טוֹב כִּי לְעוֹלָם חַסְדּוֹ: הודו

LET HIM WHO COMES BE BLESSED. Thus Yisrael answers the others from within the Sanctuary into which it has already entered with its declaration of thanksgiving. הבא is separated from בשם by the cantillation points so that the literal translation of the verse is not "Blessed be the one who comes in the Name of Hashem," but rather "Let him who comes be blessed in, or with, the Name of Hashem." Actually, it is not *in* the Name of Hashem," but rather *with* the Name of Hashem." Even the Priests, who pronounce their priestly blessing at the express command of Hashem and of whom it could thus be said that they bless *in* the Name of Hashem, actually bless *with* the Name of Hashem. It is explicitly said of them: "And they shall place My Name upon the sons of Yisrael, and as for me, I shall bless them" (*Bemidbar* 6:27). They are to make Yisrael the bearers of the Name of Hashem, to put the impress of God's Name upon all of Yisrael's affairs, so that these may be completely dedicated to God and shaped in accordance with His will. Only then will Hashem, too, bless them. Here, too, we are told: Men come before God and beseech for themselves the blessings of salvation and success in their endeavors. But Yisrael replies to them from within the Sanctuary of Hashem: *It is not from God, but only with God, with His Name, that you can seek and find this blessing. We have given you this benediction from the House of Hashem. In this House are laid down all the conditions under which you can obtain the blessing you seek: God's Law, the table and the menorah, which symbolize physical and spiritual life and growth shaped in accordance with this Law, and the altar upon which we pay our pledge of devotion to the Law.*

HASHEM IS GOD. Yisrael continues to address the nations: *True, Hashem and Hashem alone is the source of all the power and strength which we need if we are to grow and prosper. However, Hashem will*

222

Let him who comes be blessed with the Name of Hashem; we have blessed you out of the House of Hashem. Let... Hashem is God when He has given us light; keep the festival offering bound with cords until you reach the high corners of the altar. Hashem... You are my God; I shall acknowledge You; o' my God, I will exalt You. You... Avow it to Hashem, that He is good, that His lovingkindness endures forever Avow...(*ibid.*, 26-29).

prove to be such only if we will let Him guide us with His Light, if we will walk in those paths which He has shown us through His Law. Therefore, when you bring the offering with which you seek to join yourselves to us and to Hashem, keep that offering bound with cords. Keep it thus tied until you reach the high corners of the altar on which you shall first have solemnized your entry into His covenant by the consecration of your very being to the lofty goals which His Law has set for you as well as for us. Hashem becomes our God not in response to our pleas for salvation, but only after we have pledged our obedience to Him. Therefore, you will not reach God quickly with your offering. It is an easy thing to pray, but to pledge obedience, to submit to the guiding light of Divine insight, requires a solemn decision reached only after long, mature deliberation. Therefore, keep your offerings bound "with cords" until such time as you will have attained sufficient solemnity of spirit to make the resolution which will lead you to the heights of the altar of God's Law.

YOU ARE MY GOD. When mankind attains the solemnity of spirit necessary to make this decision, it will proclaim its new-found resolve in its avowal of homage to Hashem as its own God: "You are *my* God." *Henceforth, I shall pay homage to no power other than You; from this time forward You shall be "my God" to Whom I subject myself because, in Your all-surpassing majesty, You are the Master of my destiny and the Guide of all my acts.*

AVOW IT TO HASHEM, THAT HE IS GOOD. After mankind thus enters into the covenant with Hashem, Yisrael will know that the aim of its mission has been fulfilled at long last. It is only then that

יְהַלְלוּךְ יהוה אֱלֹהֵינוּ כָּל מַעֲשֶׂיךָ וַחֲסִידֶיךָ
צַדִּיקִים עוֹשֵׂי רְצוֹנֶךָ וְכָל עַמְּךָ בֵּית יִשְׂרָאֵל בְּרִנָּה
יוֹדוּ וִיבָרְכוּ וִישַׁבְּחוּ וִיפָאֲרוּ וִירוֹמְמוּ וְיַעֲרִיצוּ
וְיַקְדִּישׁוּ וְיַמְלִיכוּ אֶת שִׁמְךָ מַלְכֵּנוּ כִּי לְךָ טוֹב
לְהוֹדוֹת וּלְשִׁמְךָ נָאֶה לְזַמֵּר כִּי מֵעוֹלָם וְעַד עוֹלָם
אַתָּה אֵל:

כִּי לְעוֹלָם חַסְדּוֹ:	הוֹדוּ לַיהוה כִּי טוֹב
כִּי לְעוֹלָם חַסְדּוֹ:	הוֹדוּ לֵאלֹהֵי הָאֱלֹהִים
כִּי לְעוֹלָם חַסְדּוֹ:	הוֹדוּ לַאֲדֹנֵי הָאֲדֹנִים
כִּי לְעוֹלָם חַסְדּוֹ:	לְעֹשֵׂה נִפְלָאוֹת גְּדֹלוֹת לְבַדּוֹ
כִּי לְעוֹלָם חַסְדּוֹ:	לְעֹשֵׂה הַשָּׁמַיִם בִּתְבוּנָה

Yisrael, both in its own name and on behalf of all mankind, now
united with it, will be able to declare with all its heart and voice the
avowal of redemption with which it celebrated all the instances of
Divine deliverance it had experienced during its wanderings
throughout the centuries of world history: "Avow it to Hashem, that
He is good, that His lovingkindness endures forever."

AVOW IT TO HASHEM THAT HE IS GOOD. This psalm is called "the
Great Hallel" since it is praise emanating from His mighty acts"
(*Pesachim* 118a). Why? Because it portrays Hashem as dwelling in the
heights of the universe, giving sustenance to every living thing (*ibid.*).
It is evident from this statement that the penultimate verse of this
psalm, "Who gives food to all flesh..." is viewed as the verse in which

All Your works shall proclaim Your praise, o' Hashem our God, and let Your devoted ones, the righteous who do Your will, and all Your people, the House of Yisrael, render homage with jubilation and bless and laud and extol and exalt, praise and sanctify and glorify Your Name, o' our King. For it is good to render You homage and it is pleasant to sing to Your Name, for from eternity to eternity You are God.

Avow it to Hashem that He is good,
　　that His lovingkindness endures forever.
Avow it to the God of gods,
　　that His lovingkindness endures forever.
Avow it to the Master of masters,
　　that His lovingkindness endures forever.
To Him Who alone does great wonders,
　　that His lovingkindness endures forever.
To Him Who shapes the heavens with understanding,
　　that His lovingkindness endures forever.

the theme of the entire psalm culminates and to which all the preceding verses lead. Applying grammatical rules, one sees that this verse is the only one which contains a direct statement. All the other verses are subordinate to the summons הודו, "avow it," and therefore, they begin with the preposition "to," or else they continue the sentences thus begun through the addition of an object, such as "the sun," or of a dependent clause, such as "and brought Yisrael out."

In truth all the preceding verses portray Hashem as dwelling in the heights of the universe, in all the greatness and majesty of His universal rule both in nature and in history. This depiction of God is then connected with the statement "Who gives food to all flesh," thus teaching us to grasp in all its significance the great truth that every piece of bread a human being earns for himself and his dear ones through honest, conscientious toil is to be viewed as only another

כִּי לְעוֹלָם חַסְדּוֹ:	לְרוֹקַע הָאָרֶץ עַל הַמָּיִם
כִּי לְעוֹלָם חַסְדּוֹ:	לְעֹשֵׂה אוֹרִים גְּדֹלִים
כִּי לְעוֹלָם חַסְדּוֹ:	אֶת הַשֶּׁמֶשׁ לְמֶמְשֶׁלֶת בַּיּוֹם
	אֶת הַיָּרֵחַ וְכוֹכָבִים לְמֶמְשְׁלוֹת
כִּי לְעוֹלָם חַסְדּוֹ:	בַּלָּיְלָה
כִּי לְעוֹלָם חַסְדּוֹ:	לְמַכֵּה מִצְרַיִם בִּבְכוֹרֵיהֶם
כִּי לְעוֹלָם חַסְדּוֹ:	וַיּוֹצֵא יִשְׂרָאֵל מִתּוֹכָם
כִּי לְעוֹלָם חַסְדּוֹ:	בְּיָד חֲזָקָה וּבִזְרוֹעַ נְטוּיָה
כִּי לְעוֹלָם חַסְדּוֹ:	לְגֹזֵר יַם סוּף לִגְזָרִים
כִּי לְעוֹלָם חַסְדּוֹ:	וְהֶעֱבִיר יִשְׂרָאֵל בְּתוֹכוֹ
כִּי לְעוֹלָם חַסְדּוֹ:	וְנִעֵר פַּרְעֹה וְחֵילוֹ בְיַם סוּף
כִּי לְעוֹלָם חַסְדּוֹ:	לְמוֹלִיךְ עַמּוֹ בַּמִּדְבָּר
כִּי לְעוֹלָם חַסְדּוֹ:	לְמַכֵּה מְלָכִים גְּדֹלִים
כִּי לְעוֹלָם חַסְדּוֹ:	וַיַּהֲרֹג מְלָכִים אַדִּירִים
כִּי לְעוֹלָם חַסְדּוֹ:	לְסִיחוֹן מֶלֶךְ הָאֱמֹרִי
כִּי לְעוֹלָם חַסְדּוֹ:	וּלְעוֹג מֶלֶךְ הַבָּשָׁן

demonstration of the greatness and magnificence of God's rule. For the mighty acts of God in nature and history alike must interact if an honest man is to receive his daily bread in an honest manner from the loving Hand of Hashem. Therefore the statement of the Sages: "It is as difficult to provide man's daily sustenance as to split the Sea of Reeds" (*ibid.*). Man does not receive his sustenance through the operation of purely physical, mechanical laws alone. On the

To Him Who firmly establishes the earth upon the waters,
    that His lovingkindness endures forever.
To Him Who fashions great lights,
    that His lovingkindness endures forever.
The sun for dominion by day,
    that His lovingkindness endures forever.
The moon and the stars for dominions at night,
    that His lovingkindness endures forever.
To Him Who slays Egypt through their firstborn,
    that His lovingkindness endures forever.
And brought Yisrael out from their midst,
    that His lovingkindness endures forever.
With a strong hand and with an outstretched arm,
    that His lovingkindness endures forever.
To Him Who divides the Sea of Reeds into parts,
    that His lovingkindness endures forever.
And made Yisrael pass through the midst of it,
    that His lovingkindness endures forever.
And poured out Pharaoh and his host into the Sea of Reeds,
    that His lovingkindness endures forever.
To Him Who leads His people through the wilderness,
    that His lovingkindness endures forever.
To Him Who smites great kings,
    that His lovingkindness endures forever.
And killed mighty kings,
    that His lovingkindness endures forever.
For Sichon, the king of the Amorites,
    that His lovingkindness endures forever.
And for Og, the king of Bashan,
    that His lovingkindness endures forever.

contrary, he receives it through Hashem's free, direct intervention into the course of the development of the phenomena of nature and history in a manner resembling the parting of the Sea of Reeds.

Man owes his daily subsistence neither to accident, nor even to an automatic interaction of natural and social conditions. Instead, he owes it to the rule of God Himself Who freely commands the forces of

וְנָתַן אַרְצָם לְנַחֲלָה	כִּי לְעוֹלָם חַסְדּוֹ:
נַחֲלָה לְיִשְׂרָאֵל עַבְדּוֹ	כִּי לְעוֹלָם חַסְדּוֹ:
שֶׁבְּשִׁפְלֵנוּ זָכַר לָנוּ	כִּי לְעוֹלָם חַסְדּוֹ:
וַיִּפְרְקֵנוּ מִצָּרֵינוּ	כִּי לְעוֹלָם חַסְדּוֹ:
נֹתֵן לֶחֶם לְכָל בָּשָׂר	כִּי לְעוֹלָם חַסְדּוֹ:
הוֹדוּ לְאֵל הַשָּׁמָיִם	כִּי לְעוֹלָם חַסְדּוֹ:

nature and society and leads both to fulfill His purposes. Accordingly, we can acquire the proper understanding of the recurrent refrain "that His lovingkindness endures forever." This means that the same almighty lovingkindness for which all things are possible, as demonstrated in the outstanding acts of God which are enumerated here one by one, is always active, even in the arena of everyday life.

In order to have us think through this idea in all its true significance, verses 2 and 3 proclaim God as being the sole absolute and freely commanding Force and Power which towers high above all the forces of nature that men would worship as gods, and above all the powers in society which men honor and fear as their overlords. Hashem is the one true God among all the alleged gods and the one true Master among all the would-be masters. Not only does He possess this power, He also puts it to use (verse 4). He does not simply leave the course of nature and history to the effects of the laws of nature which He set up at the time of Creation. He intervenes even now, with His unique, free and personal will, guiding, leading and shaping all things by means of direct action. He does indeed possess this power, for heaven and earth and the heavenly bodies which influence the natural development of earthly things are all His work (verses 5-9).

And gave their land as an inheritance,
> that His lovingkindness endures forever.
As an inheritance to Yisrael His servant,
> that His lovingkindness endures forever.
Who remembered us in our lowly state,
> because His lovingkindness endures forever.
And freed us from our oppressors,
> because His lovingkindness endures forever.
Who gives food to all flesh,
> since His lovingkindness endures forever.
Avow it to the God of Heaven,
> that His lovingkindness endures forever (*ibid.*, 136).

The purpose and goal dwelling within these bodies, as well as the arrangement of the world, determining a certain sequence of developments, are His also. And He wields this power even as He has demonstrated it in Yisrael's history, judging and saving, as in the exodus from Egypt (verses 10-15); leading, protecting, nourishing and disciplining, as in the journey through the wilderness (verse 16); and overthrowing some destinies and establishing others, as in the cession of the land to Yisrael (verses 17-22). All the rest of our subsequent history has also taught us that He was near us not only at the time of the establishment of our destiny, but also throughout the course of our history (verses 23, 24). However, the greatness of God's rule, in which He judges and delivers, leads, protects, nourishes, disciplines, overthrows and establishes men and nations, and His constant care throughout the ages, which was demonstrated in such obvious ways in the history of the nations, are manifestations of the same power that is revealed in every moment of modest, quiet subsistence which He grants to any person. It is to this Divine lovingkindness — judging and saving, leading, protecting, nourishing and disciplining, overthrowing and establishing — to this constant care of His, that we owe every single crumb of our daily sustenance.

נִשְׁמַת כָּל חַי תְּבָרֵךְ אֶת שִׁמְךָ יהוה אֱלֹהֵינוּ וְרוּחַ כָּל בָּשָׂר תְּפָאֵר וּתְרוֹמֵם זִכְרְךָ מַלְכֵּנוּ תָּמִיד. מִן הָעוֹלָם וְעַד הָעוֹלָם אַתָּה אֵל וּמִבַּלְעָדֶיךָ אֵין לָנוּ מֶלֶךְ גּוֹאֵל וּמוֹשִׁיעַ פּוֹדֶה וּמַצִּיל וּמְפַרְנֵס וּמְרַחֵם. בְּכָל עֵת צָרָה וְצוּקָה אֵין לָנוּ מֶלֶךְ אֶלָּא אָתָּה. אֱלֹהֵי הָרִאשׁוֹנִים וְהָאַחֲרוֹנִים אֱלוֹהַּ כָּל בְּרִיּוֹת אֲדוֹן כָּל תּוֹלָדוֹת הַמְהֻלָּל בְּרוֹב הַתִּשְׁבָּחוֹת הַמְנַהֵג עוֹלָמוֹ בְּחֶסֶד

THE SOUL OF EVERY LIVING THING. Man — what is he in this God-filled world, among this throng of God's creatures, this chorus of God's servants? Even if the Torah were silent on this point, would not the very sight of creation reveal it to one, one's own conscience tell it to him? Is not man, too, a Divine creation? Should he not also be enlisted in His service? Man's body — every fiber was formed by Him, arranged by Him, endowed by Him with strength. His mind — a veritable universe of forces — is God's creation in every detail. His personality, this Divine spark, invisible like God, weaving and working in this little universe, controlling body and mind, and possessing the power to make use of the entire world for its purposes, is itself an *emanation of Deity*. One must learn to respect one's sanctity as a creature of God, and, in the sight of heaven and earth and the entire host of Divine servants, call himself in joyous solemnity by the name that expresses and consecrates his mission: a servant of God. Since everything, small or large, constitutes a God-given force meant to function purposefully, by given means, in its appointed place, in its assigned environment, and in compliance with His laws, taking only in order to give — could it be that man alone is excluded from this circle of life, is born only to take, to indulge or to endure, but not to function productively? Is he not to fill a post? Is he merely to be his

230

‎𝕾 THE soul of every living thing shall bless Your Name, o' Hashem our God, and the spirit of all flesh shall ever glorify and exalt Your remembrance, o' our King. From the remotest past to the most distant future, You are God, and beside You we have no King, Who redeems, and saves, delivers and rescues, sustains and has compassion; in all times of trouble and distress we have no King but You. God of the first and of the last, God of all creatures, Master of all that is begotten, proclaimed in an abundance of praises, Who guides His world with lovingkindness and His

own be-all and end-all? Is it conceivable that everything is to be of service in the world, of service to God, and only man is to be self-serving throughout?

No — surely not! One's own inner awareness tells him, and the Torah states it, that man's purpose is to be צלם אלהים — in the *likeness of God*. He is to be more than everything else, to exist for everything else. Man can only know God through His acts of love and justice — and, in turn, he too is called to *act in justice and love*, not merely to indulge or endure. Everything bestowed upon man — mind, body, fellow man, material goods, other creatures — every talent and every power — all are merely means to action, לעבדה ולשמרה, to further and to safeguard everything, with love and with justice! The earth was not created as a gift to man — he has been given the earth and is to treat it with respectful consideration because it is God's earth. Everything on it, including man's fellow creatures, are God's creation and as such each is to be respected, loved and helped to attain its purpose according to God's will. To this end one's mind is able to form the right image of all that exists; to this end one's heartstrings vibrate sympathetically with every cry of distress sounding anywhere in creation and with every glad sound uttered by a joyful creature; to this end one is made happy when the flower blossoms and sad when it wilts.

231

וּבְרִיּוֹתָיו בְּרַחֲמִים. וַיהוה לֹא יָנוּם וְלֹא יִישָׁן
הַמְעוֹרֵר יְשֵׁנִים וְהַמֵּקִיץ נִרְדָּמִים וְהַמֵּשִׂיחַ
אִלְּמִים וְהַמַּתִּיר אֲסוּרִים וְהַסּוֹמֵךְ נוֹפְלִים
וְהַזּוֹקֵף כְּפוּפִים. לְךָ לְבַדְּךָ אֲנַחְנוּ מוֹדִים. אִלּוּ
פִינוּ מָלֵא שִׁירָה כַּיָּם וּלְשׁוֹנֵנוּ רִנָּה כַּהֲמוֹן גַּלָּיו
וְשִׂפְתוֹתֵינוּ שֶׁבַח כְּמֶרְחֲבֵי רָקִיעַ וְעֵינֵינוּ
מְאִירוֹת כַּשֶּׁמֶשׁ וְכַיָּרֵחַ וְיָדֵינוּ פְרוּשׂוֹת כְּנִשְׁרֵי
שָׁמַיִם וְרַגְלֵינוּ קַלּוֹת כָּאַיָּלוֹת אֵין אֲנַחְנוּ
מַסְפִּיקִים לְהוֹדוֹת לְךָ יהוה אֱלֹהֵינוּ וֵאלֹהֵי
אֲבוֹתֵינוּ וּלְבָרֵךְ אֶת שְׁמֶךָ עַל אַחַת מֵאָלֶף אֶלֶף
אַלְפֵי אֲלָפִים וְרִבֵּי רְבָבוֹת פְּעָמִים הַטּוֹבוֹת

The law to which all forces submit instinctively and involuntarily
— to this law man too is to subordinate himself, but consciously and
of his own free will. Consciously and freely! This is man's eminent
vocation, his highest privilege. All forces are ranged in service around
God's throne. Their standing is concealed from them, and their
countenance is covered, so that they do not see the purpose of their
mission. They sense only the impetus to action, and they act in
accordance with their assigned task. But man — his countenance is
half-uncovered, his place is in part revealed to him, he is able to
conceive of himself — and consecrate himself — as God's servant. He
is able to gain an inkling of his mission, which God has attuned his
ear to perceive. Surrounded by God's servants busily at work and
sensing in himself, too, the impetus to act — would he not join their
chorus with the joyful cry of allegiance: נעשה ונשמע — "We will do
and therefore listen"? *We will act and, in carrying out the mission, try
to comprehend its intent.* Consciously and freely — thus to be first
and preeminent in this legion of God's servants.

232

creatures with compassion. And Hashem neither slumbers nor sleeps; it is He, rather, Who awakens those who sleep, Who rouses those that are stunned, Who gives speech to the mute, Who sets free those that are bound, supports the falling and raises up those that are bowed down. To You and to You alone do we avow thanks. Though our mouths were filled with song as the sea, and our tongues with joy's outpouring as the swell of its waves, and our lips with praise as the expanse of heaven, and though our eyes were brilliant like the sun and moon, our hands spread out like the eagles of the heavens, and our feet as light as the deer — we would still be unable to thank You, Hashem our God and God of our fathers, and to bless Your Name for even one thousandth of the myriad favors which You have bestowed upon

Man's purpose in life is, therefore, not the acquisition of possessions; one should not measure his achievement in life by the volume of external or internal treasures that he accumulates. Man's life's mission is concerned with what he becomes, what he makes of himself, and what he gives, not what he gets. One should measure his attainments by the extent to which he fulfills God's will with the help of his external and internal acquisitions, utilizing every single one, small or large, for truly human deeds of Divine service. One's endeavors to acquire internal and external possessions have value only because they provide the means for performing such deeds.

From the slightest mental faculty, and the nerve ganglia which serve it, to the strength of one's hand, with which he is able to bring about changes in creation and to which the entire realm of nature and every being within his reach are subject — all one's capabilities are but tools lent to him, which one day will appear before the throne of God as witnesses for or against him, testifying whether he neglected them or used them well, whether he wrought blessing with them or

שֶׁעָשִׂיתָ עִם אֲבוֹתֵינוּ וְעִמָּנוּ. מִמִּצְרַיִם
גְּאַלְתָּנוּ יהוה אֱלֹהֵינוּ וּמִבֵּית עֲבָדִים פְּדִיתָנוּ
בְּרָעָב זַנְתָּנוּ וּבְשָׂבָע כִּלְכַּלְתָּנוּ מֵחֶרֶב הִצַּלְתָּנוּ
וּמִדֶּבֶר מִלַּטְתָּנוּ וּמֵחֳלָיִם רָעִים וְנֶאֱמָנִים
דִּלִּיתָנוּ. עַד הֵנָּה עֲזָרוּנוּ רַחֲמֶיךָ וְלֹא עֲזָבוּנוּ
חֲסָדֶיךָ וְאַל תִּטְּשֵׁנוּ יהוה אֱלֹהֵינוּ לָנֶצַח. עַל כֵּן
אֵבָרִים שֶׁפִּלַּגְתָּ בָּנוּ וְרוּחַ וּנְשָׁמָה שֶׁנָּפַחְתָּ
בְּאַפֵּינוּ וְלָשׁוֹן אֲשֶׁר שַׂמְתָּ בְּפִינוּ הֵן הֵם יוֹדוּ

curse. Accordingly, there is an external, universally applicable criterion by which to judge the deeds of man — whether they correspond to the will of God. And there is an internal criterion for the greatness of man that differs from case to case — it does not measure the sum total of man's achievements, the amount of resources with which he has been endowed, but whether he has used them to the best of his ability in doing God's will. It follows that in spite of one's greatest achievements, his life may be an utter failure if his actions were not the right ones. On the other hand, a man's life may be sublimely great even though it shows only minor accomplishments, if the means allotted to him did not permit major ones. Thus, happiness and perfection consist in using to their fullest measure all of one's external and internal possessions, according to God's will — *which alone is what makes man great.*

Rabbi Chanina bar Papa taught (see *Niddah* 16b) that the angel in charge of man's coming into existence takes the seed which is to develop into a human being, brings it before the Holy One, Whose will all beings serve, and asks, "This seed — what shall become of it in life? Shall the human being growing from it be strong or weak, wise or simple, rich or poor?" The angel does not ask, however, whether the human being shall be good or bad, since everything depends on God *except for the fear of God* — that is, everything except faithfully fulfilling one's duty, utilizing the means granted to him. Therefore, our fathers and upon us. You have redeemed us from Egypt, o' Hashem our God, and freed us from the house of slavery; You have fed us in famine and satisfied us in plenty. You have delivered us from the sword, freed us from pestilence, and relieved us from severe and lasting diseases. Until now Your compassion has helped us, and Your kindnesses have not forsaken us, so Hashem our God, forsake us never. Therefore the limbs which You have apportioned for us, the spirit and soul which You have breathed into our nostrils and the tongue which You have put into our mouth, shall all render homage, bless, praise,

man cannot be judged according to what is scarcely halfway in his hands, but rather, according to that which God put entirely in his control and which, therefore, can alone constitute his greatness.

Thus comprehended, the purpose of man can be attained by anyone, at any time, with his individual measure of strength and means. Whoever in his lifetime fulfilled the will of God towards the creatures brought into his orbit, wronging none, assisting each one to the best of his ability to reach the goal which God intended for it — he was truly a man; he expressed justice and love in his life. His entire life, all of himself, his thoughts, feelings, speech and action — even his business transactions and personal enjoyments — were considered service of God. Such a life transcends *all vicissitudes*. Whether in luxury or privation, abundance or want, whether with tears of joy or sorrow, such a personality, unchanging almost like God, sees in every new blessing, as in every loss, merely another challenge to tackle anew the same unchanging task.

Thus man, in his earthly form, belongs to this world, and his earthly existence is full of significance. Just as no breath of air nor the tiniest blade of grass nor beetle exists for nought, but contributes its share, slight though it may be, which God's wisdom uses for the building of the edifice of the universe, thus, too, no pleasure, no thought, no deed, no matter how modest, is empty and futile. Those that are proper form the handiwork that man delivers into God's Hands

235

וִיבָרְכוּ וִישַׁבְּחוּ וִיפָאֲרוּ וִירוֹמְמוּ וְיַעֲרִיצוּ
וְיַקְדִּישׁוּ וְיַמְלִיכוּ אֶת שִׁמְךָ מַלְכֵּנוּ. כִּי כָל פֶּה
לְךָ יוֹדֶה וְכָל לָשׁוֹן לְךָ תִשָּׁבַע וְכָל בֶּרֶךְ לְךָ
תִכְרַע וְכָל קוֹמָה לְפָנֶיךָ תִשְׁתַּחֲוֶה. וְכָל לְבָבוֹת
יִירָאוּךָ וְכָל קֶרֶב וּכְלָיוֹת יְזַמְּרוּ לִשְׁמֶךָ. כַּדָּבָר
שֶׁכָּתוּב כָּל עַצְמֹתַי תֹּאמַרְנָה יהוה מִי כָמוֹךָ
מַצִּיל עָנִי מֵחָזָק מִמֶּנּוּ וְעָנִי וְאֶבְיוֹן מִגֹּזְלוֹ. מִי
יִדְמֶה לָּךְ וּמִי יִשְׁוֶה לָּךְ וּמִי יַעֲרָךְ לָךְ הָאֵל הַגָּדוֹל
הַגִּבּוֹר וְהַנּוֹרָא אֵל עֶלְיוֹן קוֹנֵה שָׁמַיִם וָאָרֶץ.
נְהַלֶּלְךָ וּנְשַׁבֵּחֲךָ וּנְפָאֶרְךָ וּנְבָרֵךְ אֶת שֵׁם קָדְשֶׁךָ
כָּאָמוּר לְדָוִד בָּרְכִי נַפְשִׁי אֶת יהוה וְכָל קְרָבַי
אֶת שֵׁם קָדְשׁוֹ:

הָאֵל בְּתַעֲצֻמוֹת עֻזֶּךָ הַגָּדוֹל בִּכְבוֹד שְׁמֶךָ
הַגִּבּוֹר לָנֶצַח וְהַנּוֹרָא בְּנוֹרְאוֹתֶיךָ הַמֶּלֶךְ הַיּוֹשֵׁב עַל
כִּסֵּא רָם וְנִשָּׂא:

for Him to embody in the overall structure of the universe.
Fulfillment of God's will, with one's possessions and pleasures, with
thought, word, and deed — this is the content of one's life. One must
properly understand this will, however, for therein lies the unique
greatness of man: whereas the voice of God speaks *in* or *through* all
other creatures, in the case of man it speaks *to* him, challenging him
to accept it, *voluntarily*, as the impelling force directing his work in
life.

glorify, exalt and declare the power, the holiness and dominion of Your Name, o' our King. For every mouth shall render You homage, every tongue shall swear You allegiance, every knee shall bend before You, and all that stands upright shall fall down before You; all hearts shall fear You, and all the inmost passions shall sing praises to Your Name, even as it is written, "All my limbs shall say, 'O' Hashem, who is like You, Who delivers the poor from one that is stronger than him, the poor and the defenseless from one who would rob him?'" Who is like You, who is equal to You, and who can be compared to You, o' great, strong, and awesome God, the Most High God, the Owner of heaven and earth? We shall proclaim Your praise, laud You, glorify You and bless Your Holy Name, even as it is said: "By David. Bless Hashem, o' my soul, and all that is within me, bless His holy Name."

O' God, in the abundance of Your might, great in the glory of Your Name, almighty in eternity and feared for Your awesome acts, the King Who, highly exalted, is seated upon a throne.

Go then, man, and measure yourself in comparison with a blade of grass or a peal of thunder. Considering the immensity of all the internal and external treasures which you possess and enjoy, if you do not blush with shame over your petty selfishness when faced with the angel-like grandeur of these creations, and if you do not rouse yourself with all your strength and every spark of your vitality to make such grandeur your own — then, indeed, you should go and lament the degradation which the age has brought upon you.

שׁוֹכֵן עַד מָרוֹם וְקָדוֹשׁ שְׁמוֹ. וְכָתוּב רַנְּנוּ
צַדִּיקִים בַּיהוה לַיְשָׁרִים נָאוָה תְהִלָּה: בְּפִי יְשָׁרִים
תִּתְהַלָּל וּבְדִבְרֵי צַדִּיקִים תִּתְבָּרַךְ וּבִלְשׁוֹן חֲסִידִים
תִּתְרוֹמָם וּבְקֶרֶב קְדוֹשִׁים תִּתְקַדָּשׁ:

וּבְמַקְהֲלוֹת רִבְבוֹת עַמְּךָ בֵּית יִשְׂרָאֵל בְּרִנָּה
יִתְפָּאַר שִׁמְךָ מַלְכֵּנוּ בְּכָל דּוֹר וָדוֹר. שֶׁכֵּן חוֹבַת כָּל
הַיְצוּרִים לְפָנֶיךָ יהוה אֱלֹהֵינוּ וֵאלֹהֵי אֲבוֹתֵינוּ
לְהוֹדוֹת לְהַלֵּל לְשַׁבֵּחַ לְפָאֵר לְרוֹמֵם לְהַדֵּר לְבָרֵךְ
לְעַלֵּה וּלְקַלֵּס עַל כָּל דִּבְרֵי שִׁירוֹת וְתִשְׁבָּחוֹת דָּוִד בֶּן
יִשַׁי עַבְדְּךָ מְשִׁיחֶךָ:

יִשְׁתַּבַּח שִׁמְךָ לָעַד מַלְכֵּנוּ הָאֵל הַמֶּלֶךְ הַגָּדוֹל
וְהַקָּדוֹשׁ בַּשָּׁמַיִם וּבָאָרֶץ כִּי לְךָ נָאֶה יהוה אֱלֹהֵינוּ
וֵאלֹהֵי אֲבוֹתֵינוּ שִׁיר וּשְׁבָחָה הַלֵּל וְזִמְרָה עֹז
וּמֶמְשָׁלָה נֶצַח גְּדֻלָּה וּגְבוּרָה תְּהִלָּה וְתִפְאֶרֶת קְדֻשָּׁה
וּמַלְכוּת בְּרָכוֹת וְהוֹדָאוֹת מֵעַתָּה וְעַד־עוֹלָם. בָּרוּךְ
אַתָּה יהוה אֵל מֶלֶךְ גָּדוֹל בַּתִּשְׁבָּחוֹת אֵל הַהוֹדָאוֹת
אֲדוֹן הַנִּפְלָאוֹת הַבּוֹחֵר בְּשִׁירֵי זִמְרָה מֶלֶךְ אֵל חֵי
הָעוֹלָמִים:

Dwelling in eternity, His Name is exalted and holy. And it is written: "Exult, o' righteous ones, in beholding Hashem; it behooves the upright to sing praises of the acts that reveal His might." By the mouth of the upright there is song in Your praise, by the words of the righteous You are blessed, by the tongue of Your devoted ones You are extolled, and in the midst of the holy You are sanctified.

And in the assemblies of the tens of thousands of Your people Yisrael, Your Name, o' our King, is glorified in every generation with fervent emotion. For it is the duty of all creatures to avow thanks before You, o' Hashem our God and God of our fathers, and to praise Your mighty acts, to laud, glorify, exalt and proclaim Your might, to bless, to extol You and to celebrate You in keeping with all the words and songs of praise by Your servant David, the son of Yishai, Your Anointed.

Praised be Your Name forever, o' our King, God, the King Who is great and holy in Heaven and on earth. For to You, o' Hashem our God and God of our fathers, pertain song and laud, praise and hymn, strength and dominion, victory, greatness, and might, renown and glory, holiness and kingship, blessings and [utterances of] thanksgiving henceforth and unto eternity. Blessed be You Hashem, God and King, great in hymns of praise, God of thanksgivings, Master of wonders, Who takes pleasure in hymns, King, God, the Life of all times.

*In most homes the fourth cup is drunk immediately
after Hallel, followed by nirtzah and then, the
Hadgadah songs. In some Ashkenazic communities,
however, the songs are now sung until after ki lo naeh,
(pages 250-51) and then the wine is drunk, followed
by nirtzah and the remainder of the songs.*

*One should have in mind that it is his intention to
fulfill the requirement of drinking the fourth
of the four cups of wine.*

בָּרוּךְ אַתָּה יהוה אֱלֹהֵינוּ מֶלֶךְ הָעוֹלָם
בּוֹרֵא פְּרִי הַגָּפֶן:

*The entire amount of the fourth cup is drunk (to enable
one to recite the berachah after drinking wine), within
the required period of time, while reclining to the left.*

בָּרוּךְ אַתָּה יהוה אֱלֹהֵינוּ מֶלֶךְ הָעוֹלָם עַל
הַגֶּפֶן וְעַל פְּרִי הַגֶּפֶן וְעַל תְּנוּבַת הַשָּׂדֶה וְעַל אֶרֶץ
חֶמְדָּה טוֹבָה וּרְחָבָה שֶׁרָצִיתָ וְהִנְחַלְתָּ לַאֲבוֹתֵינוּ
לֶאֱכוֹל מִפִּרְיָהּ וְלִשְׂבּוֹעַ מִטּוּבָהּ. רַחֶם נָא יהוה
אֱלֹהֵינוּ עַל יִשְׂרָאֵל עַמֶּךָ וְעַל יְרוּשָׁלַיִם עִירֶךָ וְעַל
צִיּוֹן מִשְׁכַּן כְּבוֹדֶךָ וְעַל מִזְבְּחֶךָ וְעַל הֵיכָלֶךָ וּבְנֵה
יְרוּשָׁלַיִם עִיר הַקֹּדֶשׁ בִּמְהֵרָה בְיָמֵינוּ וְהַעֲלֵנוּ
לְתוֹכָהּ וְשַׂמְּחֵנוּ בְּבִנְיָנָהּ וְנֹאכַל מִפִּרְיָהּ וְנִשְׂבַּע
מִטּוּבָהּ וּנְבָרֶכְךָ עָלֶיהָ בִּקְדֻשָּׁה וּבְטָהֳרָה (בשבת וּרְצֵה

In most homes the fourth cup is drunk immediately after Hallel, followed by nirtzah and then, the Hadgadah songs. In some Ashkenazic communities, however, the songs are now sung until after ki lo naeh, (pages 250-51) and then the wine is drunk, followed by nirtzah and the remainder of the songs.

One should have in mind that it is his intention to fulfill the requirement of drinking the fourth of the four cups of wine.

Blessed be you, Hashem our God, King of the universe, Who creates the fruit of the vine.

The entire amount of the fourth cup is drunk (to enable one to recite the berachah after drinking wine), within the required period of time, while reclining to the left.

Blessed be You, Hashem our God, King of the universe, for the vine and the fruit of the vine; for the produce of the field and for the desirable, good and spacious land which You have given to our fathers as an inheritance in favor, that they might eat of its fruit and be satisfied with its goodness. Have compassion, Hashem our God, upon Your people Yisrael, upon Yerushalayim, Your City, and upon Tzion, the Abode of Your glory, upon Your altar and upon Your Temple, and rebuild Yerushalayim, the city of holiness,* speedily in our days; bring us up into it and make us rejoice in its rebuilding. May we eat of its fruit and be satisfied with its goodness so that we may bless You for it in holiness and purity. (*On Shabbos add:*

---

*See footnote on page 191.

241

וְהַחֲלִיצֵנוּ בְּיוֹם הַשַּׁבָּת הַזֶּה) וְשַׂמְּחֵנוּ בְּיוֹם חַג הַמַּצּוֹת הַזֶּה כִּי אַתָּה יְהֹוָה טוֹב וּמֵטִיב לַכֹּל וְנוֹדֶה לְּךָ עַל הָאָרֶץ וְעַל פְּרִי הַגָּפֶן:* בָּרוּךְ אַתָּה יְהֹוָה עַל הָאָרֶץ וְעַל פְּרִי הַגָּפֶן:*

נִרְצָה

חֲסַל סִדּוּר פֶּסַח כְּהִלְכָתוֹ. כְּכָל מִשְׁפָּטוֹ וְחֻקָּתוֹ. כַּאֲשֶׁר זָכִינוּ לְסַדֵּר אוֹתוֹ. כֵּן נִזְכֶּה לַעֲשׂוֹתוֹ: זָךְ שׁוֹכֵן מְעוֹנָה. קוֹמֵם קְהַל עֲדַת מִי מָנָה. בְּקָרוֹב נַהֵל נִטְעֵי כַנָּה. פְּדוּיִם לְצִיּוֹן בְּרִנָּה:

לְשָׁנָה הַבָּאָה בִּירוּשָׁלָיִם:

---

*For wine or grape juice from Eretz Yisrael substitute: וְעַל פְּרִי גַּפְנָהּ

242

And be pleased to fortify us on this Shabbos day.) And gladden us on this day of the Festival of Unleavened Bread, for You, Hashem, are good and do good to all. To You we give thanks for the land and for the fruit of the vine.* Blessed be You, Hashem, for the land and for the fruit of the vine.*

Nirtzah

THE order of the Pesach is complete, according to its laws, all of its ordinances and statutes. Just as we merited to perform it, so may we merit to offer the sacrifice in deed. O' Pure One, Who abides on high, uplift the assembly of the community who cannot be counted (Yisrael). Soon, and in joy, may You lead the offshoots of the stock which You have planted, redeemed, to Tzion.

Next Year May We Be in Yerushalayim!

(See "Next Year May We Be in Yerushalayim," page 279).

---

*For wine or grape juice from Eretz Yisrael substitute: fruit of *her* vine.

Those who live in Eretz Yisrael say both the following songs on the night of the Pesach Seder. Those who live in chutz la'aretz say the following song only on the first night and then proceed to Ki Lo Naeh (pages 250-1). On the second night, they skip this song and proceed to Vaamartem Zevach Pesach (pages 246-7).

וּבְכֵן וַיְהִי בַּחֲצִי הַלַּיְלָה

בַּלַּיְלָה.   אָז רוֹב נִסִּים הִפְלֵאתָ

הַלַּיְלָה.   בְּרֹאשׁ אַשְׁמוֹרֶת זֶה

לַיְלָה.   גֵּר צֶדֶק נִצַּחְתּוֹ כְּנֶחֱלַק לוֹ

וַיְהִי בַּחֲצִי הַלַּיְלָה:

הַלַּיְלָה.   דַּנְתָּ מֶלֶךְ גְּרָר בַּחֲלוֹם

לַיְלָה.   הִפְחַדְתָּ אֲרַמִּי בְּאֶמֶשׁ

לַיְלָה.   וַיָּשַׂר יִשְׂרָאֵל לְמַלְאָךְ וַיּוּכַל לוֹ

וַיְהִי בַּחֲצִי הַלַּיְלָה:

הַלַּיְלָה.   זֶרַע בְּכוֹרֵי פַתְרוֹס מָחַצְתָּ בַּחֲצִי

בַּלַּיְלָה.   חֵילָם לֹא מָצְאוּ בְּקוּמָם

לַיְלָה.   טִיסַת נְגִיד חֲרֹשֶׁת סִלִּיתָ בְּכוֹכְבֵי

וַיְהִי בַּחֲצִי הַלַּיְלָה:

בַּלַּיְלָה.   יָעַץ מְחָרֵף לְנוֹפֵף אִוּוּי הוֹבַשְׁתָּ פְגָרָיו

לַיְלָה.   כָּרַע בֵּל וּמַצָּבוֹ בְּאִישׁוֹן

לַיְלָה.   לְאִישׁ חֲמוּדוֹת נִגְלָה רָז חֲזוֹת

וַיְהִי בַּחֲצִי הַלַּיְלָה:

244

Those who live in Eretz Yisrael say both the following songs on the night of the Pesach Seder. Those who live in chutz la'aretz say the following song only on the first night and then proceed to Ki Lo Naeh (pages 250-1). On the second night, they skip this song and proceed to Vaamartem Zevach Pesach (pages 246-7).

Vayehi Bachatzi Halaylah
And It Came To Pass at Midnight

Of old You worked so many miracles	at night;
At the start of the watches,	this very night;
To the righteous convert [Avraham] You gave victory when [his army] divided for him	in the night;

And it came to pass at midnight.

You judged the King of Gerar in a dream	in the night;
Frightened [Laban] the Aramean the preceding	night;
And Yisrael [Yaakov] fought an angel and overcame him	in the night;

And it came to pass at midnight.

The firstborn sons of Pasros [Egypt] You crushed at	midnight;
Their host they never found as they arose	in the night;
The soaring flight of [Sisra] the prince of Charoshes You trampled by the stars	of night;

And it came to pass at midnight.

Blaspheming [Sancheriv] schemed to raise his hand against [Yerushalayim] the cherished Abode; You let his [soldiers'] carcasses rot	in the night;
Bel [Babylon's god] and its pedestal fell prostrate in the dark	of the night;
To [Daniel] the man of [Your] delight was revealed the secret of the [king's] vision	of night;

And it came to pass at midnight.

	מִשְׁתַּכֵּר בִּכְלֵי קֹדֶשׁ נֶהֱרַג בּוֹ	בַּלַּיְלָה.
	נוֹשַׁע מִבּוֹר אֲרָיוֹת פּוֹתֵר בִּעֲתוּתֵי	לַיְלָה.
	שִׂנְאָה נָטַר אֲגָגִי וְכָתַב סְפָרִים	בַּלַּיְלָה.

וַיְהִי בַּחֲצִי הַלַּיְלָה:

	עוֹרַרְתָּ נִצְחֲךָ עָלָיו בְּנֶדֶר שְׁנַת	לַיְלָה.
	פּוּרָה תִדְרוֹךְ לְשׁוֹמֵר מַה	מִלַּיְלָה.
	צָרַח כַּשּׁוֹמֵר וְשָׂח אָתָא בּוֹקֶר וְגַם	לַיְלָה.

וַיְהִי בַּחֲצִי הַלַּיְלָה:

	קָרֵב יוֹם אֲשֶׁר הוּא לֹא יוֹם וְלֹא	לַיְלָה.
	רָם הוֹדַע כִּי לְךָ הַיּוֹם אַף לְךָ	הַלַּיְלָה
	שׁוֹמְרִים הַפְקֵד לְעִירְךָ כָּל הַיּוֹם וְכָל	הַלַּיְלָה.
	תָּאִיר כְּאוֹר יוֹם חֶשְׁכַּת	לַיְלָה.

וַיְהִי בַּחֲצִי הַלַּיְלָה:

וּבְכֵן וַאֲמַרְתֶּם זֶבַח פֶּסַח

	אֹמֶץ גְּבוּרוֹתֶיךָ הִפְלֵאתָ	בַּפֶּסַח.
	בְּרֹאשׁ כָּל מוֹעֲדוֹת נִשֵּׂאתָ	פֶּסַח.
	גִּלִּיתָ לְאֶזְרָחִי חֲצוֹת לֵיל	פֶּסַח.

וַאֲמַרְתֶּם זֶבַח פֶּסַח

	דְּלָתָיו דָּפַקְתָּ כְּחוֹם הַיּוֹם	בַּפֶּסַח.
	הִסְעִיד נוֹצְצִים עֻגוֹת מַצּוֹת	בַּפֶּסַח.
	וְאֶל הַבָּקָר רָץ זֵכֶר לְשׁוֹר עֵרֶךְ	פֶּסַח.

וַאֲמַרְתֶּם זֶבַח פֶּסַח

246

[Belshatzar] drank himself drunk with the
    sacred [Temple] vessels, was slain   that very night;
[Daniel] saved from the lion's den,
    interpreted the fearful phantasms   of night;
[Haman] the Agagi nursed hatred in his heart
    and wrote [lethal] edicts   in the night;

And it came to pass at midnight.

You aroused Your victory over him by
    disturbing [Achashverosh's] sleep   at night;
The wine-press [of our enemies' destruction]
    You will tread for [Jewry that asks]
    "Watchman! What will be   of the night?"
[God] will exclaim like the watchman and say,
    "Morning has come [for Jewry]
    and also [for Esav]   the night";

And it came to pass at midnight.

O' bring the [Mashiach's] day [of Redemption]
    which is neither day nor   night;
Make it known, exalted God, that Yours is the day,
    and even Yours   the night;
Appoint sentries for Your city, for all the day and all   the night;
Brighten as with the light of day the darkness of   night;

And it came to pass at midnight.

Va'amartem Zevach Pesach
Say Then: It Is the Feast of Pesach

The power of Your mighty deeds
    You wondrously displayed   on Pesach;
Above all festivals did You elevate   Pesach;
To the oriental [Avraham] You revealed the
    [miraculous exodus at] midnight   of Pesach;

Say then: It is the feast of Pesach.

At his door You knocked in the heat of midday   on Pesach;
He served the sparkling angels cakes of matzah   on Pesach;
And ran to the cattle, a harbinger of the ox,
    [the festive offering] related   to Pesach;

Say then: It is the feast of Pesach.

247

זֹעֲמוּ סְדוֹמִים וְלוֹהֲטוּ בָּאֵשׁ   **בַּפֶּסַח.**

חֻלַּץ לוֹט מֵהֶם וּמַצּוֹת אָפָה בְּקֵץ   **פֶּסַח.**

טָאטֵאתָ אַדְמַת מוֹף וְנוֹף בְּעָבְרְךָ   **בַּפֶּסַח.**

וַאֲמַרְתֶּם זֶבַח פֶּסַח

יָהּ רֹאשׁ כָּל אוֹן מָחַצְתָּ בְּלֵיל שִׁמּוּר   **פֶּסַח.**

כַּבִּיר עַל בֵּן בְּכוֹר פָּסַחְתָּ בְּדַם   **פֶּסַח.**

לְבִלְתִּי תֵּת מַשְׁחִית לָבֹא בִפְתָחַי   **בַּפֶּסַח.**

וַאֲמַרְתֶּם זֶבַח פֶּסַח

מִסְגֶּרֶת סֻגְּרָה בְּעִתּוֹתֵי   **פֶּסַח.**

נִשְׁמְדָה מִדְיָן בִּצְלִיל שְׂעוֹרֵי עֹמֶר   **פֶּסַח.**

שׂוֹרְפוּ מִשְׁמַנֵּי פוּל וְלוּד בִּיקַד יְקוֹד   **פֶּסַח.**

וַאֲמַרְתֶּם זֶבַח פֶּסַח

עוֹד הַיּוֹם בְּנוֹב לַעֲמוֹד עַד גָּעָה עוֹנַת   **פֶּסַח.**

פַּס יַד כָּתְבָה לְקַעֲקֵעַ צוּל   **בַּפֶּסַח.**

צָפֹה הַצָּפִית עָרוֹךְ הַשֻּׁלְחָן   **בַּפֶּסַח.**

וַאֲמַרְתֶּם זֶבַח פֶּסַח

קָהָל כִּנְּסָה הֲדַסָּה צוֹם לְשַׁלֵּשׁ   **בַּפֶּסַח.**

רֹאשׁ מִבֵּית רָשָׁע מָחַצְתָּ בְּעֵץ חֲמִישִׁים   **בַּפֶּסַח.**

שְׁתֵּי אֵלֶּה רֶגַע תָּבִיא לְעוּצִית   **בַּפֶּסַח.**

תָּעֹז יָדְךָ וְתָרוּם יְמִינְךָ כְּלֵיל הִתְקַדֶּשׁ חַג   **פֶּסַח.**

וַאֲמַרְתֶּם זֶבַח פֶּסַח

The men of Sedom kindled Your wrath,
    and were set aflame with fire   on Pesach;
Lot was saved from their midst,
    and baked matzos at the close   of Pesach;
You swept clean the ground of Moph and
    Noph [Egypt] When You passed through   on Pesach;
Say then: It is the feast of Pesach.

God, You crushed every firstborn's head on
    the watchnight   of Pesach;
O' Great One, yet over Your firstborn You skipped
    by [to spare him] because of
    the blood [marking the doors]   of the Pesach;
So as not to let the destroyer enter my doorways   on Pesach;
Say then: It is the feast of Pesach.

The locked shut [city of Yericho] fell at the time   of Pesach;
Midyan was wiped out through a barley cake,
    the omer offering   of Pesach;
The stalwart men of Pul and Lud [Ashur]
    were burned in a great blaze   on Pesach;
Say then: It is the feast of Pesach.

"Yet today" [Sancheriv planned] to arrive at Nov
    [and besiege Yerushalayim] till [he had his
    downfall when] came the time   of Pesach;
An unseen hand wrote to prophesy the
    destruction of Tzul [Babylon]   on Pesach;
While they set the watch, prepared the table,   on Pesach;
Say then: It is the feast of Pesach.

Hadassah [Esther] assembled the [Jewish] community
    for a three-day fast   on Pesach;
The head of the wicked house [Haman] You
    destroyed on a fifty-foot gallows   on Pesach;
Double misfortune o' bring instantly on Utzis [Edom] on Pesach;
May Your Hand be strengthened, and Your right
    Hand exalted, as on that night
    when You sanctified the Festival   of Pesach;
Say then: It is the feast of Pesach.

כִּי לוֹ נָאֶה. כִּי לוֹ יָאֶה:

אַדִּיר בִּמְלוּכָה. בָּחוּר כַּהֲלָכָה. גְּדוּדָיו יֹאמְרוּ לוֹ. לְךָ וּלְךָ. לְךָ כִּי לְךָ.
לְךָ אַף לְךָ. לְךָ יהוה הַמַּמְלָכָה. כִּי לוֹ נָאֶה. כִּי לוֹ יָאֶה:

דָּגוּל בִּמְלוּכָה. הָדוּר כַּהֲלָכָה. וָתִיקָיו יֹאמְרוּ לוֹ. לך ולך וכו'.

זַכַּאי בִּמְלוּכָה חָסִין כַּהֲלָכָה טַפְסְרָיו יֹאמְרוּ לוֹ לך ולך וכו'.

יָחִיד בִּמְלוּכָה כַּבִּיר כַּהֲלָכָה לִמּוּדָיו יֹאמְרוּ לוֹ לך ולך וכו'.

מֶלֶךְ בִּמְלוּכָה נוֹרָא כַּהֲלָכָה סְבִיבָיו יֹאמְרוּ לוֹ לך ולך וכו'.

עָנָו בִּמְלוּכָה פּוֹדֶה כַּהֲלָכָה צַדִּיקָיו יֹאמְרוּ לוֹ לך ולך וכו'.

קָדוֹשׁ בִּמְלוּכָה רַחוּם כַּהֲלָכָה שִׁנְאַנָּיו יֹאמְרוּ לוֹ לך ולך וכו'.

תַּקִּיף בִּמְלוּכָה תּוֹמֵךְ כַּהֲלָכָה תְּמִימָיו יֹאמְרוּ לוֹ לך ולך וכו'.

*Those who do not drink the fourth cup until this point,
do so now, according to the instructions on page 240-41.
They then say the berachah after drinking wine and
continue to recite "The order of the Pesach service,"
etc., until "Next year in Yerushalayim!" and
then continue from here.*

אַדִּיר הוּא

אַדִּיר הוּא יִבְנֶה בֵיתוֹ בְּקָרוֹב בִּמְהֵרָה בִּמְהֵרָה בְּיָמֵינוּ בְּקָרוֹב אֵל
בְּנֵה אֵל בְּנֵה בְּנֵה בֵיתְךָ בְּקָרוֹב.
בָּחוּר הוּא גָּדוֹל הוּא דָּגוּל הוּא הָדוּר הוּא וָתִיק הוּא זַכַּאי הוּא
חָסִיד הוּא יִבְנֶה בֵיתוֹ בְּקָרוֹב. בִּמְהֵרָה בִּמְהֵרָה בְּיָמֵינוּ בְּקָרוֹב.
אֵל בְּנֵה אֵל בְּנֵה. בְּנֵה בֵיתְךָ בְּקָרוֹב:
טָהוֹר הוּא יָחִיד הוּא כַּבִּיר הוּא לָמוּד הוּא מֶלֶךְ הוּא נוֹרָא הוּא
סַגִּיב הוּא עִזּוּז הוּא פּוֹדֶה הוּא צַדִּיק הוּא יִבְנֶה בֵיתוֹ בְּקָרוֹב.
בִּמְהֵרָה בִּמְהֵרָה בְּיָמֵינוּ בְּקָרוֹב. אֵל בְּנֵה אֵל בְּנֵה. בְּנֵה בֵיתְךָ
בְּקָרוֹב.

250

Ki Lo Na'eh, Ki Lo Ya'eh

For To Him It Is Becoming; For To Him It Is Fitting

Mighty in majesty, truly supreme, His companies [of angels] say to Him: To You, again to You; to You, for to You; to You, indeed to You; to You, Hashem, belongs all sovereignty. For to Him it is becoming; for to Him it is fitting.

Excelling in majesty, truly resplendent, His faithful [in Jewry] say to Him: *To You etc.*

Pristine in majesty, truly powerful, His [angelic] princes say to Him: *To You etc.*

Unique in majesty, truly omnipotent, His disciples [in Jewry] say to Him: *To You etc.*

Ruling in majesty, truly held in awe, His surrounding [Heavenly] companions say to Him: *To You etc.*

Humble in majesty, truly a Redeemer, His righteous ones [in Jewry] say to Him: *To You etc.*

Holy in majesty, truly compassionate, His chorus of angels say to Him: *To You etc.*

Forceful in majesty, truly all-sustaining, His perfect ones say to Him: *To You etc.*

Those who do not drink the fourth cup until this point,
do so now, according to the instructions on page 240-41.
They then say the berachah after drinking wine and
continue to recite "The order of the Pesach service,"
etc., until "Next year in Yerushalayim!" and
then continue from here.

Adir Hu

Mighty Is He

May He build His House soon! Speedily, yes speedily, in our days, soon! Build, o' God; build, o' God; build Your House soon!

Foremost is He, great is He, supreme is He
May He build...

Resplendent is He, faithful is He, worthy is He, kindly is He
May He build...

Pure is He, unique is He, omnipotent is He, learned is He, sovereign is He, awesome is He, sublime is He, powerful is He, the Redeemer is He, righteous is He
May He build...

251

קָדוֹשׁ הוּא רַחוּם הוּא שַׁדַּי הוּא תַּקִּיף הוּא יִבְנֶה בֵּיתוֹ בְּקָרוֹב.
בִּמְהֵרָה בִּמְהֵרָה בְּיָמֵינוּ בְּקָרוֹב. אֵל בְּנֵה אֵל בְּנֵה. בְּנֵה בֵּיתְךָ
בְּקָרוֹב:

*Those who live in chutz la'aretz and have not yet
counted the Omer after maariv on the second
night of Pesach do so now.*

בָּרוּךְ אַתָּה יהוה אֱלֹהֵינוּ מֶלֶךְ הָעוֹלָם אֲשֶׁר
קִדְּשָׁנוּ בְּמִצְוֹתָיו וְצִוָּנוּ עַל סְפִירַת הָעוֹמֶר:
הַיּוֹם יוֹם אֶחָד לָעוֹמֶר:

יְהִי רָצוֹן מִלְּפָנֶיךָ יְיָ אֱלֹהֵינוּ וֵאלֹהֵי אֲבוֹתֵינוּ שֶׁיִּבָּנֶה בֵּית
הַמִּקְדָּשׁ בִּמְהֵרָה בְּיָמֵינוּ וְתֵן חֶלְקֵנוּ בְּתוֹרָתֶךָ. וְשָׁם נַעֲבָדְךָ בְּיִרְאָה
כִּימֵי עוֹלָם וּכְשָׁנִים קַדְמוֹנִיּוֹת:

אֶחָד מִי יוֹדֵעַ

אֶחָד מִי יוֹדֵעַ. אֶחָד אֲנִי יוֹדֵעַ. אֶחָד אֱלֹהֵינוּ שֶׁבַּשָּׁמַיִם וּבָאָרֶץ:
שְׁנַיִם מִי יוֹדֵעַ. שְׁנַיִם אֲנִי יוֹדֵעַ. שְׁנֵי לֻחוֹת הַבְּרִית. אֶחָד אֱלֹהֵינוּ
שֶׁבַּשָּׁמַיִם וּבָאָרֶץ:
שְׁלֹשָׁה מִי יוֹדֵעַ. שְׁלֹשָׁה אֲנִי יוֹדֵעַ. שְׁלֹשָׁה אָבוֹת. שְׁנֵי לֻחוֹת הַבְּרִית.
אֶחָד אֱלֹהֵינוּ שֶׁבַּשָּׁמַיִם וּבָאָרֶץ:
אַרְבַּע מִי יוֹדֵעַ. אַרְבַּע אֲנִי יוֹדֵעַ. אַרְבַּע אִמָּהוֹת. שְׁלֹשָׁה אָבוֹת. שְׁנֵי
לֻחוֹת הַבְּרִית. אֶחָד אֱלֹהֵינוּ שֶׁבַּשָּׁמַיִם וּבָאָרֶץ:
חֲמִשָּׁה מִי יוֹדֵעַ. חֲמִשָּׁה אֲנִי יוֹדֵעַ. חֲמִשָּׁה חֻמְשֵׁי תוֹרָה. אַרְבַּע
אִמָּהוֹת. שְׁלֹשָׁה אָבוֹת. שְׁנֵי לֻחוֹת הַבְּרִית. אֶחָד אֱלֹהֵינוּ
שֶׁבַּשָּׁמַיִם וּבָאָרֶץ:
שִׁשָּׁה מִי יוֹדֵעַ. שִׁשָּׁה אֲנִי יוֹדֵעַ. שִׁשָּׁה סִדְרֵי מִשְׁנָה. חֲמִשָּׁה חֻמְשֵׁי

Holy is He, compassionate is He, the Almighty is He, puissant is He
May He build...

*Those who live in chutz la'aretz and have not yet
counted the Omer after maariv on the second
night of Pesach do so now.*

Blessed be You, Hashem our God, King of the universe, Who has sanctified us by His commandments and commanded us concerning the counting of the Omer.

Today is the first day of the Omer.

May it be Your will, Hashem, our God and God of our fathers, that the Temple be speedily rebuilt in our days, and give us our portion in your Torah, so that we may serve You there with awe as in the days of old and as in former years.

Echad Mi Yodei'a
Who Knows One?

Who knows one? I know one. Our God is One, in heaven and on the earth.

Who knows two? I know two. The tablets of the covenant are two, our God is One, in heaven and on the earth.

Who knows three? I know three. The Patriarchs are three, the tablets of the covenant are two, our God is One, in heaven and on the earth.

Who knows four? I know four. The Matriarchs are four, the Patriarchs are three, the tablets of the covenant are two, our God is One, in heaven and on the earth.

Who knows five? I know five. The books of the Torah are five, the Matriarchs are four, the Patriarchs are three, the tablets of the covenant are two, our God is One, in heaven and on the earth.

Who knows six? I know six. The Mishnah sections are six, the books

תּוֹרָה. אַרְבַּע אִמָּהוֹת. שְׁלשָׁה אָבוֹת. שְׁנֵי לֻחוֹת הַבְּרִית. אֶחָד אֱלֹהֵינוּ שֶׁבַּשָּׁמַיִם וּבָאָרֶץ:

שִׁבְעָה מִי יוֹדֵעַ. שִׁבְעָה אֲנִי יוֹדֵעַ. שִׁבְעָה יְמֵי שַׁבַּתָּא. שִׁשָּׁה סִדְרֵי מִשְׁנָה. חֲמִשָּׁה חֻמְשֵׁי תוֹרָה. אַרְבַּע אִמָּהוֹת. שְׁלשָׁה אָבוֹת. שְׁנֵי לֻחוֹת הַבְּרִית. אֶחָד אֱלֹהֵינוּ שֶׁבַּשָּׁמַיִם וּבָאָרֶץ:

שְׁמוֹנָה מִי יוֹדֵעַ. שְׁמוֹנָה אֲנִי יוֹדֵעַ. שְׁמוֹנָה יְמֵי מִילָה. שִׁבְעָה יְמֵי שַׁבַּתָּא. שִׁשָּׁה סִדְרֵי מִשְׁנָה. חֲמִשָּׁה חֻמְשֵׁי תוֹרָה. אַרְבַּע אִמָּהוֹת. שְׁלשָׁה אָבוֹת. שְׁנֵי לֻחוֹת הַבְּרִית. אֶחָד אֱלֹהֵינוּ שֶׁבַּשָּׁמַיִם וּבָאָרֶץ:

תִּשְׁעָה מִי יוֹדֵעַ. תִּשְׁעָה אֲנִי יוֹדֵעַ. תִּשְׁעָה יַרְחֵי לֵדָה. שְׁמוֹנָה יְמֵי מִילָה. שִׁבְעָה יְמֵי שַׁבַּתָּא. שִׁשָּׁה סִדְרֵי מִשְׁנָה. חֲמִשָּׁה חֻמְשֵׁי תוֹרָה. אַרְבַּע אִמָּהוֹת. שְׁלשָׁה אָבוֹת. שְׁנֵי לֻחוֹת הַבְּרִית. אֶחָד אֱלֹהֵינוּ שֶׁבַּשָּׁמַיִם וּבָאָרֶץ:

עֲשָׂרָה מִי יוֹדֵעַ. עֲשָׂרָה אֲנִי יוֹדֵעַ. עֲשָׂרָה דִבְּרַיָּא. תִּשְׁעָה יַרְחֵי לֵדָה. שְׁמוֹנָה יְמֵי מִילָה. שִׁבְעָה יְמֵי שַׁבַּתָּא. שִׁשָּׁה סִדְרֵי מִשְׁנָה. חֲמִשָּׁה חֻמְשֵׁי תוֹרָה. אַרְבַּע אִמָּהוֹת. שְׁלשָׁה אָבוֹת. שְׁנֵי לֻחוֹת הַבְּרִית. אֶחָד אֱלֹהֵינוּ שֶׁבַּשָּׁמַיִם וּבָאָרֶץ:

אַחַד עָשָׂר מִי יוֹדֵעַ. אַחַד עָשָׂר אֲנִי יוֹדֵעַ. אַחַד עָשָׂר כּוֹכְבַיָּא. עֲשָׂרָה דִבְּרַיָּא. תִּשְׁעָה יַרְחֵי לֵדָה. שְׁמוֹנָה יְמֵי מִילָה. שִׁבְעָה יְמֵי שַׁבַּתָּא. שִׁשָּׁה סִדְרֵי מִשְׁנָה. חֲמִשָּׁה חֻמְשֵׁי תוֹרָה. אַרְבַּע אִמָּהוֹת. שְׁלשָׁה אָבוֹת. שְׁנֵי לֻחוֹת הַבְּרִית. אֶחָד אֱלֹהֵינוּ שֶׁבַּשָּׁמַיִם וּבָאָרֶץ:

שְׁנֵים עָשָׂר מִי יוֹדֵעַ. שְׁנֵים עָשָׂר אֲנִי יוֹדֵעַ. שְׁנֵים עָשָׂר שִׁבְטַיָּא. אַחַד עָשָׂר כּוֹכְבַיָּא. עֲשָׂרָה דִבְּרַיָּא. תִּשְׁעָה יַרְחֵי לֵדָה. שְׁמוֹנָה יְמֵי מִילָה. שִׁבְעָה יְמֵי שַׁבַּתָּא. שִׁשָּׁה סִדְרֵי מִשְׁנָה. חֲמִשָּׁה חֻמְשֵׁי תוֹרָה. אַרְבַּע אִמָּהוֹת. שְׁלשָׁה אָבוֹת. שְׁנֵי לֻחוֹת הַבְּרִית. אֶחָד אֱלֹהֵינוּ שֶׁבַּשָּׁמַיִם וּבָאָרֶץ:

שְׁלשָׁה עָשָׂר מִי יוֹדֵעַ. שְׁלשָׁה עָשָׂר אֲנִי יוֹדֵעַ. שְׁלשָׁה עָשָׂר מִדַּיָּא. שְׁנֵים עָשָׂר שִׁבְטַיָּא. אַחַד עָשָׂר כּוֹכְבַיָּא. עֲשָׂרָה דִבְּרַיָּא. תִּשְׁעָה יַרְחֵי לֵדָה. שְׁמוֹנָה יְמֵי מִילָה. שִׁבְעָה יְמֵי שַׁבַּתָּא. שִׁשָּׁה סִדְרֵי מִשְׁנָה. חֲמִשָּׁה חֻמְשֵׁי תוֹרָה. אַרְבַּע אִמָּהוֹת. שְׁלשָׁה אָבוֹת. שְׁנֵי לֻחוֹת הַבְּרִית. אֶחָד אֱלֹהֵינוּ שֶׁבַּשָּׁמַיִם וּבָאָרֶץ:

of the Torah are five, the Matriarchs are four, the Patriarchs are three, the tablets of the covenant are two, our God is One, in heaven and on the earth.

Who knows seven? I know seven. The days of the week are seven, the Mishnah sections are six, the books of the Torah are five, the Matriarchs are four, the Patriarchs are three, the tablets of the covenant are two, our God is One, in heaven and on the earth.

Who knows eight? I know eight. The days of circumcision are eight, the days of the week are seven, the Mishnah sections are six, the books of the Torah are five, the Matriarchs are four, the Patriarchs are three, the tablets of the covenant are two, our God is One, in heaven and on the earth.

Who knows nine? I know nine. The months of childbirth are nine, the days of circumcision are eight, the days of the week are seven, the Mishnah sections are six, the books of the Torah are five, the Matriarchs are four, the Patriarchs are three, the tablets of the covenant are two, our God is One, in heaven and on the earth.

Who knows ten? I know ten. The Ten Commandments are ten, the months of childbirth are nine, the days of circumcision are eight, the days of the week are seven, the Mishnah sections are six, the books of the Torah are five, the Matriarchs are four, the Patriarchs are three, the tablets of the covenant are two, our God is One, in heaven and on the earth.

Who knows eleven? I know eleven. The stars [in Joseph's dream] are eleven, the Ten Commandments are ten, the months of childbirth are nine, the days of circumcision are eight, the days of the week are seven, the Mishnah sections are six, the books of the Torah are five, the Matriarchs are four, the Patriarchs are three, the tablets of the covenant are two, our God is One, in heaven and on the earth.

Who knows twelve? I know twelve. Twelve are the tribes of Yisrael, the stars are eleven, the Ten Commandments are ten, the months of childbirth are nine, the days of circumcision are eight, the days of the week are seven, the Mishnah sections are six, the books of the Torah are five, the Matriarchs are four, the Patriarchs are three, the tablets of the covenant are two, our God is One, in heaven and on the earth.

Who knows thirteen? I know thirteen. God's attributes are thirteen, the tribes of Yisrael are twelve, the stars are eleven, the Ten Commandments are ten, the months of childbirth are nine, the days of circumcision are eight, the days of the week are seven, the Mishnah sections are six, the books of the Torah are five, the Matriarchs are four, the Patriarchs are three, the tablets of the covenant are two, our God is One, in heaven and on the earth.

חַד גַּדְיָא

חַד גַּדְיָא. חַד גַּדְיָא. דְּזַבִּין אַבָּא בִּתְרֵי זוּזֵי. חַד גַּדְיָא חַד גַּדְיָא:

וְאָתָא שׁוּנְרָא וְאָכְלָא לְגַדְיָא דְּזַבִּין אַבָּא בִּתְרֵי זוּזֵי. חַד גַּדְיָא חַד גַּדְיָא:

וְאָתָא כַלְבָּא וְנָשַׁךְ לְשׁוּנְרָא. דְּאָכְלָא לְגַדְיָא. דְּזַבִּין אַבָּא בִּתְרֵי זוּזֵי. חַד גַּדְיָא חַד גַּדְיָא:

וְאָתָא חוּטְרָא וְהִכָּה לְכַלְבָּא. דְּנָשַׁךְ לְשׁוּנְרָא. דְּאָכְלָא לְגַדְיָא. דְּזַבִּין אַבָּא בִּתְרֵי זוּזֵי. חַד גַּדְיָא חַד גַּדְיָא:

וְאָתָא נוּרָא וְשָׂרַף לְחוּטְרָא. דְּהִכָּה לְכַלְבָּא. דְּנָשַׁךְ לְשׁוּנְרָא. דְּאָכְלָא לְגַדְיָא. דְּזַבִּין אַבָּא בִּתְרֵי זוּזֵי. חַד גַּדְיָא חַד גַּדְיָא:

וְאָתָא מַיָּא וְכָבָה לְנוּרָא. דְּשָׂרַף לְחוּטְרָא. דְּהִכָּה לְכַלְבָּא. דְּנָשַׁךְ לְשׁוּנְרָא. דְּאָכְלָא לְגַדְיָא. דְּזַבִּין אַבָּא בִּתְרֵי זוּזֵי. חַד גַּדְיָא חַד גַּדְיָא:

וְאָתָא תוֹרָא וְשָׁתָה לְמַיָּא. דְּכָבָה לְנוּרָא. דְּשָׂרַף לְחוּטְרָא. דְּהִכָּה לְכַלְבָּא. דְּנָשַׁךְ לְשׁוּנְרָא. דְּאָכְלָא לְגַדְיָא. דְּזַבִּין אַבָּא בִּתְרֵי זוּזֵי. חַד גַּדְיָא חַד גַּדְיָא:

וְאָתָא הַשּׁוֹחֵט וְשָׁחַט לְתוֹרָא. דְּשָׁתָה לְמַיָּא. דְּכָבָה לְנוּרָא. דְּשָׂרַף לְחוּטְרָא. דְּהִכָּה לְכַלְבָּא. דְּנָשַׁךְ לְשׁוּנְרָא. דְּאָכְלָא לְגַדְיָא. דְּזַבִּין אַבָּא בִּתְרֵי זוּזֵי. חַד גַּדְיָא חַד גַּדְיָא:

וְאָתָא מַלְאַךְ הַמָּוֶת וְשָׁחַט לְשׁוֹחֵט. דְּשָׁחַט לְתוֹרָא. דְּשָׁתָה לְמַיָּא. דְּכָבָה לְנוּרָא. דְּשָׂרַף לְחוּטְרָא. דְּהִכָּה לְכַלְבָּא. דְּנָשַׁךְ לְשׁוּנְרָא. דְּאָכְלָא לְגַדְיָא. דְּזַבִּין אַבָּא בִּתְרֵי זוּזֵי. חַד גַּדְיָא חַד גַּדְיָא:

וְאָתָא הַקָּדוֹשׁ בָּרוּךְ הוּא וְשָׁחַט לְמַלְאַךְ הַמָּוֶת. דְּשָׁחַט לְשׁוֹחֵט. דְּשָׁחַט לְתוֹרָא. דְּשָׁתָה לְמַיָּא. דְּכָבָה לְנוּרָא. דְּשָׂרַף לְחוּטְרָא. דְּהִכָּה לְכַלְבָּא. דְּנָשַׁךְ לְשׁוּנְרָא. דְּאָכְלָא לְגַדְיָא. דְּזַבִּין אַבָּא בִּתְרֵי זוּזֵי. חַד גַּדְיָא חַד גַּדְיָא:

One should continue to occupy himself with the story
of the Exodus and the laws of Pesach until
sleep overtakes him.
Many recite Shir Hashirim which expresses the
overwhelming love between Hashem and His
chosen people, Yisrael.

Chad Gadya
An Only Kid

An only kid, an only kid, which my father bought for two zuzim. An only kid, an only kid.

And the cat came, and ate the kid, which my father bought for two zuzim. An only kid, an only kid.

And the dog came, and bit the cat, that ate the kid, which my father bought for two zuzim. An only kid, an only kid.

And the stick came, and beat the dog, that bit the cat, that ate the kid, which my father bought for two zuzim. An only kid, an only kid.

And the fire came, and burned the stick, that beat the dog, that bit the cat, that ate the kid, which my father bought for two zuzim. An only kid, an only kid.

And the water came, and extinguished the fire, that burned the stick, that beat the dog, that bit the cat, that ate the kid, which my father bought for two zuzim. An only kid, an only kid.

And the ox came, and drank the water, that extinguished the fire, that burned the stick, that beat the dog, that bit the cat, that ate the kid, which my father bought for two zuzim. An only kid, an only kid.

And the slaughterer came, and killed the ox, that drank the water, that extinguished the fire, that burned the stick, that beat the dog, that bit the cat, that ate the kid, which my father bought for two zuzim. An only kid, an only kid.

And the Angel of Death came, and slew the slaughterer, who killed the ox, that drank the water, that extinguished the fire, that burned the stick, that beat the dog, that bit the cat, that ate the kid, which my father bought for two zuzim. An only kid, an only kid.

And then came the Holy One, Blessed be He, and smote the Angel of Death, who slew the slaughterer, who killed the ox, that drank the water, that extinguished the fire, that burned the stick, that beat the dog, that bit the cat, that ate the kid, which my father bought for two zuzim. An only kid, an only kid.

*One should continue to occupy himself with the story
of the Exodus and the laws of Pesach until
sleep overtakes him.*

*Many recite Shir Hashirim which expresses the
overwhelming love between Hashem and His
chosen people, Yisrael.*

The Four Cups of Redemption

(continued from Prologue)

1. The first cup: to deliverance from burdens!

והוצאתי אתכם מתחת סבלת מצרים "I shall bring you out
from under the burdens of Egypt."

When the conditions for physical survival compel a man to
toil without respite, to crush mountains merely to gain a little
breathing space, then "man shall be bowed down and brought
low..." (*Yeshayahu* 2:9, 5:15). His spirit becomes subservient to
his overburdened body. He must exhaust the last "spark" of his
soul to help him carry the oppressive load. The body groans
and with it the spirit — he has no time to listen to the call of
freedom. The herald comes in vain: "...and they did not listen
to Moshe because of impatience of spirit and hard labor"
(*Shemos* 6:9).

Relief from burdens is not the *result* of freedom; it is its
prerequisite. Only when a man has discharged his physical
load and escaped from material burdens can he come to himself
— to breathe freely, reflect and arrive at a happy awareness of
self.

The first cup, then, is consecrated to the One Who brought
us out from under the Egyptian load, Who took the bricks off
our shoulders, and taught us to walk upright (see *Vayikra*
26:13).

Look at these Jews seated at their great global celebration!
You can see their table of freedom set in the mansions of the rich
and the tenements of the poor alike. Look at them all sitting at
ease. Indeed, this is how they have reclined through centuries
past, even in the dark days of oppression, and, thank God, so
they recline even today — as long as the spirit of Jewish
freedom endures in their hearts. All still recline despite the
tensions of the times, ridding themselves of their anxieties and
servitude; all are free, all feel like royal princes.

The One Who removed the bricks of Egypt from their backs
freed them from material burdens forever. He has seen to it that
even the poorest Jew can preserve His spiritual heritage. By

giving us Shabbos and Festivals, He has ensured us one-fifth of our lives to restore ourselves, to free ourselves from day-to-day worries, to reflect with renewed vitality and tranquility of mind. He has endowed us, on these Sabbath and Festival days, with an "extra soul" to strengthen our spiritual life (see *Beytzah* 16a).

And, so, the Jews have merited what no other nation has attained. Oppressed and despised more than any other people, they have yet preserved the flame of their soul and risen, more than any other people, above all material distress. The One Who lifted away the burdens of our forefathers has ever encouraged and comforted even the poorest among us, and He speaks to each and every individual in Yisrael, even to this day: "Cast upon Hashem what has been placed upon you, and He will provide for you" (*Tehillim* 55:23). And, thus, like a royal prince at the coronation feast, even the poorest man in Yisrael raises his cup joyfully as a free man and offers his blessing to the One Who has given him "feasts of rallying and seasons for delight," to the One Who has kept him alive and preserved him until this anniversary of the liberation of Yisrael.

Now look once more at these Jews who, dismissing all worry and sadness from their hearts, have joyfully drunk their toast to the Name of God! During this Festival of their freedom, they have nothing to be ashamed of. They can readily show their table to the world! For their escape from oppression was significant not only as it relates to *them*. Their feast is not held solely for *their* own benefit. God has sent them to all of suffering mankind to proclaim liberty and lighten its load.

"Whoever is hungry, let him come and eat": If men have learned to share their bread with the hungry, to alleviate suffering, to bring help and succor to the hovels of the poor, it is because they have learned this lesson from the Torah and its Jews. If the non-Jewish laborer has succeeded in obtaining his day off when he can relax, straighten his back and breathe and reflect freely; if, among those people who are blessed with prosperity, serious thought is given to the welfare of the poor; if men — understanding, as did Pharaoh, that the heavier the load on man's shoulders, the less his mind can soar aloft (see

259

Shemos 5:9) — acknowledge their responsibilty to raise moral and spiritual standards as much as material ones, it is because the Torah and its practice have shed their light on the world for these past two thousand years.

And when the first cup is filled at this world-wide festive banquet, and the God Who frees man from all burdens is acknowledged, thanked and blessed, then let all miserable, wretched mankind throughout the world arise — every prisoner in his cell, every sick man on his bed, every poor man in his hovel — everyone who has become ennobled through love for his fellowman — let them all respond together, with a resounding "Amen" to this blessing of Yisrael's Festival, to the kiddush, the sanctification of the season of our freedom.

2. The second cup: to liberation from slavery!

והצלתי אתכם מעבדתם "And I shall deliver you from their bondage."

To be weighted down by a heavy load is not the most deadening of oppressions. The removal of such physical burdens is merely the first stage in achieving freedom; it only paves the way toward liberation. A man may bear the heaviest of loads, but if he has *taken* that load *upon himself*, of his *own free will*, or if it has been decreed by his Father in Heaven that this be his fate in order to train and test him, to temper his strength — true, he may groan under its weight and it may bring him to his knees, but he still remains a free man.

Conversely, all a man's days may be fun and frolic; he may be adorned with gold and fed on honey. But deprive him of self-determination by *giving* him everything, prevent him from acquiring anything through his own efforts, never allow him to set his own goals, forbid him to choose his own means, turn him into someone else's plaything at the mercy of the wishes and whims of another mortal — then this honey-fed, gold-clad man is transformed into a fearful, trembling slave. Remove from his heart the faith in a just, compassionate, free and powerful God Who reveals Himelf in nature and history and gives guidance to human life, and substitute in its place blind forces controlling the physical world and human destiny according to a predetermined and unchangeable pattern — then, no matter how luxurious his way of life, his dignity, his destiny and his freedom are all lost.

Such was the life of the Jewish slave in Egypt. Not only was he robbed of his freedom, but he was a slave to a fearful hatred, burdened with a back-breaking load and overwhelmed with bitterness: "we were slaves unto Pharaoh in Egypt"!

In Egypt, freedom had been buried, human dignity doomed. There were no free men in Egypt. The towering pyramids, the astounding sculptures and works of art, the lives perpetuated in statue and painting, the hieroglyphics of the tombs and inscriptions proclaiming the fame of the Pharaohs — all are mute testimony to the abject slavery that *all* Egyptians suffered. How could those wonders of the world have been created if not through subjugation to godlike arbitrariness and tyrannic power over people's energy and activities? Only a population that surrenders its destiny to become a mere instrument for the glorification of its rulers would thus sacrifice life and body to forced labor. Only a people trapped in a caste system where social, economic and physical life were divided into the rigidly, arbitrarily separated spheres of the various deities, could worship its rulers as absolute gods. Any consciousness of an all-embracing Maker and Father Who ennobled all creatures with His mark of Divine origin had been forgotten.

Such was the character of the Egyptian caste system. Its search to discover the secrets of nature and society resulted only in the perception of deterministic forces locked in blind conflict, fettered in eternal obedience to the laws of nature. The Egyptians idealized the unrestrained expression of man's basest instincts, symbolized by animal worship and expressed by materialism, to which altars were built and society dedicated. Hence, no one was considered simply a human being or even an Egyptian. Rather, a man was defined and ranked according to his own particular caste and professional guild. All of Egyptian life was coerced into this framework, and, as Egyptian paintings depict to this day, even the king had to kneel before the very class of royalty into which he was born!

It was this people, consisting entirely of subservient classes, that sought to subjugate the free sons of Avraham and turn them into slaves. Indeed, in the rigidly stratified society of the Egyptian state, a class of slaves was missing — slaves to be trampled underfoot by the rest, to serve as their "footstool." Had the diabolic plan succeeded, the free origin of the Hebrews would soon have been forgotten, and each son of Avraham would have been considered "predestined" to remain a slave to the monarch in perpetuity, as it says: "We, our children, and our children's children still would have been enslaved to Pharaoh in Egypt."

However, this design was not to succeed. For His purpose God chooses the Hebrews, the very class of slaves who were doomed to servitude for generations. There, in the state based on an oppressive, self-perpetuating caste-system, He proclaims to mankind the message of eternal freedom, of the inherent mark of Divinity upon all men who are created in His image and are His children for all time.

Holding the despised Hebrew slave in His care, He sends His messenger to the very throne of Egypt's sovereign ruler: *Yisrael are My firstborn (their brothers — all mankind — will follow eventually in their steps, since through Yisrael I will champion the cause of all men).* "Send out My People, that they may serve Me" *Mortal human beings are all brothers to one another; I alone am their ruler! Your own son, whom you believe to be born to divine kingship, will perish if you dare deny these slaves their relationship to God!*

Trembling seizes Pharaoh's house, the gods of Egypt are shaken. All now see the Master, the One and Only God setting the deified natural forces back into their place within His Divine order. They see the Creator Whom their wise men have never discovered and Whom their sorcerers have denied.

At last, as the ten plagues come upon them, they see Him in the Nile River, the center of their idolatry, and in all its creatures. They see Him revealed in the earth and in the animals of the woods, in the air and everything it brings forth, from flashes of lightning to swarms of insects. He stands revealed through all of these, as He sends them forth as His

262

emissaries, as "a mission of messengers of evil." Each plague that smites the people and the land is a "mission" from a free, omnipotent God, showing the dismayed king and his priests that there is One God Who has remained unknown to them, One Whom their scribes have ignored and their priests overlooked, One Who is beyond their calculations.

The supernal arm that despises enslavement, that mocks artificial class divisions, is revealed, outstretched equally over the exalted king on his high throne and the laborer at his bench, in order to champion the cause of the lowly slaves whose Divinely implanted nobility is about to be trampled in the dust. Their broken spirit arouses the "glow of His anger." (See commentary, page 118.) He abandons His state of hiding and embarks on a process of crossing through the veil of His concealment, revealing Himself before them all. They see His "excess of wrath" break forth in a flash of justice, they experience God's "condemnation," and in their dire "stress" they see the impotence of man: All that had been meant to bring blessings, now becomes a "mission of messengers of evil." The Finger raised by the Sovereign Judge is revealed to king and priests. They are seized with terror — and the slave goes forth to freedom.

He remains free even after the king has shaken off his fright, as if awakening at dawn from a dream. The Finger of God is quickly denied and forgotten, but soon His strong Hand will descend decisively. With his best officers, the king of Egypt sets out to return the redeemed People to their former slavery. He pursues and overtakes them; he has already drawn his sword; but the sea flees from the presence of the God of Yaakov (see *Tehillim* 114). The redeemed People go forth to freedom — and Pharaoh's hosts are drowned in the depths of the sea.

They remain free, despite the vicissitudes of their fate, for two thousand years. In every new oppression and every new exile, despite all the plotting of generations of men seeking to exterminate them, that "which stood by our fathers and by us" — the lesson they learned from the days of Pharaoh — enabled them to endure all the afflictions that hatred can devise and all

263

the terrors that force can impose. This was their lot through the centuries. Mountainous burdens were thrust on their shoulders, their human dignity was trampled underfoot. Attempts were made to convert them by force, to make them assimilate with the nations of the world. Yet their faith remained unshaken, their courage undaunted, because they maintained their human dignity and did not forget the One Who had redeemed them from bondage. They suffered every conceivable restriction and oppression, they were despoiled and pillaged — but to the mentality of slaves they never returned. They descended into dungeons and went up to the stake — and they entrusted their grandchildren to the Redeemer of their fathers. The flames enveloped them, and they died...as free men.

And therefore, the second cup is drunk in honor and praise of the One Who delivered us from bondage, Who freed us from the fear of men and the forces of nature, and Who has preserved our souls from the mentality of slavery. We raise our cup in gratitude to the One Who inspired our hearts to dedicate our lives to the proclamation of our faith, Who sent us forth to announce to the world man's dignity, his everlasting freedom, and the mark of Godliness in every human being.

At the great banquet, Jews everywhere raise their glasses to the One Who saved them from bondage. Their song makes itself heard far beyond the circle of the Jewish people. All free men the world over, all who thirst for freedom, all who fight for human rights, all who seek the dignity of man — all can join in the blessing of Yisrael and participate in the joyous hymns; for when Yisrael's freedom was born so was their own. Those who went forth from Egypt restored the forgotten consciousness that all men have One Father, all possess equal rights, because all were created in the image of God, their Creator.

The charter attesting to the rights of every man, the charter of man's inherent freedom and Divine dignity, was transmitted to mankind by those who went out from Egypt. Through this charter, the hearts of men and the minds of leaders and nations were enlightened by the realization that there can be no hope or deliverance for society unless there is freedom and independence for every individual. As a result, society expectantly awaits salvation: it directs its hopes towards the days to come, when its Father in Heaven will bless all His children, when all men will form a single community, dwelling on earth in freedom and peace.

Indeed, it is this faith in their eventual salvation that sustains mortal beings. It alone is the vision that inspires their striving and thinking. The Torah and the history of Yisrael's liberation from Egypt furnish the same hope to the black slave in the plantation as to the Western thinker in his book-lined study.

And, so, when history achieves its ultimate goal; when, in the course of time, Messianic hopes will come to fruition as saplings grow into trees, gently and imperceptibly, as it says: "Behold, I bring my servant *Tzemach* (from צמח — to grow)" (*Zecharyah* 3:8); when the Father of mankind sends His "second Moshe," ending the persecution of His People upon earth and wiping away all tears (see *Yeshayahu* 25:8) — then will the Exodus be remembered and acknowledged as the root from which the redemption of Yisrael and all mankind has stemmed: "that you may remember the day you came forth out of the land of Egypt *all* the days of your life — which refers to the days of the Mashiach as well" (see Haggadah, p. 71).

3.   The third cup: to redemption!

זרוע נטויה ובשפטים גדולים "I shall redeem you with an outstretched arm and with great punishing judgment."

Relief from the burdens of suffering is merely the root, deliverance from slavery only the trunk, of the tree of freedom. Redemption alone is the branch upon which the fruit completing this tree of life can come to perfect ripeness. A liberation which merely strikes off the shackles remains a negative attainment at best. It removes the obstacles from the path of a man seeking to fulfill his calling in life; it clears the ground for the image of God to flourish within him. But for his liberation and his vocation to reach their ultimate fruition, merely lifting the yoke and breaking the fetters is not enough. Man must become aware of the Source of his freedom. He must acknowledge that his deliverance is God's gift, so that his liberation will make him feel constantly attached to God, enlisted in and consecrated to Him.

If one removes man's burden of oppression and slavery but deludes him into believing that freedom from the terrors of man and nature means freedom from *any* master or lawgiver anywhere and that he has no need to feel gratitude or responsibility to anyone, then one has deceived him about the meaning of his freedom and the nature and extent of his independence. If one conceals from him that he has been freed on this earth in order to serve God, then not only does one prevent him from reaching his Divine destiny on earth, but also robs him of the very foundation upon which his freedom is based. Denying him allegiance to God means denying him the only certain means of preserving this freedom for all time, for his allegiance is his guarantee that no chain can fetter his spirit ever again and that freedom will be intrinsic to his soul. Only God, the Master and Essence of freedom, can grant real freedom to man. Only God, Who created every immutable law and stands above every compulsion and necessity, He alone, by binding Himself to us, can elevate us into the realm of His own absolute freedom, can make us truly free.

Indeed, if one removes God from the heart of man, then he has already destroyed his freedom. Outwardly, he may have been released from his burdens and chains, but soon his unrestrained, base instincts will become his worst tyrannical masters, and he will flounder, a slave to his passions, lusts and desires. It is this inner subjugation that has always given rise to despotism and slavery in society, to the subservience of men to the deities of nature and idolatrous priesthood — forces far removed from the light of truth which, enslave both spirit and soul. The person and the society which has not received its freedom from God will repeatedly and helplessly sink back into slavery.

And, so, the third cup is raised to praise the One Who not only removed the burdens from our shoulders and the chains from our hands and feet, but Who revealed Himself to us as the Source and Creator of our freedom. He taught us to understand freedom as geulah,* — ransoming, buying back — which denotes leaving the subjection of tyrants in order to enter into the service of the Almighty.

Yisrael's historical experience, then, renewed the primal bond, woven of respect and love, by which every man of pure thoughts feels connected to God as His creation, child and servant. It revived the awareness that one's closeness to God is the only enduring basis of freedom. Yisrael's geulah sealed God's bond with our People for all time, and, through Yisrael, this bond was sealed with all mankind — which is destined for redemption in the future.

When Yisrael were about to go forth to freedom, they were still afraid of the dark terrors of nature and brute force. They were still slaves, helpless in the face of tyranny, incapable of removing a single drop of the poison of oppression from their lot. The angel of death stalked the streets, the drawn sword in his hand, raised against both the noble and the lowly, the free man and the slave. Man was powerless to resist and mortal danger loomed over Yisrael — ruin to the community, death to the individual. They were rescued from this double perdition only because they *gave* themselves to God; they dedicated themselves to Him with all their hearts — men and women alike — with the very lives of their sons and daughters.

At this point, God revealed Himself as their Goel, their Kinsman, Guardian and Redeemer, taking up the cause of these despised humans who had been treacherously betrayed, whose rights had been trampled upon. Now He revealed His "outstretched arm" to despots and His stern "punishing judgments" to the forces of violence — and Yisrael were redeemed.

Not through their own strength, but thanks to their God, did Yisrael go out to freedom. Neither muscular strength nor physical might enabled them to go free. The basis of their

---

* See commentary, page 158.

freedom was and is devotion to God. Today, too, if one abandons this basis, myriad forces and tyrants will threaten him. But if one lets himself be led by God, if one places one's trust in Him, loves Him, respects Him, makes Him the "only One" for him — then all the tyranny of society and all the forces of nature will lose their power over him. God's "outstretched arm" will strengthen him when he is powerless; His "punishing judgments" will vindicate him in justice. God will impose statute and law on nature, an orderly arrangement over all its forces. "...And against all the gods of Egypt I will execute judgment..." (*Shemos* 12:12). He will raise one above all the determinism of the laws of nature to the realm of His freedom: "...I, Hashem" (*ibid.*).

Even after their liberation from Egypt when they offered their Pesach Sacrifice, in the freedom of their own land, Yisrael ate it together with the "bread of dependence," matzah, and the bitter herbs, maror, in order to remind themselves and impress upon their hearts that the way to preserve their freedom is the same as the way which gained them their freedom — dedication to God. If the Jew disdains dedication to God, as symbolized by the Pesach Sacrifice, then the bread of slavery and the herbs of bitterness await him yet again.

Today, in their dispersion, the Jews are denied the opportunity to offer the Pesach Sacrifice. All the outward benefits which their freedom eventually brought them were forfeited. Their homeland was reduced to ruins and their Temple to ashes because they did not dedicate themselves to God — in order to preserve the Divinely bestowed benefits of their freedom — with the same degree of devotion as did their forefathers. Sadly, all that remains of their former status are pale symbolic reminders.

And, yet, behold the scattered Children of Yisrael: In every corner of the world they sit reclining at their banquet as free men! As the redeemed and rescued of *God*, they celebrate the Festival of their independence; to Him they raise their cups.

But what is the central dish at this "Independence Night" dinner? The bread of slavery and bitter herbs! The meal starts with matzah and ends with matzah. The bread of slavery — all they had at the time of their redemption — is Yisrael's ultimate encouragement in their current dispersion. It teaches their children and grandchildren that at the time of redemption, no material wealth was necessary. At the time of their redemption, they were merely slaves, without property or even a homeland or Sanctuary. As slaves they emerged into freedom; the sanctity of their hearts was their territory, their conviction the bond uniting them, the lintel of their home their altar, and dedication to God their salvation. They had neither state nor Temple, their hands were empty but for bitterness and the bread of bondage, yet God became their Redeemer solely because of their devotion.

Now look once more at this Divinely redeemed People. Their banquet, served with bitter herbs and slavery's bread, spans the earth wherever man resides and recurs throughout centuries of history. Sanctioned by God Himself, it is one great, loud and lasting protest voiced against all those who would rob man of God and, thereby, his freedom.

Perhaps the day will come when all the things bestowed upon mankind for its benefit and liberation will become corrupted into their very antithesis. Mankind, instead of assuring its members their legitimate rights of development and paving the way to a blissful existence, will serve them the tear-drenched bread of slaves and bitterness. In blind reaction, provoked to self-assertion, the masses will try to save themselves by breaking down all restraints and rescinding every law, believing they can find freedom in lawlessness or destruction. Tyranny and anarchy will fight for world dominion, and, as they toss their bloody dice between them, mankind will be the loser at every throw.

At such a time, science, too, will become solely destructive. It will not hold its torch aloft to spread the light of God's truth and justice, His righteousness and lovingkindness, His morality and nobility. Science will not try to bring mankind to its senses by revealing God's wonders in nature, His deeds in history and His workings in the heart of man. It will not seek to

269

ennoble the spirit of man so as to enable him to discern God in the world of nature and the Divine image in his own soul. It will not pave the way for mankind's redemption by spreading the awareness of God. Instead, science will frantically blind itself with its own brightness and, in a macabre dance of death, will lead benighted mankind into sepulchral darkness. The light of God's truth — justice, duty, love, morality, even human dignity — all will have been extinguished, leaving no more than the smoke of delusion rising from the gray embers of a perished past. At that time, any new ideology aspiring to the redemption of mankind will be mocked as a madman's unscientific illusion. Mankind will vainly exhaust its strength in a blind upsurge of uncurbed desires and uncontrolled conflicting drives, until the strongest force will prevail — violence will conquer all and a deathly silence end the slavish tumult.

Finally, religion will be called upon to spread healing and salvation, but the soiled hands of its priests will do the opposite. At such a time, they will take their position between the living and the dead — not to restore the dying to life, but to lead the living into death. They will extinguish the last glimmer in the night, banish the last hope of the sick. They will bring despairing mankind not to God, but to an idol of their own fabrication. Nor will they act only as intermediaries, leading these sorrowing hearts to a direct relationship with this god; rather, they will insist that man submit to their mediation, since they *must* intervene and intercede. And, thus, they will transform the liberation of the human heart, which can only be accomplished before God, into a travesty.

Should this day ever come when everything will have become unpalatable, lethal poison — still, across the face of the earth, mankind will return and rediscover its redemption at the hallowed Jewish table. There, violence will learn to surrender to the mighty arm of the eternal Judge, and humanity will recognize the nature of true freedom and the way it may be found.

With matzah and bitter herbs in one hand and the cup of

270

redemption in the other, the People of Yisrael proclaim to the world at their banquet: neither slavery nor bitterness reduces one to subjection; nor do licentiousness and luxury mean liberation. True freedom grows in a different climate. Only a person who has become spiritually free through the freedom bestowed upon him by God will be independent in his actions as well. Independence ceases to be a dream only if it is understood as dependence on God and not as self-determination. As long as man cannot learn to be spiritually free even while eating the bread of slavery and tasting bitterness, he can fall prey to new deprivation and new oppression time and time again. The yoke of human servitude can be broken once and for all by only one thing — the spirit. To the benighted spirit the call of redemption goes out: *Do you believe that Yisrael's redemption was based on concrete proofs, which can be weighed and measured? Then you are mistaken! With nothing but the bread of slavery and bitter herbs they have remained free in the past and are still free now — the living exemplification of redemption upon earth. Their annual banquet is a testimonial, and each individual member a witness, to the truth of His existence, the reality of the One Whom you deny and all the Divinely bestowed benefits that you scorn.*

All the greatness of your material riches and splendor have passed as a shadow from the arena of history. But this People, with no land under their feet for centuries, possessing nothing but God and His spiritual riches — they alone have outlived all others. They alone celebrate the anniversary of their enduring redemption. This People gave themselves to God, and He redeemed them. And this God Who redeemed them, this God to Whose existence they testify, is neither a tangible idol nor the fancy of idle dreams. He is Hashem, the God of heaven and earth, Who dwells above the stars and yet enters the simple homes of men and the hearts of the poor. He can be found everywhere. He can be approached by anyone at any time, for He requires neither intermediary nor priest.

Do you see? — Here at the feast of the redeemed, no priest consecrates the meal, passes the cup or breaks bread. This People has no need for priests. Where the heart reaches out to God, all are priests and ministers of holiness. Every hovel is a sanctuary, every table an altar, every head of the family a priest of God, and all their sons and daughters are acolytes in His ministry.

And, now, at the conclusion of their meal of slave's bread, as they praise the Redeemer Who has liberated *them* — would that the significance of Jewish freedom and Jewish redemption become universally understood. By answering "Amen" to this praise with a cup raised to geulah, mankind would win *its* redemption.

4.   One last time the cups are filled, as the fourth cup is dedicated to the election of Yisrael as God's People.

ולקחתי אתכם לי לעם "I shall take you to Me for a People."

The first three cups were raised to give praise for deliverance from burdens, for liberation and for redemption, as it was granted to Yisrael to experience them. While these values have been, and still are, promised to every human being as the inalienable possession of all mankind, the fourth cup is raised in praise of the election of Yisrael. Over this cup we give expression to the unique status of Yisrael in the world, its Divine mission among the nations, its destiny and vocation in history:

"When Yisrael went forth from Egypt,

the House of Yaakov from a people of alien tongue,

Yehudah became His sanctuary,

Yisrael His sphere of dominion" (*Tehillim* 114:1-2).

Yehudah became His living sanctuary because Yisrael's fate gives proof to God's existence; Yisrael became His sphere of dominion because their way of life is permeated by God's rule.

And I shall take you to Me for a People ... said the Redeemer of Yisrael. This is the purpose and ultimate goal of the previous deliverance from burdens, liberation and redemption. Yisrael dedicate themselves to God, and God designated them as His

272

sanctuary and His domain: He made them His People.

How great a destiny is implied in those few words *to Me for a People*. How firm and unshakeable the decision *I shall take you!* The Torah, the entire Jewish heritage, is one great elaboration upon these words "to Me for a people." Jewry's entire history, spanning more than three thousand years, is the actualization of this decision that "I shall take you."

To have the entire life of a nation regulated and supported by God, dependent upon Him, motivated and blessed through His Presence — this indeed is the ideal of Torah and mitzvos that He put before His redeemed People. In the fulfillment of God's will, they will find their spiritual bond and their national unity. Thus they will become a nation that dedicates all the thoughts, feelings and actions of its individuals, families and communities to the implementation of His will. Here will they find their sole duty, individual happiness, national honor and lasting peace.

Jewish history serves as the educational process leading to this ideal. Through it one thing becomes certain: whether they remain faithful or they backslide on their way towards this ideal, whether they draw near or pull away, hesitate or persevere, "Hashem will never cast off His People nor will He forsake His inheritance" (*Tehillim* 94:14). Hashem will be with them through the centuries of trials and darkness, through pain and deprivation, until they reach their pinnacle of perfection, the goal set before them by the Torah, and the fullness of joy that it promises.

True, this ideal has not yet been fully realized. We have straddled the fence. Until now, the idea of being God's People to the exclusion of everything else has not permeated all of our thoughts. We have shown, over and over again, that to be God's People does not quite satisfy us. We are still eyeing other nations, and their shimmering glamor has not yet lost its temptation for our hearts. Hence the days of our trials are not over and as yet we are not able to proclaim that after the long night of our trials, the dawn of our long awaited day has arrived. Nevertheless, even in these dark pre-dawn hours of fate,

Yisrael need not be ashamed of their past. Indeed, Yisrael may be proud, for, on its unparalleled course through world history, Yehudah has nevertheless become His sanctuary and Yisrael His realm.

Look now at the elect holding their great feast all over the world. Despite all they have suffered, they still joyfully fill their cups to praise God for having chosen and exalted them as His People. They have the right to be called "God's People"; they have paid a high price for this title. In days of prosperity they may have demurred at their Divine calling, but during times of distress they have fulfilled their mission brilliantly. To an astonished world they have demonstrated what it means to remain true to one's duty and conviction, to be loyal to God. Their historical martyrdom, recurring over thousands of years, has proven their desire to remain Jews, to cling to their God and Master even unto death. Even in the lowliest corner assigned to them, they have fought for the right to establish a Jewish home so that they could lead a Divinely guided family life, one composed of purity and morality, acts of charity, and mental and spiritual development through the study of the Torah. In order to lead such a life, they were prepared to sacrifice pleasures and honors, to bear oppression and the contempt that accompanies being misunderstood. For the sake of a Torah guided family life they have suffered every torture hatred could devise. While a demented world danced, sneering, over the graves of their fallen, they carried before them their shining beacon, implanting in the heart of mortal man the steadfast faith that a better mankind will emerge in the future, that the Kingdom of God will be established on earth, and the vision of the prophets will come true — a vision of truth and justice, holiness and righteousness, kindness, forgiveness and reconciliation.

Because of this, Yisrael now raise their fourth cup to the One Who proclaimed thousands of years ago, "I shall take you to Me for a People" — and He has kept His word throughout millennia. In consequence of this, they now intone their national hymn of Hallel, expressing in it all their song and sadness, their struggle and victory, their protracted trial and confident hope, praising His encompassing Presence and everlasting Providence.

הללויה. The first part of Hallel has already been recited, to accompany the cup of "redemption," affirming that Hashem is not only the God of the Heavens, but that He looks down to the earth to lift the lowly from the dust and the defenseless from the dunghill; and He bestows on man the happiness of family joy (הללויה). We have furthermore declared earlier, that Yehudah became His sanctuary and Yisrael His realm, that all the world's forces retreated before the might of the God of Yaakov (בצאת ישראל).

Now, over the cup raised to our Divine 'election,' the hymn recalls the sorrowful periods that the Chosen People encounter, when it seems as if they have been forsaken. It tells of the years of darkness when Yisrael hears the contemptuous jeering of the nations: "Where now is their God?". Yisrael cries out from its night of affliction but still clings to its faith that Hashem alone is the One God, Who wills and speaks, Who sees and hears, perceives and intervenes in the process of history. In His thoughts the future of mankind is conceived. And so they exclaim: "Hashem, not to us, but to Your own Name give honor," that the entire world may know Your love and Your truth. Before Your reality, all those figments of man's imagination, which he vainly endowed with spurious attributes of volition, speech, thought and power, shrink into nothingness, and they perish together with their adherents (לא לנו).

No matter what may befall them, our People are sure that the One Who remembered them once will return and remember them time and time again, and He will bless them with ever-increasing favor in each generation. He will preserve them as the Eternal People, who will never perish but will wander over the earth in order to proclaim God's might and Providence wherever they go (יי זכרנו).

With this knowledge, Jewry also cherishes those hours of trial, the times of trouble and sorrow, when out of distress they call upon the Name of God and He hears them! They know that even while He is sitting in judgment, He is merciful. Our People are prepared to seem like an uncomprehending simpleton; Yisrael will gladly submit to the adversities of their times even if at the moment they do not understand the precise place of their pain or anguish in the process of history.

They willingly allow themselves to be called a naive People — for God protects the unaware and lifts them up again from the depths. With this knowledge they can attain serenity and presence of mind even in the hour of their agony. They know Hashem watches over them as of old; He delivers not only their souls from death but also their eyes from tears and their feet from stumbling. They walk on before God, they alone continue in the land of the living, over all the graves of the past. They alone, in the depths of their degradation, remain firmly convinced of the truth of their mission. Even in their flight to the ends of the earth, they still have the courage to decry the rest of mankind for being mistaken and deluded (אהבתי).

Therefore, at those times when they remember the bounties that God has bestowed on them, they raise their cups to give praise and thanks for their salvation in all its many forms and joyfully proclaim the Name of Hashem. All the dispersed Children of Yisrael pledge allegiance to their Divine mission and promise to persevere until God will again gather them in. They are well aware that whenever they face apparent annihilation, it is of fateful importance to God's plans for humanity, and they are grateful for their meaningful mission, however trying it is.

They realize that, by virtue of their faithful service to Him, they are liberated from all other bonds, and they vow to fulfill their assignment in exile until that day when Hashem will gather them "in the courts of the House of Hashem in your midst, o' Yerushalayim" (מה אשיב).

Eventually, the fruits of their having been elected will ripen. Then the glorious culmination of Yisrael's destiny will make God's love and truth radiate out upon all mankind. Not only Yisrael, not only the House of Aharon, but all who are God-fearing among the nations of the world will be called to acknowledge God's lovingkindness and truth and to join the people of Yisrael in its homage: "Avow it Hashem that He is good, that His lovingkindness endures forever (הללו, הודו)."

Then Yisrael will rise up as the Divine herald, to make manifest and clear the revelation of God — which will be openly established by the culmination of their fate in world history. For the entire history of the Jewish People is a testimony to Hashem's almighty Providence. It is a lasting proof that struggles are ultimately won by virtue of the inner strength and stamina which recognition of God and acknowledgment of His holy Name accord. The People of Yisrael, thrust into the turmoil of the ages, have been able to stand up to their enemies thanks to their one sole weapon: their belief in the Name of God. There is hardly a nation in history that has not oppressed Yisrael. But "in the Name of God," our People faced them all and emerged victorious. "True, you have struck me again and again that I might fall," Jewry can exclaim to the nations of the world, "but Hashem helped me." *He gave me the strength to resist and the inspiration to sing* — "and this has become my salvation."

And, so, out of Yisrael's history a paean of praise rises from the tents of *all* the righteous: Only "the right Hand of Hashem does valiantly." Only "the right Hand of Hashem has ever proven exalted." Hence, Jewry shall not die but shall live to recount the works of God. Yes, God will send them trials for the sake of educating them, but He does not turn them over to death, and wherever righteousness can be found on earth, there the gates will be opened for Yisrael to enter and avow their debt of thanks to Him, all the righteous following in their wake.

Those "builders" who ostensibly provided for mankind's welfare disdained Yisrael, but now it is Yisrael who will become the "chief cornerstone" of humanity's new structure. This will become unmistakably clear as Hashem's doing, so "marvelous" to human eyes. This will be the day that Hashem had made, culminating in the unification of the generation, the day when every human joy and salvation will be solely within God; through His sanction will men's endeavors be crowned with success (מן המצר, אנא). Then, in the Name of Hashem, Yisrael will welcome all and everyone and direct them to these blessings which can be found only in the House built by God's law and in His light. Therefore, the nations, too, will have to "keep the festival offering bound"; they will have to restrain their impulsive eagerness to claim Hashem's favor until the altar again rises in majesty in Tzion, until all submit to the guiding light of Divine insight (ברוך הבא).

"You are my God; I shall acknowledge You; o' My God, I will exalt You." This is the song that Yisrael chants in the chorus of mankind. It is Yisrael's anthem, which has accompanied our People through the centuries and the millennia. During these long, endless years, whenever a ray of hope shed its light on our fathers in the blackness of their fate, they soared on the wings of this song to a vision of God's transcendency in history. On this night of Pesach, at their world-wide banquet, this song reverberates from the lips of the Chosen People; and it shall sound and resound on earth until it becomes reality and all mankind joins with Jewry to drink the cup of ultimate salvation. Together they will aspire to the light of God; they will not only be freed from physical burdens and liberated from spiritual misconception but will also be elected to the service of God. And at last they will join in the hymn. "Avow it to Hashem that He is good, that His lovingkindness endures forever"— הודו ליי כי טוב כי לעולם חסדו.

278

Next Year May We Be in Yerushalayim

The object of our prayers, of the yearning of the Jewish spirit, is the Temple, the Abode of God and of His Divine Word. The Temple and all it contains are the symbols showing us the correct way — and this path can only be tread upon in the city of Yerushalayim and the Land of Yisrael. "Take your shoe off of your foot, for the place on which you are standing is holy" (*Yehoshua* 5:15). Thus spoke the captain of Hashem's hosts, drawn sword in his hand, to the first Jewish army-general at the beginning of the conquest of the Land. The Land belongs to the Sanctuary. The whole Land was a mountain of God, upon whose summit radiated the Torah-Sanctuary, surrounded by the tribes of Yisrael. "You bring them home and plant them in the mountain of Your inheritance, the place prepared for Your habitation, which You, o' Hashem, have established, the Sanctuary, o' God, of which Your Hands have laid the foundation" (*Shemos* 15:17).

God's majesty rested on this Sanctuary for as long as there was still a ray of hope that this people would hold on to the Land solely for the sake of the Sanctuary and all it symbolized, that this People would find their "light" and their "table," the spiritual and material welfare of their national life, in the Torah. His Cherubim hovered protectively over the People and over the Land for as long as there was hope that their political achievements served the aims of the Torah and that only one goal would reign supreme in national life: the Torah.

As long as the last trace of this hope persisted, that the Divine glory could become radiantly revealed in the midst of temporal bliss (indeed, this is the etymology of the word ירושלים: It is where Hashem is destined to be revealed, יראה, in peace and salvation, שלם, hence ירו-שלם, Yerushalayim), God continued

279

to send His Spirit and His Word by way of His prophets from the Temple and to dwell in the midst of His People in spite of their abominations (see *Vayikra*, 16:16), expecting them, still, to come to their senses and return to their God and their salvation. However, once the one remaining bond, the bond tying national life to the Torah, was broken; once Yisrael pursued peace in the sense of earthly well-being totally divorced from the shalom, the peace flowing out of the light of Divine radiance; once this people severed the city and the Land from the Sanctuary and set out its "table" not for the Torah but for "fate" — "who prepare a table for Fortune" (*Yeshayahu*, 65:11) — then the Cherubim departed from the state, abandoned the Land, and left the Temple. The same fate which can befall all other temporal political systems buried this state and its Temple. The Torah had to go into exile, following the expatriate People, and it took up its abode in their homes, in their family life. Its triumphs were reaped in the realm of the glorious deaths of its martyrs and in the bliss of Jewish family life — but the optimal vigor of its full potential, the salutary flourishing of a *national* life sustained by God, the fullest implementation of Yisrael's Divine destiny, ירו – שלם — this had to be relegated to the future.

It is over this "Galus HaShechinah," this exile of the majesty of God, as our ancestors called it with true insight, the stunting of the Torah's growth, that Jewish tears are shed and Jewish hearts grieve. We mourn not our own Galus, but the Galus of the Torah!

Are we, then, to cease our grieving and dry our tears now that nations are becoming more humane and more egalitarian? Now that they are undoing the fetters on the hands and feet of the Galus-weary Jews, emancipating them, now that Yisrael are taking their place in the union of the non-Jewish nations — does it mean that the Torah is any less in exile? Does it mean that the Shechinah has ceased its Galus? Does it mean that the Torah has found its native soil, the ground in which it can strike roots, blossom and bring the fruits of blessing and redemption — for the sake of which it was planted as the "everlasting tree of life" — to full maturation? Or are there still new and harsher trials in store for it? Will it have to endure new and more bitter Galus suffering; does a new and more painful exile threaten it?

Even in the darkest centuries of the Galus, when the Roman sword rent the curtain of the Temple and the Divine majesty departed from the Jewish State and with it this Jewish State itself vanished from the earth, the Shechinah escaped, the Torah escaped and found sanctuary in Jewish family life; the Jewish home and every Jewish dwelling remained a temple, every Jewish table remained an altar and every Jewish heart the priestly preserve of the "lamp of Hashem" and the striving for Divine perfection.

Yes, the barriers are coming down, the chains are falling off, the Jewish home is emerging from obscure shadow into the open daylight. Nations accept the sons of Yisrael into their society. Will Yisrael take with them their Godliness from the ghetto to the court, from the tenement to the mansion, from the cheder to the salon, from the sweatshop to the office, from the shul into the "temple"? Are they prepared to take along the ancient Shechinah, the old Torah sanctity, into their newly found life of free and equal citizenship? Or is the last, harshest phase of the Galus HaShechinah still imminent? Is the Presence of God, the sanctity of the Torah, now to be exiled from family life also, from the Jewish homes and the Jewish hearts, as once Jews were exiled from national life? Would that these questions were still questions!

But, what else? Should Yisrael enter into full citizenship with ambivalent feelings, with dual loyalty? If the states of the world are revoking their restrictions, accepting Jews unreservedly and without conditions into their circle, should not Yisrael fully emerge into their national life, should they not find their exclusive satisfaction in belonging to their country, should they not cease to pine for far-away places and latter-day salvation?

Fools! Go, ask the states whose cause you so zealously espouse, ask the states themselves whether they have attained the pinnacle of their aspirations, if they have already discovered the magic wand of paradise, bringing the world eternal joy and peace. Ask them how much consolation they are bringing into the slums, how much joy to the poor. Have they been able to lift up the downtrodden, to banish wretchedness, crime and vice, to give strength to the feeble, compassion to the strong, self-respect to the lowly and humility to the highly-placed? Ask them whether they have been able to banish the curse from this earth, when God had intended that it be blessed, whether they have already discovered even the rudiments of a political system where justice joins up with mercy and where saintliness and earthly joy can dwell side by side without conflict.

Does the telegraph convey only — or even mostly — tidings of joy and peace throughout the world? Does the locomotive transport only wares of blessing and salvation from one land to another? Does the light of knowledge, the magic of technology bring the world to the peak of happiness? Has the formula been found for resolving the contradictions of science so that, like the seven-branched menorah of Tzion, the heavenly lights are turned towards the earthly and the earthly towards the heavenly, fusing into *one* flame which illuminates on high? Has the formula been found for turning man-made bread into the show-bread of God's blessing, each person having sufficient for himself and the wherewithal to help his neighbor as well as the incense of contentment and cheerfulness that goes with it? Has the way been found to inspire the warring factions of political parties, to give them an ideal that transcends their sectarian interests, that is inviolable and equally inspiring and justified to all of them, so as to bring to human society the true olive branch of freedom and bliss?

Is it really Judaism alone which longs for salvation? Does only Yisrael's happiness depend on the resurrection of Tzion? Alas, the Jewish People, persecuted and despised as they may be, are not the most unfortunate. The entire world thirsts for redemption. Grief and misery, reigning in both huts and palaces, arouse Messianic longings in every heart. It is not only Yisrael whose redemption depends upon the rebuilding of

Tzion, and, surely, their confident expectation that the redemption will indeed come about is not the least valuable dowry which the Jew brings with him into the comity of nations.

There was a time, once before, when the world craved redemption — it was when Tzion fell. The pagan world had decayed, the gods were hearing their death knell, and pain obsessed the human heart. Innocence and human dignity were ridiculed, bestial lust and shameless indulgence ruled the day, madness and infirmity ascended the thrones, tyrants revelled on earth and so did slaves, but *men* groaned and died. Mankind had lost its Divine image — it longed for a new God.

If only Tzion had stood then — Tzion in the bloom and blessing of its millennium, Tzion in its eternal youth. If only the many nations had gone to the house of Yaakov and said: "Come let us go up to the mountain of Hashem, to the House of the God of Yaakov and He will teach us of His ways and we will walk in His paths, for from Tzion..." (*Yeshayahu* 2:3). But only silence was heard... It was not to be. Tzion fell.

Before it fell, a spark went forth from the holy lamp of Tzion. It was carried out into the despairing pagan world by feeble hands. Yet, even this single, isolated Jewish spark seemed, to those who bore it, too radiant for the heathen world. These Jews forgot to trust in the power of the Divine, they forgot that it did not need human assistance, that it knew its time, the time when the human spirit would rise to the perception of its faint glimmer. They took pity on their perishing fellow men, could not endure the sorrow of the breaking hearts and, in their commiseration with them, the Jews dimmed the bright light of Judaism's spark, lowering it down to the twilight shade of the heathen heart.

Even so, this lonely spark which had fallen from the lamp of Tzion, even while in heathen camouflage, disguised virtually beyond recognition, still, in spite of its distortion, it became the *remedy* for the world, dragging moribund mankind back from the abyss and leading it on the way to recovery. History is nothing but the struggle of this Jewish spark to divest itself of its pagan shroud, its struggle against the heathen obscuration of its light and against the very heathen foundations upon which it had been placed. They meant to rescue men's spirits, men's hearts, but what about this *world*? In their despair they abandoned it, relinquished man's world to "perdition." They had produced a new *faith* for mankind, but, lacking courage, they said nothing of its *Law* — and yet it is only the Law which can bring full salvation.

The spark is fighting — and conquering. The cloak falls down, the props are breaking, a new agony convulses the world. They can perceive it, they can sense it, they are learning: the redemption of the world will not be brought about by belief, not even by the purest of faiths. The redemption of the world means: *Law*. Faith may indeed illuminate the soul and comfort the heart, but to wed justice with mercy, saintliness with joy, subsistence with peace; to reconstruct paradise on earth, to satisfy man's soul in this world — this feat can be accomplished by one medium only: Torah and mitzvos.

The day will come when the yearning for this Law will awaken and on that day Tzion will stand ready, for at such a time:

> "...In the end of the days, it will come about:
> That the mountain of Hashem's House will be established
> On the top of the mountains,
> And it shall be exalted above and people shall flow unto it.
> And many nations shall go and say:
> 'Come let us go up to the mountain of Hashem
> And to the House of the God of Yaakov
> And He will teach us of His ways
> And we will walk in His paths,'
> For out of Tzion shall go forth the Torah
> And the Word of Hashem from Yerushalayim.
> And He shall judge between many peoples
> And shall admonish mighty nations, very far off
> And they shall beat their swords into plowshares
> And their spears into pruning-hooks,
> Nation shall not lift up a sword against nation
> Neither shall they learn war any more.

And they shall sit every man under his vine
And under his fig-tree
And none shall make them afraid
For it is the Mouth of Hashem of hosts that has spoken."

(Michah 4:1-4)

Next year may we be in Yerushalayim!

טבלת זמנים לחג הפסח

השנה	סוף זמן אכילת חמץ למג״א	סוף זמן אכילת חמץ לגר״א	סוף זמן שריפת חמץ, ביטולו ומכירה לגוי למג״א	סוף זמן שריפת חמץ, ביטולו ומכירה לגוי לגר״א	חצות היום בערב פסח	הדלקת הנרות בערב שבת	שקיעת החמה בערב פסח
תש״מ	9.07	9.37	10.25	10.39	11.42		5.59
תשמ״א	8.55	9.27	10.16•	10.32•	11.37		6.11
תשמ״ב	9.02	9.34	10.21	10.35	11.40		6.04
תשמ״ג	9.07	9.40	10.11	10.42	11.43		5.58
תשמ״ד	8.57	9.29	10.18	10.30	11.37		6.10
תשמ״ה	9.04	9.30	10.23	10.35	11.40	5.22	6.02
תשמ״ו	8.51	9.20	10.13	10.25	11.36		6.15
תשמ״ז	8.57	9.29	10.17	10.33	11.38		6.08
תשמ״ח	9.06	9.36	10.24	10.38	11.42	5.20	6.00
תשמ״ט	8.54	9.25	10.15	10.30	11.37		6.12
תש״נ	9.01	9.33	10.21	10.37	11.39		6.05
תשנ״א	9.09	9.39	10.17	10.41	11.42	5.18	5.58
תשנ״ב	8.56	9.28	10.17	10.33	11.37	5.30	6.10
תשנ״ג	9.04	9.30	10.23	10.35	11.40		6.02
תשנ״ד	9.09	9.41	10.26•	10.45•	11.43		5.56
תשנ״ה	8.57	9.29	10.17	10.44	11.38	5.28	6.08
תשנ״ו	9.04	9.35	10.22	10.47	11.41		6.01
תשנ״ז	8.51	9.25	10.12	10.31	11.36		6.13

• שריפה בששי, וביטולו בשבת

כל הזכויות שמורות

286

לאופק ירושלים (לפי השעון הרגיל)

שונות	זמן מוצאי ז' דפסח לר"ת	זמן מוצאי ז' דפסח	זמן מוצאי א' דפסח לר"ת	זמן מוצאי א' דפסח	עלות השחר בליל פסח	חצות ליל פסח	צאת הכוכבים בליל פסח לר"ת
שנת הביעור	7.20	6.38	7.15	6.34	3.54	11.42	7.13
	7.35	6.52	7.30	6.47	3.28	11.37	7.29
עירוב תבשילין בחו"ל ערב פסח	7.25	6.44	7.21	6.39	3.44	11.40	7.18
	7.17	6.37	7.12	6.33	3.58	11.43	7.10
שנת הביעור	7.34	6.51	7.28	6.46	3.31	11.37	7.28
עירוב תבשילין ערב ז' פסח	7.24	6.43	7.19	6.38	3.47	11.40	7.19
עירוב תבשילין בחו"ל ערב פסח	7.40	6.56	7.34	6.52	3.21	11.36	7.33
שנת הביעור	7.30	6.48	7.25	6.44	3.35	11.38	7.25
עירוב תבשילין ערב ז' פסח	7.21	6.39	7.16	6.35	3.52	11.41	7.15
עירוב תבשילין בחו"ל ערב פסח	7.36	6.53	7.30	6.48	3.27	11.36	7.30
	7.28	6.45	7.22	6.41	3.41	11.39	7.21
עירוב תבש· ערב ז' פסח; שנת הביעור	7.17	6.37	7.13	6.33	3.57	11.42	7.12
עירוב תבשילין ערב ז· פסח	7.34	6.52	7.29	6.47	3.30	11.37	7.28
	7.25	6.43	7.19	6.38	3.47	11.40	7.19
שנת הביעור	7.16	6.35	7.11	6.32	4.01	11.43	7.11
עירוב תבשילין ערב ז· פסח	7.31	6.49	7.26	6.45	3.35	11.38	7.25
עירוב תבשילין בחו"ל ערב פסח	7.22	6.41	7.17	6.37	3.50	11.41	7.17
	7.40	6.54	7.33	6.50	3.24	11.36	7.30

טבלה זו נערכה בקירוב ע"י הרה"ג שריה דבליצקי שליט"א

287

טבלת זמנים לחג הפסח

PER VILNA GAON	PER MAGEN AVRAHAM	SUNRISE	DATE	YEAR
	END EATING CHAMETZ			
סוף זמן אכילת חמץ				
לפי הגר"א	לפי מגן אברהם	הנץ החמה	תאריך	השנה
9.53	9.19	5.42	3/31/80	תש"מ
9.41	9.04	5.14	4/18/81	תשמ"א
9.48	9.13	5.31	4/7/82	תשמ"ב
9.55	9.21	5.47	3/28/83	תשמ"ג
9.42	9.05	5.17	4/16/84	תשמ"ד
9.49	9.15	5.34	4/5/85	תשמ"ה
9.38	9.00	5.06	4/23/86	תשמ"ו
9.44	9.08	5.21	4/13/87	תשמ"ז
9.53	9.18	5.41	4/1/88	תשמ"ח
9.40	9.03	5.12	4/19/89	תשמ"ט
9.47	9.11	5.28	4/9/90	תש"נ
9.55	9.20	5.46	3/29/91	תשנ"א
9.41	9.04	5.15	4/17/92	תשנ"ב
9.49	9.15	5.34	4/5/93	תשנ"ג
9.57	9.23	5.51	3/26/94	תשנ"ד
9.43	9.07	5.20	4/14/95	תשנ"ה
9.51	9.16	5.37	4/3/96	תשנ"ו
9.38	9.02	5.09	4/21/97	תשנ"ז

* זמן צאת הכוכבים לפי שיטת רבינו תם מחושב על יסוד של שעה וחצי אחרי שקיעת החמה (בארץ ישראל בא' בתקופת ניסן), דהיינו זמן הליכת ד' מילין באשר זמן הליכת מיל הוא כ"ב וחצי דקות. עיין חוק יעקב וגר"א או"ח סי' תנ"ט באריכות, ובקונטרס "בעניני זמן בין-השמשות ועה"ש" בספרי "זמני היום בהלכה" (עמ' טז-יט).

טבלה זו נערכה ע"י הרב יהודה ב"ר י"א הלוי לוי   כל הזכויות שמורות

288

NIGHT-FALL PER R. TAM*	LIGHT CANDLES	NOON AND MID-NIGHT	END BURNING CHAMETZ	
			PER VILNA GAON	PER MAGEN AVRAHAM
			סוף זמן שריפת חמץ	
צאת הכוכבים על־פי ר׳ תס•	זמן הדלקת הנרות	חצות היום וחצות הלילה	לפי הגר״א	לפי מגן אברהם
8.03	6.01	12.00	10.57	10.40
8.29	6.20	11.55	10.48	10.30
8.13	6.08	11.58	10.54	10.36
7.59	5.58	12.01	10.59	10.42
8.26	6.18	11.56	10.49	10.31
8.10	6.06	11.59	10.54	10.37
8.36	6.25	11.54	10.46	10.28
8.21	6.15	11.57	10.51	10.33
8.05	6.02	12.00	10.57	10.39
8.30	6.21	11.55	10.48	10.29
8.15	6.11	11.58	10.53	10.35
8.01	5.59	12.01	10.58	10.41
8.27	6.19	11.56	10.49	10.30
8.10	6.06	11.59	10.54	10.37
7.57	5.56	12.02	11.00	10.43
8.23	6.16	11.56	10.50	10.32
8.07	6.04	11.59	10.55	10.38
8.33	6.23	11.55	10.47	10.29

* Nightfall according to Rabbeinu Tam has been calculated here on the basis of 90 minutes after sunset (in Eretz Yisrael at the equinox), corresponding to a 4-mile walk, reckoning 22 1/2 minutes per mile. For explanation, see *Chok Ya'akov*, and G'RA (the Vilna Gaon) on *Shulchan Aruch Orach Chayim*, §459; and Leo Levi, *Jewish Chrononomy*, Hebrew part, pp. 16–19.

Sources for Commentaries and Essays

The Pesach Seder	Collected Writings vol. I pp. 67-87
The Search for Chametz	Horeb § 197-200
The Pesach Sacrifice	Collected Writings vol. I pp. 103-111
Kaddesh	The Hirsch Siddur pp. 292-93
And It Was Evening...	Bereishis 1:31
And the Heaven...	Bereishis 2:1
God Blessed the Seventh Day...	Bereishis 2:3
Blessed Be	Bereishis 9:27; Collected Writings vol. II pp. 187-88
Who Creates the Flames of the Fire	Gesammelte Schriften vol. II pp. 471,472
Maggid	Horeb § 207-209
Bread Of Dependence	Shemos 12:8,39; Devarim 16:3
The Second Cup is then Poured...	Gesammelte Shriften vol. II pp. 411-413
We Were Slaves unto Pharaoh...	Bereishes 15:9-21; Shemos 20:2; 12:19-20
The Recital of the Morning Shema	Devarim 6:4
The Time for the Recital...	Devarim 6:7
And I Did Not Succeed in Proving...	Devarim 16:3
Commentary on the Four Sons	Collected Writings vol. I pp. 46-65
I Took Your Father Avraham...	The Nineteen Letters: Letter Eight
To Esav I Gave Mount Seir...	Bereishis 36:31
The Holy One, Blessed Be He...	Bereishis 15:9-21
And He Went down to Egypt...	Devarim 26:5
And Sojourned There as a Stranger...	Devarim 26:5; Shemos 1:14
And Now Hashem Your God Has Made You...	Devarim 1:10; Bereishis 15:5
And the Children of Yisrael Were Fruitful...	Shemos 1:7
And I Passed over You...	Collected Writings vol. I. pp. 5-6
The King of Egypt Died...	Shemos 2:32
And God Heard Their Groaning...	Shemos 2:24-25
I Hashem	Collected Writings vol. I pp. 30-31
And This Staff Shall You Take...	Shemos 4:2
An Alternative Explanation	Collected Writings vol. I pp. 40-41
Rabbi Yehudah Made a Mnemonic...	Shemos 7:15

He Lets Break Forth against Them... — Collected Writings vol. I pp. p. 41

He Brought Us out of Egypt... — Collected Writings vol. I pp. 39-40

And Slew Their Firstborn... — The Psalms 136:10-15

And Provided Our Needs in the Desert...

And Gave Us Shabbos — Shemos 15:25; 16:2,4

Gesammelte Shriften vol. I pp. 170-73

And Fed Us with Mannah... — Gesammelte Shriften vol. I pp. 180-83; 185-88

And Gave Us the Torah... — Collected Writings vol. I pp. 211-16

The Paschal Lamb... — Collected Writings vol. I pp. 6-12

The Matzah Which We Eat... — Collected Writings vol. I pp. 12-18

The Maror Which We Eat... — Collected Writings vol. I pp. 18-20

Let Us Therefore Recite... — Shemos 15:2

The First Chapters of the Hallel — The Psalms 113-14

And We Shall Thank You... — The Psalms 33:3

For Our Redemption... — Gesammelte Shriften vol. II pp. 319,320

Rochtzah — Horeb § 163

Who Has Sanctified Us by His Commandments... — Devarim 8:10

Matzah — Horeb § 205

Shulchan Orech — Horeb § 181

To Eat the Flesh of the Paschal Lamb... — Shemos 12:6-7

The Paschal Lamb Is Eaten Neither Half-Cooked... — Shemos 12:9

It is not Taken from One Group... — Shemos 2:23

Whoever Breaks a Bone... — Shemos 12:46

The Paschal Lamb May Be Eaten... — Shemos 12:10

The Paschal Lamb in Egypt... — Shemos 12:7

A Song of Ascents — The Psalms 126

Birkas Hazimun — The Hirsch Siddur pp. 704-705

Birkas Hamazon — Horeb § 673

He Gives Food to All Flesh — The Hirsch Siddur pp. 696-97

Yaaleh Veyavo — The Hirsch Siddur pp. 146-47

Last Chapters of the Hallel — The Psalms 115-18

Avow It to Hashem... ("The Great Hallel") — The Psalms 136:1

The Soul of Every Living Thing — The Nineteen Letters: Letter Four

Next Year May We Be in Yerushalayim — Collected Writings vol. I pp. 344-48